SUDAN'S UN

/ AFRICAN
/ ARGUMENTS

African Arguments is a series of short books about contemporary Africa and the critical issues and debates surrounding the continent. The books are scholarly and engaged, substantive and topical. They focus on questions of justice, rights and citizenship; politics, protests and revolutions; the environment, land, oil and other resources; health and disease; economy: growth, aid, taxation, debt and capital flight; and both Africa's international relations and country case studies.

WILLOW BERRIDGE, JUSTIN LYNCH,
RAGA MAKAWI & ALEX DE WAAL

Sudan's Unfinished Democracy

The Promise and Betrayal of a People's Revolution

HURST & COMPANY, LONDON

IAI International African Institute

Published in collaboration with the International African Institute.
First published in the United Kingdom in 2022 by
C. Hurst & Co. (Publishers) Ltd.,
New Wing, Somerset House, Strand
London WC2R 1LA

A Cataloguing-in-Publication data record for this book is available from the British Library.

ISBN: 9781787385351

www.hurstpublishers.com

Printed in Great Britain by Bell and Bain Ltd, Glasgow

This book is dedicated to the Sudanese who put their lives on the line in the struggle for freedom and change, and especially those who did not live to see the day when their dreams of democracy and justice were within grasp.

CONTENTS

PREFACE AND ACKNOWLEDGEMENTS

This book is a collaboration between four individuals who have different engagements with Sudan. Willow Berridge is a historian specialising in postcolonial Sudan. Justin Lynch is a journalist and humanitarian worker who has lived in Sudan throughout the events described in this book. Raga Makawi is a democracy activist and editor who was closely involved with the democratic uprising. Alex de Waal has been engaged with Sudan as a researcher, activist and conflict mediator since 1984.

Each of us brings a different set of perspectives, insights and styles. We have all contributed to every chapter. However, Chapter 2 is primarily the work of Alex de Waal, Chapters 3 and 4 are mostly by Justin Lynch, and Chapter 5 is chiefly by Willow Berridge; Raga Makawi has contributed throughout. What we have tried to do is to write a book that combines in-the-moment narrative that captures immediacy and indeterminacy, with historical and political science that places events in context. We have sought to combine structure and agency, top-down and bottom-up analyses. The first four chapters combine an in-depth analysis of unfolding political developments with reflections on the role of political economy, gender dynamics and international policy-making. Chapter 5 reaches into Sudan's history and contrasts today's revolutionary experiences with those of Sudan's recent past, particularly the 1964 and 1985 revolutions. The final chapter offers some reflections on the challenges facing Sudan's still uncertain efforts at democratisation.

We would like to thank all those who have given their time to us during the production of this book: in particular, Abdalla Hamdok and Yasir Arman; and Yousra Mohammed who helped with sourcing information to inform the trajectory of the women's rights agenda post-revolution. We are also very grateful to the team at Hurst, including Lara Weisweiller-Wu, Kathleen May and Alice Clarke, for their tireless work towards the production of this book. In particular, we would like to give our thanks to our editor, Stephanie Kitchen, for her continuing patience and numerous helpful and thoughtful contributions. Without the team at the LSE Conflict Research Programme, which hosted the event from which this project evolved, the book would never have reached fruition. Particular thanks go to Rim Turkmani and Azaria Morgan. Willow Berridge is also indebted to the team at the Society for the Study of the Sudans (UK), including Azim el-Hassan and Mawan Muortat, for hosting her webinar contribution based on Chapter 5, which was a source of valuable feedback. Others whose thoughts and feedback have helped shape our perspectives as the book developed include Edward Thomas, Jean-Baptiste Gallopin, Rachel Ibreck, Abdel Wahab Al-Effendi, Abdul Mohammed, Amar Jamal, Abdalla Ahmed Aidroos and Ali Abdel-Rahman.

The book benefited from the financial support of the World Peace Foundation.

LIST OF ABBREVIATIONS

AUHIP	African Union High-Level Implementation Panel
CPA	Comprehensive Peace Agreement
DUP	Democratic Unionist Party
FFC	Forces of Freedom and Change
HIPC	Heavily Indebted Poor Countries Initiative
IGAD	Inter-Governmental Agency on Development
JEM	Justice and Equality Movement
JPA	Juba Peace Agreement
NCF	National Consensus Forces
NCP	National Congress Party
NIF	National Islamic Front
NISS	National Intelligence and Security Service
NSS	National Security Service
PCP	Popular Congress Party
PDF	Popular Defence Forces
PSC	Peace and Security Council
R-ARCSS	Agreement on the Resolution of the Conflict in South Sudan
RSF	Rapid Support Forces
SAF	Sudan Armed Forces

SCP	Sudanese Congress Party
SLA	Sudan Liberation Army
SLM	Sudan Liberation Movement
SPA	Sudan Professionals Association
SPLA/M	Sudan People's Liberation Army/Movement
SPLA/M-N	Sudan People's Liberation Army/Movement-North
SRF	Sudan Revolutionary Front
SST	State Sponsor of Terror
SSU	Sudan Socialist Union
SUNA	Sudan News Agency
TFA	Transitional financial arrangements
TMC	Transitional Military Council
UNAMID	United Nations–African Union Mission in Darfur
UNITAMS	United Nations Integrated Transition Assistance Mission in Sudan

1. Sudan in regional context

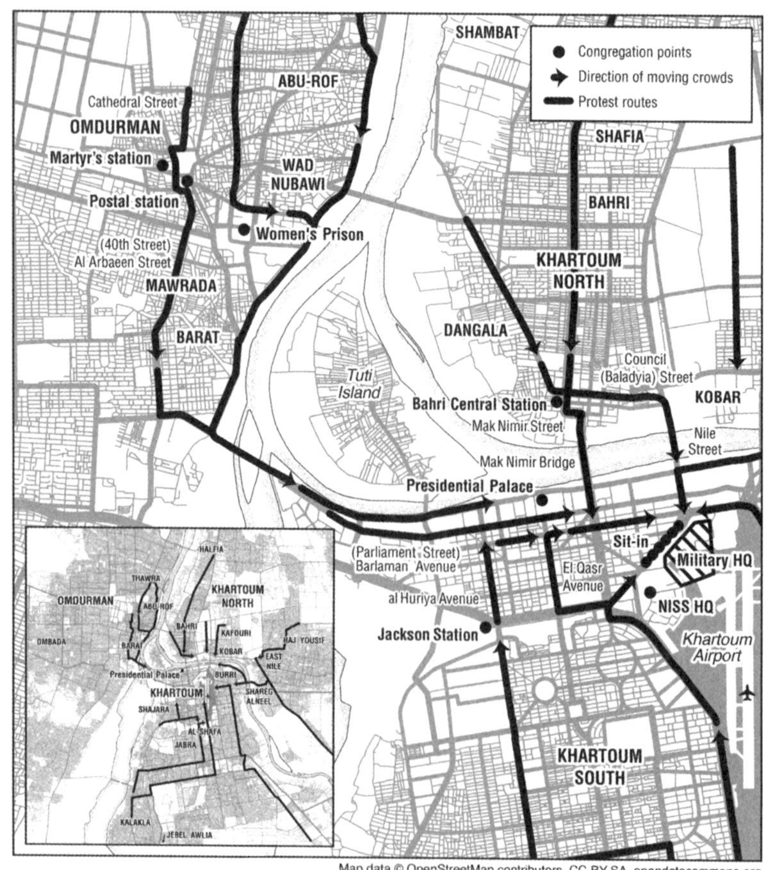

2. The uprising in Khartoum

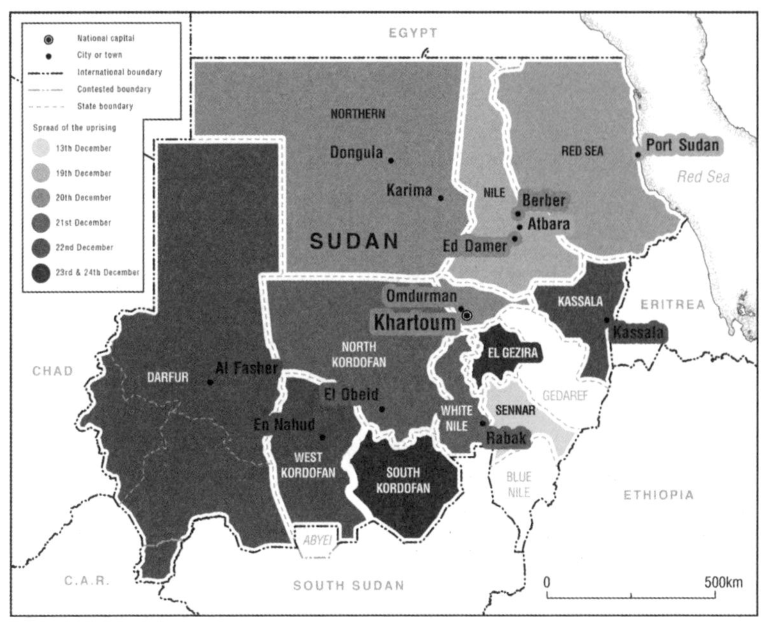

3. Sudan's uprising showing progression of the protests

1

FREEDOM AND CHANGE

Samahir Mubarak walked through the empty streets of Khartoum and was crestfallen. She thought she would be marching against the regime of Omar al-Bashir alongside a million people. Instead, she wandered alone. She watched a boy kick up dirt as he walked to the middle of the road. It was 6 April 2019.

Samahir is an emblem of those who brought revolution to Sudan in the twenty-first century. Educated, female, young and devoted to a cosmopolitan civic ideal of what her country could be, she personifies everything that the authoritarian regime of al-Bashir was trying to repress. She was a dedicated member of the pharmacists' union and a spokesperson for the Sudan Professionals Association (SPA), which was organising protests against the government in Khartoum and other major cities. The extent to which people like Samahir represented the Sudanese people as a whole, and instigated the Sudanese revolution, is a question to which we will return. Ever since al-Bashir had seized power 30 years earlier, as the front man of an Islamist military junta, there had been armed and unarmed resistance, but the 2019 demonstrations carried with them a more tangible sense than before that real change was within grasp.

The boy in the middle of the road inhaled sharply and yelled, 'Freedom, peace, justice!' Samahir looked around, hoping it was a signal. The boy shouted again. Still, nothing happened. Samahir wondered if the resistance had been broken; whether the protests had dissipated, like so many before. Perhaps Sudan was trapped. Then the boy shouted a third time: 'Freedom, peace, justice!'

Protestors emptied out of their homes and flooded the streets. Women tilted their heads and howled up at Khartoum's cloudless April skies. It was the hottest time of the year. '*Madaniyya!*' they chanted—a word signifying the values of civilian rule, dignity and democracy, perhaps best translated as 'civicness'. It was a rallying call for the resistance, along with '*Tasgut, bas!*', which meant 'Just fall!'—the demand that the ugly, ageing kleptocrat in army uniform who had ruled the country for a generation should depart. 'Down with the rule of thieves!', they shouted. Well over half Sudan's population had been born since 1989. Only those aged over 51 actually had the chance to vote in an election that mattered, meaning that the political leaders active during Sudan's previous democratic experiment were now into the typical age of retirement. The protestors wanted the regime swept away, after which—they dreamed—anything would be possible.

Young men crooned back, waving their arms in the air. Samahir joined this crowd. If the chanting had not been so loud she would have heard the thuds of sandals trudging in the streets, a sound that promised freedom. Samahir let the current of people carry her to the centre of the inflection point of Sudan's revolution. She ended up outside military headquarters where hundreds of thousands of people were congregating in what would be called the 'sit-in', an encampment at the army headquarters in central Khartoum that was both a direct challenge to the military kleptocrats and also a living expression of the protestors' ideals for a transformed Sudan.

The military headquarters wasn't the formal seat of state power. The Republican Palace lay a further two miles away—an elegant but fading colonial-era building whose doors opened right onto the corniche of the Blue Nile, next to a new Chinese-built extravaganza, whose ceilings were so high they made even the most egotistical person feel diminutive. Visiting heads of state would drive to this twin palace, their police-escorted motorcades bringing the city centre to a halt. But real power was exercised from within the vast pharaonic compound of the military headquarters where coercion was directed and cash handed out—and where the fate of Sudan was ultimately decided. The headquarters was dominated by three hulking office blocks, one square, one supposedly shaped to resemble a ship, the third resembling a rather squat aeroplane. Adjacent were buildings hidden behind a thick wall that hid the nerve centre of the security and intelligence services. Inside the walls was cramped, with a mini-city of its own shops, banks, fuel stations and offices. Tucked inside was also a portly house that was al-Bashir's private residence and political office, where twice weekly he held an open house for commissioned military officers and sundry other well-connected petitioners. The protestors had chosen correctly. The compound was ringed by a wall with mock battlements and Ottoman-style gatehouses. It couldn't withstand a real siege. And the army wasn't prepared for a civic siege either.

The story of how protestors like Samahir overthrew al-Bashir is both a distinctively Sudanese playbook for how to overthrow a reviled regime, and also a version of a widely followed script for non-violent protest movements reprised around the world. The heart of the movement was the SPA, a gathering of trade unions that initially had more modest aims—mainly, better wages. The SPA took on the role of coordinating a flourishing network of neighbourhood resistance committees, already established or rapidly coming into being and sharing non-violent methods and democratic ideals, united by their determination to bring down al-Bashir, his cabal and cronies. Each resistance committee was a collection of 20 to 50 people in a neighbourhood, mostly young, which acted similar to a social club.[1] Many of the SPA leaders were in the diaspora, with networks and skills that proved essential to the resistance, but by the same token less well placed for the challenges that followed. Sudan's civic revolutionaries were ill-prepared for the state power that suddenly fell within their grasp. '*Tasgut, bas!*' was fit for purpose, but a limited purpose only. The palpable energy of people's power seemed to promise that anything was possible.

It was not just idealism that powered the uprising. There was also deprivation and hunger. The booming economy of the first decade of the 2000s, when Sudan was pumping oil, had collapsed into chaotic austerity. Inflation was high, jobs were fewer, fuel and bread were becoming scarce. The army devoured most of the national budget. Critics on the left decried the 'deep state': the network of security men, business godfathers and their cronies that wielded real power.[2]

In the two and a half years since the April 2019 revolution, the structural problems of Sudan's political economy remain. The economic crisis has deepened. Sudanese politics still functions as a competitive marketplace in which those skilled in political horse-trading can turn the turbulence of events to their advantage. Democratic institution building has been diluted by encounters with transactional politics and empty state coffers. The inequalities of wealth and political influence, long shaped by geography and skin colour, could not be swept aside so easily despite revolutionary chants in solidarity with a more unified Sudan and against the centre's exclusionary ethnic politics: 'You arrogant racist—all the country is Darfur!' Some of Sudan's civic revolutionaries bemoan the missed opportunities, accusing their colleagues of betraying their ideals; others concede that their aspirations were unrealistic and the challenges too great. At the time of writing the flame of democracy in Sudan is flickering.

How the Revolution Began

The main act of the Sudanese revolution is the confrontation between the civic uprising and al-Bashir: the people facing a tyrant. Since he came to power in 1989, few Sudanese liked al-Bashir or were ready to sacrifice for him—many loathed him, the greedy and cruel men around him, and the apparatus they had built. But dissatisfaction does not make a revolution. Rather, the story of Sudan's civil uprising is the tale of how that anger and resentment were organised into coalitions and mobilised into collective action. The demonstrations, organised with local groups that sprang up neighbourhood by neighbourhood, rapidly came to be coordinated by the SPA, which bottled the demand for change and repackaged it into a structure that could topple a dictator. The SPA did not begin Sudan's revolution and has never claimed ownership over it. Instead, the group shepherded change by being the most prominent body that organised protests. The story of Sudan's civic uprising starts from humble roots. Protestors were deeply passionate about the transformation they envisaged. Others backed the uprising but with a note of caution—they had seen this script before, and it had not ended well. In Chapter 5 of this book we turn from an account of the events of 2018–21 to a historical and comparative perspective, including showing how the exemplary civic uprisings of 1964 and 1985 had raised high hopes, but had then disappointed.

Al-Bashir was a chameleon dictator. While he stayed close to his oldest friends in the army throughout his three decades in power, his shades of Islamist green shifted over the years, and his alliances changed dramatically.[3] Unlike most long-standing autocrats, al-Bashir never succeeded in cultivating a cult of personality—on the few occasions on which he tried to do so the efforts were widely ridiculed. He made few public speeches. Campaign posters for the elections of 2010 showed airbrushed images of the president in a variety of costumes, looking far younger than his age, and invited humorous debunking. Just as significantly, al-Bashir was well aware of the limits of his power and only in his final days did he succumb to hubristic miscalculation. For the first ten years (1989–99) al-Bashir was in office but the Islamist movement headed by Sheikh Hassan al-Turabi set the political agenda.[4] The Islamists even ran their own foreign policy for six years, until their entanglement in terrorism became an imminent threat to the regime, and al-Bashir began to assert some control—the beginnings of his accumulation of real power. In 1997–99 al-Turabi tried to reduce the president to a figurehead and almost succeeded, until at the last moment the apparently cornered al-Bashir played his highest card: he declared a state of emergency and dismissed his rival.[5] Over the next six years, al-Bashir consolidated executive power in his office, but the strategic decisions over the future of the country—the formula contained in the 2005 Comprehensive Peace Agreement (CPA)—were made by Vice President Ali Osman Taha, al-Turabi's former deputy. During the six years that followed the CPA, of cohabitation with the Sudan People's Liberation Movement (SPLM), al-Bashir both accumulated power and dispersed institutional authority, in the classic manner of a 'big tent' patrimonial leader. And his final eight years were consumed with power-politicking as the bill for the previous years' blunders became due.

Al-Bashir and his cabal of soldiers and security men began and ended their years in power on the same note. When they and the civilian Islamists mounted their coup in June 1989—calling it the 'National Salvation Revolution'—they saw their main threat as organised civil society. Their first and most ruthless steps were to ban and dismantle independent trade unions and professional associations, sending many of their leaders to infamous 'ghost houses' and others into exile.[6] In their place the Islamists created new associations for lawyers, teachers, doctors, engineers and others, under the same names, but run entirely by their own cadres.[7] It was a façade of civil society that aimed over the years to become all-pervasive, a hegemonic project known as *al tamkeen*, and an attempt to abolish any form of organised resistance.[8] The unions with real constituencies went underground and operated in secret. They continued to mobilise against the new regime's price hikes and reduction of the minimum wage, but were violently repressed.[9] After the 2005 CPA and the unbanning of political parties, these individuals came out into the open once again, but their former organisations struggled to compete against the regime-sanctioned unions and associations. But the quasi-liberalisation of the CPA's interim period was dialled back as soon as South Sudan's independence approached.

Scarcely noticed at the time, popular protests erupted in northern cities during the week of the referendum in southern Sudan in January 2011. After 55 years of second-class status within a united Sudan, southern Sudanese voted for independence. It was a humiliation for the leadership and a crippling economic blow, as the south took with it three-quarters of the country's oil. Al-Bashir and his security chiefs feared that the recriminations over the loss of the south and the economic shock from the loss of oil revenue spelled a crisis in Khartoum. Moreover, civic uprisings were bringing down the regimes in Tunisia and Egypt during those very weeks. The Sudanese leadership saw off the protests[10] but, in doing so, it continued running the economy as if they were still an oil-rich country and kept the subsidies of wheat and fuel untouched.

The seeds of the SPA were planted around November 2011 when opposition politicians and underground union leaders decided to unify some of the labour groups.[11] The idea was based on the historical power that unions once had and the knowledge that, if they formed an alliance, it would be mutually beneficial. Their goals were specific to boosting wages and labour rights. Doctors could combine forces with teachers and make each other's protests stronger. Some say the first key moment of the modern SPA was a small protest in 2012 outside a government ministry.[12] Ahmed Rabie, a teacher, was one of six people to show up at the protest. The government hadn't faced these kinds of protests since the mid-1990s, but it had the apparatus for repression well prepared. The National Intelligence and Security Service (NISS) had studied the way in which civic leaders in Tunisia and Egypt had mobilised using social media. Based on this research, the security men had caught up with the protestors' tactics. They also used the same old methods of arrest, detention, torture, and threat of disappearance.

Rabie and the six activists were brave but not suicidal. They rushed out of a van, snapped a photo with signs demanding better pay, and then scurried back into the vehicle. A lot of the early protests were like that: lonely, small, forgotten.

After the protest in 2012, the collective of unions didn't have a name but it continued coordinating for workers' rights. There was no leader. The structure was a coalition of six groups: lawyers, doctors, professors, engineers, teachers and journalists. Each of the six unions had two representatives in a council, who then voted for six to eight members of a secretariat who executed the decisions of the council. The consensus-based approach worked because issues were uncontroversial and mostly centred around when to call a protest. The alliance remained underground out of a fear of infiltration by agents from NISS.

Autocrats commonly trade repression against welfare—the classic 'bread and circuses' strategy. In 2010, al-Bashir's electoral message could have been distilled to, 'Forget my early years of human rights violations, remember only the prosperity brought by oil.' In the years after Sudan began exporting oil in 1999, the national budget grew by a factor of 13. Khartoum and the main cities benefited from a boom in construction, consumption and employment. The boom couldn't last, and neither could the political strategy built on it. When South Sudan seceded, the government had to tighten its belt. Al-Bashir knew the likely consequences so he prevaricated as long as he could.[13]

In September 2013, the government introduced its first round of austerity measures. As expected, the usual suspects—students and youth groups, unions and professional associations—mounted protests. The NISS was well prepared with the ingredients for turning political protest into general mayhem. One tactic was inserting agents provocateurs among the protestors, who turned to smashing shop windows and burning petrol stations, prompting many urbanites to have misgivings. Another tactic took advantage of young people's naïve over-confidence in social media, which allowed security agents to spread deadly disinformation. The demonstrations were put down with lethal force, with more than 200 people killed.[14]

Failure can be a better teacher than success. Five years later, NISS used the same tactics, but the SPA had learned its lesson. The SPA leaders took the errors of 2013 as a cautionary tale: they mourned the human toll and regretted the blind alley of rioting. They didn't want to send young men and women to their deaths without anything to show for it.[15]

The early years of the still-unnamed labour collective were more of an ad hoc alliance than a revolutionary organisation. Progress happened in fits and starts. The group organised small protests for years where perhaps a dozen people would show up. Arrests of union members and leaders were common. 'We had a lot of difficulties getting organised,' said Mohamed Yousif, a professor and influential member in the group. Yousif was a wizened old man with grey hair sprouting in every which direction—perhaps one for each protest he'd taken part in. He had formerly been a member of the SPLM and had played a role in the campaign to vote al-Bashir out of office in the 2010 elections, an effort that foundered as much on opposition infighting as on the resolve of the ruling National Congress Party (NCP) that it wouldn't yield. He said, 'People would disappear.' But the labour groups slowly rebuilt and refined their tactics. History will remember the SPA for its role in deposing al-Bashir, but this wouldn't have been possible without those years of trial and error. The body learned that the more specific and immediate an issue the more traction the group received. Low pay and corruption attracted support. Abstract ideas like justice did not unify as many people.

The government had put itself in a trap of raised expectations. It had used the windfall from oil to put more than a million people on the government payroll, spend lavishly on construction contracts, import cheap consumer goods, and entrench a system of patronage politics that was expensive beyond Sudan's means.[16] Instead of using the short-lived oil revenues to build a sustainable economy around farming and manufacturing, the NCP (and equally, its partner in kleptocracy, the SPLM) squandered the money. Most fatally for its own political prospects, Sudan's ruling party racked up an impossible bill for fuel and food subsidies. Like a reckless drug dealer, it got high on its own supply. It begged, borrowed and stole to feed its habit. And the vanities of al-Bashir and his system were exposed, one by one.

By 2018, Sudan's economy was contracting even faster than it had grown in the heady oil boom years. It ranked 167 out of 187 on the Human Development Index. Corruption had swallowed the investment budget, and the exorbitant expenses of the new dams on the Nile compelled al-Bashir to dismantle the corporation that built them. The Khartoum refinery—another sponge for absorbing money—was so poorly managed that Sudan had to start importing refined fuel. But that year's military budget was three times more than the education and health budget combined. That summer, the unions finally united into the SPA with its explicit goal of increasing the minimum wage. The founding platform of the organisation was formal labour laws, which reveals its demographic base. Its membership was overwhelmingly middle-class workers—teachers, journalists, health workers, all of them financially stressed—in Khartoum and other towns, its leadership from the upper echelons of the professions—doctors, engineers, lawyers and professors. Meanwhile, nearly 90% of economic activity occurred in the informal sector.[17]

The narrow class basis of the SPA was a limitation but also an important strength. Bonds between organisation members were strong. They thought alike, they didn't need to spend time on wider questions of political philosophy. The SPA's campaign to increase the minimum wage began in August 2018. It produced a study about stagnating and depreciating wages[18] followed by a press conference to present the findings of the study and set a list of reform demands. That served as its effective introduction to Sudan, where two of its members spoke, the leather-faced Yousif and a young doctor who struggled to grow facial hair, named Mohamed Nagi al-Assam. Hardly anyone attended. The press conference received little media attention. The SPA's plan to deliver a list of demands to the government centred around the minimum wage was overtaken by events and the petition was never presented.

Spontaneous protests against the regime began a few weeks later in 2018. Demonstrations started in the town of ad-Damazein on 13 December, with just a few dozen people. Protestors closed down roads from Sinnar to Sinja. They were rounded up by the security forces and thrown in prison. These demonstrations were not unique in Sudan, in fact they happened almost every week in some part of the country. Frustration had been boiling for years. But what made this small street protest spark an uprising was the fact it was married to a coalition that could shepherd the movement. On 17 December, the doctors' union issued a statement in support of the social movement starting to take shape, directing doctors across Sudan to support and contribute to its success. Two days later, on 19 December, a much larger protest broke out in Atbara, north of Khartoum. Atbara is the historic centre for labour activism in Sudan, the central depot for Sudan Railways and the headquarters for the railway workers' union, once the engine of the Sudan Communist Party.[19] They adopted the symbol of a loaf of bread, because it was becoming unaffordable. 'Down with the rule of thieves!', they shouted. There, protestors initiated the practice of burning down the NCP headquarters. The charred offices became a symbol of 'liberated' cities—no longer under the control of the intertwined forces of the NCP and NISS. News of the demonstrations spread on social media across Sudan. Within days there were other demonstrations in Port Sudan, Dongola in the Northern state, al-Damar, Berber and Sinnar respectively, spreading to other cities.

The SPA hadn't expected the protests to spread like this. It was an organisation focused on improving workers' rights but its leaders spotted an opportunity. It faced the first of a series of questions that would quickly define the course of the revolution. Should it stick to its agenda of boosting workers' rights or change course and call for the downfall of the entire system? Still without a hierarchical leadership structure, it was divided over what to do. Some wanted to keep the organisation focused on improving the minimum wage. Members who experienced the trauma of the 2013 protests and felt guilt about the deaths of young protestors were unconvinced that these marches would be different. They believed that more young people would die without anything to show for it. Perhaps it was better to work inside the system that was. But others believed that the best way to improve workers' rights was to achieve the long-cherished goal of removing the government altogether. While al-Bashir and his cronies stayed in power, they would surely stifle or subvert any reform. The organisation called for a protest on 25 December with the question of whether or not to call for the president's removal still undecided. The idea was that people at the protest would decide the way forward, and the decision was indicative of an important trait the organisation had.

The SPA's history is one of avoiding confrontation among its members out of fear that such confrontation will create lasting fissions in the group. The SPA is an organisation of consensus. The leaderless structure meant that any large divides within the organisation simply remained unresolved until the answer was overwhelmingly apparent—which sometimes wouldn't happen at all. SPA leaders watched the 25 December march and saw that people demanded al-Bashir should leave: the slogan '*Tasgut, bas!*' was heard. It was a critical inflection point because the group changed its mission to civic revolution.

After the December march the group posted a 'timetable' for when and where demonstrations would happen each week on social media, mainly Facebook and Twitter. The advent of technology and the presence of a largely tech-savvy mobilised youth population enabled a turning point in popular organisational tactics with the SPA publishing on 6 April the first protest map showing the routes for processions. It served as a common tool and reference point for dissidents across the country of when and where to organise. And it helped organise other forms of protest as well, online and in neighbourhoods. Resistance committees formed in urban neighbourhoods across the country, replicating the structures of the Popular Committees whereby al-Bashir's party and security apparatus had tried to control the cities, but this time providing a more democratic and energetic alternative. But many senior SPA members still feared the marches would not succeed. They believed the regime was too strong. Leaders recall looking at the marches in Khartoum and seeing a few hundred or thousand show up and worrying that it was not enough. Revolutionaries try to convince us that they act without fear, because victory is imminent. Privately, many recalled their doubts about the efficacy of these early protests. They were not armed insurrectionists for whom killing and dying were a routine part of political calculus. Each dead protestor was one life lost too many. Etched in their memory was the bloody failure of the 2013 protest.[20]

At the time, the president and his inner circle were preoccupied with their internal politicking. They understood well the principles and practice of transactional politics and how to position themselves and survive inside the regime, with its intrigue, greed and back-stabbing. But they underestimated the protests, thinking they could buy off the masses with some concessions on the price of bread, intimidate them with a show of force, and play political games with the leaders—once they had figured out who they were and what their purchase price was. They even went as far as enlisting sharia edicts on the religious cost of enforcing public order through blood shed for the greater good, a principle of good and righteous governance under Islam. The SPA leaders were outsiders to this political culture but they knew enough to be pessimistic. They overestimated the regime and underestimated the protestors.

Geographies of Wealth, Power and Protest

Who were these protestors? Like the Sudanese nation itself, they were diverse, contradictory and enigmatic. Those who have studied the Sudanese uprising are intrigued and are still searching for answers.[21] We can begin by looking at how they are shaped by Sudan's social geography.

For two centuries, Khartoum has dominated the land of Sudan, extracting resources from its hinterland and investing the proceeds in the city. The country itself has been a microcosm of empire, and politics a metropolitan affair. Peripheral convulsions might displace millions and kill hundreds of thousands, without disturbing the governing class. Regime change has always happened within the capital.

Sudan's uprising was decentralised but a majority of senior leaders clustered around one neighbourhood. Burri lies just to the east of Khartoum city centre, in the elbow of the Blue Nile as the river makes its last westward turn before merging with the White Nile. It is divided from the old colonial city by a raised railway line that spans the main thoroughfare into the neighbourhood. Pictures of protestors and their murals on that bridge were to become iconic images. To the north, the railway crosses the Blue Nile corniche and then the river itself; in the other direction lie the military headquarters and the airport. Adjacent to the seat of state power, Burri has a historical role in Sudan's revolutions. It is an old working-class neighbourhood, the site of the city's largest private military hospital, and is where the police headquarters are located. The colonial military barracks were there—both the locus of nationalist plotting in Sudan's original nationalist uprising of 1924 and its suppression. After independence in 1956 the barracks, still with the graffiti of Tommies scoured into the brickwork, became dormitories for students at the University of Khartoum, while the bachelor junior faculty had their digs in a nearby subsidised housing complex, one of the neglected treasures of the city's modernist architecture, known as the 'pink palace' on account of its lurid colour. The students who marched in 1964 started from here; the lecturers who were so central in the 1985 uprising conspired there.

Khartoum is a constantly half-built city, suspended between construction and decay. Public spaces are dusty and often littered with debris and rubbish, the streets unpaved. Islamic banking doesn't allow for mortgages, so houses are constructed whenever their owners can assemble enough money for the next stage. Many private houses still have the concrete skeletons of additional stories yet to be completed, or piles of construction materials outside their gates, sometimes for years on end. Burri is like that: a mixture of humble houses prematurely weathered by sand and sun, high-rise apartment blocks and smart villas with shiny gates, interspersed with vacant lots—stakes in the future, purchased as an investment by someone who hasn't mustered the funds to begin pouring concrete foundations. It shows the hopes and disappointments of seven decades of Sudan's booms and busts, a concrete testament to how a new type of middle class whose intermittent income—determined by its precarious position in the global economy—sculpts the landscape of growing cities. In the 2000s, this corner of Khartoum became the most desirable of the city's inner suburbs. The 'garden city' to which it is joined enjoyed the smartened-up corniche, the villas built for visiting heads of state, and offices of telecom companies, as well as high-end residential villas and apartment complexes, eventually home to the SPA's headquarters during the first phase of the transitional period. Burri was becoming gentrified.

To the south is the prosperous neighbourhood known as Riyadh, built on the remittances of migrants from Saudi Arabia, also home to the leaders of the Islamic Movement. Across the river is Khartoum North, the nation's decrepit industrial centre and also the stronghold of the Democratic Unionist Party. Driving westward from Burri, one passes the army compound, the grid of the colonial city, said to be modelled on a Union Jack, with the university, ministries and palace, and commercial centre, before reaching the White Nile and the bridges to Omdurman, which is the historic centre for the Mahdists. Together these places mark the nodal points of the 'community of the state',[22] the socially cohesive but politically fractious class whose members rose to prominence in the late colonial period and who have ruled every one of Sudan's postcolonial governments. It is a community of internal tolerance, but one which excludes others—some subtly, some overtly—on the basis of geographical origin and skin colour. After generations of preferential access to education, members of this class will automatically rise to the top of any meritocratic system. Possessing both financial capital and the social connections needed to readily get business permits and land leases, they have benefited from Sudan's tiered labour system.

People from neighbourhoods such as Burri are also among the elite of the Sudanese diaspora. The Sudanese expatriate community is spread between the Arab states, Europe and North America, with a scattering elsewhere in the world. The first wave that travelled abroad were professionals and skilled construction workers drawn by offers of large salaries in the oil-rich Gulf states in the 1970s.[23] Sudan lost a huge proportion of its doctors, engineers and professors. A second exodus followed the economic implosion and political repression of the 1980s and especially the 1990s. Again, it was the professional classes that were most represented in the flight abroad.[24] In the last 15 years a third wave has followed, driven by war and deprivation in Darfur and elsewhere, braving the hazards of crossing the Sahara and the Mediterranean. Unlike the older diaspora, these migrants are mostly poor. It is from the more affluent, multilingual, skilled second-generation diaspora that many of the SPA's leaders were drawn.

Burri is the contemporary, cosmopolitan face of the community of the state, connected to each of the other nodes with its particular historic resonance and political colouring, but also semi-detached, its own microcosm of modernity. Not everyone in Burri is well off, but the neighbourhood shows few signs of the ruthless, predatory engine of material extraction that makes possible its relative affluence and its civic order.

In all directions, further out, Khartoum has expanded hugely, with mile after mile of dusty lower-income neighbourhoods and semi-planned squatter settlements. Khartoum has acted as a giant magnet drawing Sudanese people from every corner of the vast country. The reason is simple: the country's elite have invested their capital in the capital and neglected the peripheries. Worse, the Sudanese economic model has exploited the lands and peoples of those peripheries in a kind of giant Ponzi scheme, always drawing in new natural and human resources to feed its profits.[25] In the colonial era, the centrepiece of the economy was the Gezira scheme, the world's largest irrigated farm. Flying into Khartoum from the south is like flying over the Netherlands: an enormous artificial landscape of rectangular fields divided by irrigation dykes. The tenants on this scheme were Sudan's rural labour aristocracy; the labourers were migrants from as far away as Nigeria, more commonly from the western peripheries.[26] To the east and west of the Niles, the country's fertile clay plains were ploughed for the commercial farming of sorghum, the prairie-like fields expanding relentlessly decade by decade, eating up pastures, smallholder farms and bushland. This is a slow-motion dustbowl. The owners of the commercial leases grow sorghum (and sometimes sesame or groundnuts) as a monocrop, harvesting bounties and profits for a few years until the fertility of the land is exhausted. They hire farm managers, bulldozers, tractors and foremen, who in turn hire seasonal workers, many on the spot, others bussed in from the peripheries. The colonial authorities classified the peripheries, namely the southern provinces, Darfur, southern Kordofan and parts of Blue Nile, as 'closed districts' where government was bare-bones law and order—plus labour recruitment. Sudan was in fact its own microcosm of the economics of colonialism: a single country that contained both impoverished rural labour reserves (derisively referred to in southern Africa as 'Bantustans') and profitable enclaves of commercial investment.[27]

This economic model has gone through different permutations over the decades. It was colonial–capitalist, a developmental state run by technocrats, unbridled capitalism, socialist central planning, the 'breadbasket of the Arab world' drawing in Middle Eastern investors, then Islamist, and back to unbridled capitalism. At every stage it works by expanding the frontier of exploited land, relying on the bounty of nature. It is profitable by paying its workers as little as possible—enough to sustain a single man or woman, not a whole family, and thereby relying on subsidies from village farming or (occasionally) humanitarian aid. The labour force has soaked up West African migrants, poor villagers from the peripheries, refugees from the wars in Ethiopia and Eritrea, and, above all, displaced Sudanese and southern Sudanese from the civil wars and the unending mayhem of the peripheries. It's ecologically and socially unsustainable.[28]

The profits from this double over-exploitation support an urban lifestyle that resembles the middle class in Egypt or the Arabian Gulf. They eat imported wheat, drive imported cars, live in air-cooled villas and apartment blocks. This consumption economy draws the immiserated millions from the peripheries to the nation's capital, where they reproduce the country's economic and racial hierarchy within the span of a few hours' drive. The low-income neighbourhoods also generate their new, revolutionary projects, replicas of the de facto autonomous republics of rebel-held strongholds in Darfur and the Nuba hills within the boundaries of the capital. The city authorities and the security services, nervous of what such discontent might mean within marching distance of the seat of state power, developed policing mechanisms, notably the 'Popular Committees' that report to the party and intelligence officers. In turn, canny discontents subvert these structures to remain opaque to those in power. The most effective subversion was the spread of locally run neighbourhood or resistance committees.

Sudan's oil boom from 1999 to 2012 was a dazzling accentuation of this pattern. It enriched a few and fuelled an elite dream of becoming a petro-state. Oil put the established system into overdrive. Burri's twin on the western edge of old Khartoum—al-Mogran—was transformed into a mini-Dubai, with glittering skyscrapers for banks and oil companies. Burri's own residents included those who benefited from the spin-off boom in legitimate businesses: private hospitals, internet companies, construction and import–export firms.

And when the oil was gone, Sudan struck gold—a resource curse of a different kind. The artisanal gold mines drew hundreds of thousands, even millions, of young men to abandon agriculture and work in drudgery and to try their luck. Informal artisanal mining continued even in the areas where the Khartoum commercial elite, which couldn't grab the gold seams quickly enough, awarded concessions to foreign contractors.[29] In the far peripheries the prize went to the ruling militiamen who, like the sorcerer's apprentice, returned to their metropolitan master as a terrifying agent of vengeance.[30] That story will be picked up in the following chapter.

Sudan's layered, precarious urban terrain was both exploited and subverted by the protestors. The protestors knew their physical and social geography well, and they created a new cityscape as they took control of the streets, built their barricades and redirected traffic, used private spaces for public mobilisation, slipped in and out of alleyways to escape and outflank the security forces, and redecorated the walls and bridges of Khartoum. One commentator has called it 'nonviolent guerrilla cartography'.[31] Burri's neighbourhood was where Sudan's most influential 'resistance committee' emerged. These committees made common cause with those elsewhere in Khartoum and beyond, and were intimately linked to the diaspora leadership. The question that all needed to face was: what could hold them together?

Generations of Opposition

The SPA were the first of 22 signatories on the Declaration of Freedom and Change, issued on 1 January 2019.[32] The declaration had three goals. The first goal was 'The immediate and unconditional end of General Omar al-Bashir's presidency and the conclusion of his administration.' The second goal was the formation of a Transitional National Government to bring about peace, democracy, justice, women's rights, economic development: a nine-point catch-all manifesto that combined the claims of all the signatories. The third goal was the most immediately relevant to the uprising: an end to violations against peaceful protestors, removing all restrictions on freedoms of speech and expression, and bringing perpetrators of violence to trial.

None of these demands was new. Sudanese opposition parties had been making them for decades. For example, a constitutional conference had been the demand of the opposition in the 1980s. So, too, the demand for restructuring the civil service and the armed forces to be representative of the nation, a long-standing agenda from the peripheries championed by the SPLM and by Darfuri Islamists. The declaration can be read as a distilled version of the different transformative agendas espoused by the opposition. They wanted a civic revolution to remove the military from politics. They wanted peace and the rehabilitation of the war-ravaged areas. They wanted a nation-wide change bringing equal status to all the diverse peoples of the country. They wanted an end to kleptocracy and a modern open and competitive economy. There were numerous revolutions rolled into one—how they would fit together was a question that could be postponed.

Missing from the list was the agenda of abolishing Islamic law and establishing instead a secular state. It is an odd omission given that the SPA and the street protestors raged against a regime that was, in name and in its personnel, deeply Islamist.

In the list of signatories to the Declaration of Freedom and Change lay a core contradiction within the revolution. Although the SPA was the most powerful group, it decided to work in collaboration with just about the entire Sudanese political spectrum except the NCP and its fully paid-up clients. The list is a roll-call of three generations of Sudanese political leaders. The array of parties ranged from Sudan's conservative movements to the radically liberal but had one common goal—to overthrow al-Bashir. The question was: would that be enough to smooth over the fractious disagreements inside their new coalition, the Forces of Freedom and Change (FFC)?

After the SPA, the second on the list is the National Consensus Forces (NCF), a coalition of political parties including the National Umma Party, the Sudan Communist Party, and the Sudanese Ba'ath Party. Missing from this coalition is the Popular Congress Party (PCP)—al-Turabi's Islamists—who had split from them some years earlier. These represent the inter-generational continuity of the community of the state. These parties had come together in 2009 to call for democratic change. The Umma leader, Sadiq al-Mahdi, an aristocratic democrat, had over 40 years tried to reconcile whether he was champion of Sudan's modern nationalism or the Imam of the Mahdist Ansar sect. Twice prime minister (in the 1960s and 1980s), he refused, on a point of principle, any government office to which he was not elected. The Communists and Ba'athist parties were small, their leaders drawn from the leftist generation in which party discipline was among the highest virtues. Through dedication to mastering the procedures of setting meeting agendas and keeping minutes, they exercised influence far beyond their limited and ageing constituencies. The Sudan Communist Party had been banned in 1965, been in government from 1969 to 1971, and then savagely repressed;[33] it was unbanned in 2005. Four years after that it held its first congress for four decades and re-elected the same leadership; or, to be exact, those who were still alive. 'The Communist party aren't really communist—they just like to read a lot of books,' one SPA member joked. Indeed, their members' attachment was sentimental first and ideological second, if at all. The NCF was chaired by Farouk Abu Issa, who had served as foreign minister from 1969 to 1971, and whose name was forever associated with the 'Night of the Barricades' during the 1964 Revolution. The leaders of these parties are often seen as encapsulating the 'October generation'. We will reflect on their influence and legacy in Chapter 5.

Further down the list are some groups that belong with them as part of the 'modern forces', notably the trade unions and professional groups that led the 1964 protests, including the Alliance of Jezira and Managil Farmers and the Congress of University of Khartoum Alumni. Also signing up were political parties that hadn't joined the NCF for one reason or another, including the Unionist Alliance, the Republican Party and the Liberal Party. The Unionists were, even more than the National Umma Party, a legacy party. Formed around the Khatmiyya Sufi sect and led by the senior members of the al-Mirghani family—revered as the leaders of that sect—the Unionist party card was something one acquired at birth. The al-Mirghani family considered those from their sect who had become communists or Islamists as prodigal sons who would return one day and they were ready to indulge such political wanderings provided that the sect, its leaders and its estates were treated with respect.

For this older generation of civilian leaders, the question of religion and the state was unresolved. They were mostly urban secularists. However, the Islamisation of politics in Sudan since the 1980s had tapped into a popular sentiment that equated secularism with communist-style political atheism, which meant that their attitudes wouldn't achieve broad support. Those who led previous uprisings in 1964 and 1985 had burned themselves on this issue and tried to keep it safely insulated. This explains why the FFC didn't touch it in its foundational declaration.

The third name on the declaration is the Sudan Call, a coalition formed in 2014 that includes the National Consensus Forces, the Alliance of the Sudanese Civil Society Organisations and the Sudan Revolutionary Front (SRF). The SRF is itself a coalition of provincial armed groups: the SPLM–North (Malik Agar and Yasir Arman), the Justice and Equality Movement (JEM), and the Sudan Liberation Movement (SLM) (Minni Minawi). The SPLM–N and SLM are the direct inheritors of the tradition of leftist armed revolution spearheaded by the SPLM, founded with the goal of smashing the inherited racial hierarchy and its associated predatory capitalist system. Despairing of achieving this, or never truly believing it was possible in the first place, the main component of the SPLM went its own way to create the separate state of South Sudan. Also in this group is the JEM—the disaffected Islamists, who joined the SLM in insurrection in Darfur in 2003. The JEM manifesto was the 'Black Book', which enumerated the unequal distribution of power and wealth in Sudan by listing the origins of every political office holder or senior civil servant along with the inequities in budgetary provisions between centre and periphery. The JEM remedy was a simple equal sharing out of jobs and money. Overall, the SRF and the JEM are the generation that came of age in the 1983–2005 civil war, and, like the 1964 generation, fissiparous and quarrelsome, divided by personal ambition as much as by material interest or ideology.

The fact that the armed groups signed on to the declaration was important, as their predecessors (the Anyanya in 1964, the SPLM in 1985) had not been part of those civic revolutions. The fact that they stayed in the background was also significant: they didn't openly link their ongoing armed rebellions to the scrupulously non-violent movement in the cities, and therefore, while the regime attempted in the early days of the uprising to claim the uprising was being led by MOSSAD-backed rebels, they couldn't make this claim stick.[34] However, the way in which their cause of racial and geographical equality slipped down the protestors' agenda was to become a problem. These protagonists and their issues will recur in the following chapters.

The third political generation represented in the declaration is a kaleidoscope of activist organisations formed in the previous ten years. The oldest of these is the No to Women's Oppression Initiative, set up in 2009 in solidarity with the journalist Lubna al-Hussein, who wore trousers in public as a provocation to the continuing Islamism of the Popular Police and the courts applying the public order and decency codes, and won wide-ranging sympathy for her demand for equal rights and single-minded exposure of the Islamists' relentless petty-mindedness. Others could be called the Arab Spring generation, inspired to replicate those uprisings in Sudan. Prominent among them was Girifna ('We have had enough') and Change Now, both organisations of young people who were active in the 2013 protests. An alliance of 22 political and civic women's groups called MANSAM (Women of Sudanese Civic and Political Groups) signed. So did the Binaa Sudan Party, a recently formed 'transpartisan' party that sought technical, non-political solutions to the country's problems, and the Forum of Sudanese Tweeters. These groups—urban, linked to the diaspora, often led by women—were a new force in Sudanese politics, and played to a tune that the gerontocrats behind the walls of the military headquarters simply couldn't understand.

Although represented in principle and name, women's demands and the scope of their political participation after the revolutionary moment faded was tokenistic. International reporting of women's role was generous and often uncritical, and it concealed the gender hierarchies at play in politics and on the street. Women's physical presence in the street during the protests, their opinions and testimonies voiced as part of the revolutionary rhetoric and their feminist artistic expressions on murals, failed to translate into political credit during the months-long negotiations that gave birth to the transitional alliance. Overlooked and undermined within the community of the state, women of Sudan struggle to find alternative methods to push through their empowerment agendas, though inter-generational fissures, geographies of class and ethnicity, seem to have rewritten the terms of emancipation in the most unlikely ways, away from traditional feminist norms and more in line with a universal narrative of liberalisation.[35] These social shifts in gender relations will be explored in greater depth in Chapter 5.

The final signatory, number 22 on the list, was the Association of the Families of the Ramadhan Martyrs, which subsequently grew by orders of magnitude to absorb the families of youth who were killed in the 3 June massacre. In January 2019, this was a small but resolute group of families, whose sons had been summarily executed in June

1990 after al-Bashir and al-Turabi uncovered a coup plot. The plotters were Ba'athists. More importantly, they were well connected in the Khartoum elite, including the military. The killing of the 28 soldiers wasn't the largest massacre of the al-Bashir era by any stretch, but it represented an egregious violation of the code whereby members of the social elite did not kill one another, whatever their political differences. It was, reportedly, an atrocity that al-Bashir regretted. He certainly did his utmost to avoid repeating it, but the question always lingered: to what lengths would the president go to hold on to power in the face of a truly dangerous challenge? In putting their name to the Declaration of Freedom and Change, the families not only kept alive the names of the murdered officers but reminded Sudanese of the red line that al-Bashir and his henchmen had crossed on that day 28 years previously. In turn, their high standing among the community of the state meant that they dominated the agenda for transitional justice[36] after the fall of al-Bashir.

The SPA was keen for the older two generations of political opposition to sign on to the declaration, but they also wanted to keep them at arm's length. Everyone knew that the NCP had tolerated the old parties because they were so fractious and disorganised that it hardly needed to rig the polls: its superior organization and funding allowed it to coast to a landslide victory. And the parties were susceptible to being bought out outright by al-Bashir, who played off factions of opposition movements against each other. By the same token, individual SPA members kept their family ties and affections for those parties, even to the extent that they retained their membership. This was a familiar inconsistency from Sudan's previous revolutions, frustrating to those who wanted a more thorough cleansing of the country's political system, but a quietly valued source of socio-political resilience. Radical political disagreements could be managed by overlapping social and political affiliations. In the meantime, all could unite around the goal of removing al-Bashir.

This type of capillary association with the old and more liberal establishment wasn't possible with the provincial armed groups. The odd phrasing of the declaration's point 2.2 reflects this reality: 'Reach out to warring parties to address lingering issues and security arrangements.' The rebel movements had observer status in the uprising.

Two armed groups were not within the ambit of the declaration and they were the ones with the strongest constituencies. One was the SPLM–N of Abd al-Aziz al-Hilu, which had tenaciously held the mountains and allegiances of many of the Nuba people of southern Kordofan against military assault and political sell-out. Perhaps the most incorruptible man in Sudanese politics, and by the same token the most stubborn, Abd al-Aziz was a veteran SPLM commander who held fast to the SPLM's founding manifesto calling for a secular state, and who also demanded the right of self-determination for the marginalised peoples of Sudan. The 2005 CPA had awarded that right to the southern Sudanese, leading to their independence six years later, but for Abd al-Aziz and many Nuba, withholding self-determination from people who had similar historical, religious, ethno-cultural and political claims, was a double standard that could not be countenanced. The people of the Nuba and Blue Nile had, he argued, been betrayed by the CPA that included only a vague 'popular consultation' on their future status, an exercise which ultimately failed, leading to a new war in 2011. Abd al-Aziz argued, with impeccable logic, that secularism and self-determination were two sides of the same coin: he could concede on one, but only on the condition that the other was firmly guaranteed. He would neither concede on both nor agree to a formula that postponed the discussion to an unspecified future date and a process in which, he feared, the Nuba would once again be sold short. Abd al-Aziz's uncompromising position on these two issues struck right to the heart of the debate, unresolved since the creation of the first modern Sudanese nationalist movement almost a hundred years before, about the nature of the Sudanese nation and state. The 1924 White Flag League was led by a detribalised black Sudanese officer, Ali Abd al-Latif. Elena Vezzadini calls it 'Sudan's lost nationalism'—lost twice over, in the defeat of the movement and the manner in which its agenda and legacy were subsequently lost to the narrative of Sudan's political history.[37]

The other rebel who was outside the fold was Abd al-Wahid al-Nur of the Sudan Liberation Movement and Army (SLM/A). One of the founders of the armed Darfur resistance in 2003, Abd al-

Wahid had refused compromise but had gained a reputation as a 'hotel guerrilla' flitting from one exile to another, his ambition far surpassing his political skill, but nonetheless retaining the backing of fighters in Darfur's Jebel Marra Mountains and displaced people in Darfur's vast camps.

In the meantime, the SPA focused on the one consensus demand: *Tasgut, bas!* Al-Bashir must go. This agenda was its strength in the short term and its weakness thereafter. As a result, the SPA also embraced a leaderless structure. The power of the organisation was not in its authority at the top but in the numbers it was able to mobilise at the bottom.

The SPA was really an assemblage of smaller groups. The political ecology of repression meant that natural selection moulded an effective revolutionary structure—dispersed, resilient and usually opaque to the intelligence services. It meant that the fire of al-Bashir's persecution forged organisations to be structured in ways that could survive in the brutal heat: groups that were leaderless, small and cellular in structure. A mapping of the revolutionary associations would look like a tangled yarn ball. Each union within the SPA had smaller committees, to deal with matters such as spokespeople and recruitment. Then there were committees to liaise between each union, including social media committees for the SPA, the recruitment of other unions and for planning what to do after al-Bashir fell. Critically, neighbourhood groups were forming across Khartoum and then across the country with the goal of toppling the regime. They called themselves resistance committees. Personal ties made them work: individuals' networks were used to bring protestors on to the streets when called, and to support them on march days. The SPA was careful to keep its organisation secret so that it could not be infiltrated. Most meetings were done virtually. Members of the central SPA committee used foreign WhatsApp numbers to keep their Sudanese identities hidden. Email accounts with fake names were created. Many members in senior positions actually didn't know each other; each committee organised on its own and they operated a shadow system where each role had a readied line of succession. The SPA was a faceless organisation that posted the protest schedule on social media, with only a handful of visible members who served as spokespeople and who were mostly living outside the country.

Elusive Nationalism, Chameleon Revolutions

The Declaration of Freedom and Change was issued on New Year's Day 2019. The timing was a conscious appeal to Sudanese awareness of their history and was the first in a series of anniversaries that resonate among the country's democratic activists and which punctuate the calendar year. Each of these dates evokes memories or, more precisely, a shared story of what earlier generations of activists achieved, and what they failed to achieve.

New Year's Day is Sudan's independence day, achieved in 1956. It is celebrated, of course, but independent Sudan's foundational event itself was also anticlimactic and ambiguous. Sudan removed the British as the result of a parliamentary manoeuvre by then-Prime Minister Ismail al-Azhari, seeking (with only temporary success) to forestall the collapse of his coalition. Until today, Sudanese cannot agree on whether this date represents the creation of a new nation, the resurrection of an old one (the Mahdist state of the late 19th century) or a false dawn in which one form of occupation was replaced by another (the southern Sudanese, who mark 9 July 2011 as their independence). Al-Azhari promised that Sudanese self-determination was something else entirely, namely a step towards the 'unity of the Nile Valley', that is union with Egypt.

These are the dimensions along which Sudanese nationalism has been contested: a vision for the future, an inheritance from the past, and a geography of belonging or exclusion. Sudan's nationalists and revolutionaries have disagreed on which of these dimensions is most important, as well as on what they mean. The country's three great civic revolutions have each been inspired by a vision of a transformed Sudan; each has been captured by those who wanted to preserve a historical legacy; none has properly confronted the unresolved politics of identity.

Meanwhile, there is also a forgotten revolution: the uprising of 1924, which was the forerunner of all secular nationalist movements in Sudan. Among the reasons for its neglect has been the identity of its leaders. Ali Abd al-Latif was a soldier who had mixed northern and southern heritage, and the members of the White Flag movement were ethnically heterogeneous, united in their demand for self-determination.[38] At that time, the British used the term 'Sudanese' in an ambiguous manner, one sense referring to inhabitants of the territory, and another to those who were neither 'Arab' nor members of a specified tribal entity. In this latter sense, 'Sudanese' belonged to an emergent but subordinate class, notably men of junior rank in the army, who were black. Over the following decades, the name 'Sudanese' migrated across the social and colour spectrums to become associated with the dominant class. This shift shows how Sudanese identity has historically been reassembled. The mason's marks of that construction were bared for all to see during the 2019 uprising. Some of these are scars acknowledged by all, but others not. As the Sudanese–South Sudanese scholar and diplomat, Francis Deng, memorably insisted: 'What is not said is what divides us.'[39]

The meanings of 'nationalism', 'self-determination' and 'Sudanese' have themselves changed over a century, just as the context of those words has transformed. Nonetheless, in the challenges posed by Ali Abd al-Latif and the colonial authorities' response we can trace the lineage of the groups that contest for power today.

The British suppressed Sudan's first nationalist movement. In its wake it formalised and intensified a neo-traditional form of governance known as 'native administration' that turned local chiefs and provincial aristocrats into district despots, also providing local government on the cheap. It was a 'care and maintenance'[40] system that doubled as pre-emptive counter-nationalism: people defined by tribe weren't likely to organise as militant modernists. But British rule also needed subaltern technocrats, and, especially after expelling Egyptians in the wake of the 1924 uprising, those had to be Sudanese. The colonial investment of infrastructure and production was restricted to the central, riverain areas of northern Sudan: the vast Gezira irrigation scheme, the middle reaches of the Nile, Khartoum, and a corridor to Port Sudan. Investment in training a subaltern class of bureaucrats, technicians and teachers was concentrated on those areas too, so that Sudan's late colonial modernity acquired its particular geographical and racial contours.

They became known as the '*effendiya*' class, united by an ethos of technocratic economic development and institution-building. When these men looked at Sudan, they saw a landscape replete with possibility: the Nile could be re-engineered for transformational irrigation projects, the savannas could be ploughed for mechanised farms, the towns along the railway line could build their modern industries.[41] The term 'modern forces' that came to the fore during the 1964 revolution arose from that lineage.

In the aftermath of the 1924 revolution, the British also switched their strategic political alliances. Until then, they had most feared a revival of Mahdism, the Islamic revivalist movement that had swept to power in the 1880s, defeating Egypt and killing the British general Charles Gordon in Khartoum. After the challenge of a modernising nationalism identifying with Egypt's call for self-determination, the British co-opted the neo-traditional patrician class, notably Sayyid Abdel Rahman al-Mahdi, posthumous son of the man who had defeated the imperialists a generation earlier.[42] The mechanism of co-option was blatantly mercenary: the spiritual and political leader would become Sudan's leading agricultural capitalist. His traditional rival—the leader of the Khatmiyya sect, Sayyid Ali al-Mirghani, who had sided with the Egyptians in the previous generation—had precisely the same conservative–capitalist political–economic interests, in his case mostly in trade. The two formed the biggest political parties, the Umma Party and the Nationalist Unionist Party. They are sometimes referred to as 'sectarian' parties because of their close ties to particular religious orders: the neo-Mahdist Ansar and Khatmiyya Sufi sects, respectively.

The *effendiya* class was trained in Gordon Memorial College (founded in 1902) and three prominent secondary schools, Hantoub (Wad Medani), Wadi Sayyidna (Omdurman) and Khor Tagat (al-Ubayyid).[43] These modernisers were not, for the most part, revolutionaries. Rather they retained their familial and political ties to the sectarian parties. Ideological incompatibilities were muted by social affinities, mutual tolerance and the practice of postponing the hardest decisions.

Sudan achieved self-government in 1953 with a parliamentary system. State institutions were 'Sudanised', which meant the takeover of jobs held by colonial officials by members of this *effendiya* class. There were few from Darfur and the Nuba Mountains and just a handful from southern Sudan. They saw themselves as stewards of Sudan's developmental state. Their core concern was to bolster Gross Domestic Product through economic activities that were easily measurable, and as such they prioritised developing the export-orientated cotton economies that had first emerged in the Anglo–Egyptian colonial period (1899–1956), and they marginalised pastoralist and smallholder livelihoods that were less readily quantifiable.[44] The cotton economy, as well as the railway sector that supported the export of cotton, came to be increasingly unionised and, alongside the growing professional class, constituted the main support base for the Sudan Communist Party.

In December 1955, Prime Minister Ismail al-Azhari tried to hold together his fractious parliamentary coalition with a vote for immediate independence. He won the vote and the Union Jack was hauled down for the last time at midnight on 31 December, making New Year's Day 1956 Sudan's independence day. But, as mentioned, there wasn't agreement on what independence meant. Al-Azhari's government didn't last long and his successor, Abdalla Khalil (himself a former soldier), arranged for the army to step in and take power in 1958. General Ibrahim Abboud became Sudan's first Sudanese military ruler, a neo-colonial authoritarian.

It should be no surprise that Sudanese don't agree on the meaning of 'revolution'—*thawra* in Arabic. They use it in a protean manner. Postcolonial Sudan has had other, more sanguinary revolutions, some of them counter-revolutions, depending on one's political leaning. The 1958 military coup was an establishment counter-revolution, relatively efficient in its metropolitan repression but the driver of the escalating war in southern Sudan. There are two other dates, celebrated (at least officially for as long as the protagonists were in power) and mourned (widely and unofficially). One is 25 May, the date of the 1969 'May Revolution', led by a coalition of communists and radical 'Free Officers'. This was a leftist coup in the Nasserite mould, which attempted a far-reaching social revolution. The second date is 30 June, the day in 1989 when Brigadier Omar al-Bashir seized power, proclaiming the 'National Salvation Revolution.' This was a social revolution in the Islamist mould, a reactionary counter-revolution as far as the democratic and civic forces were concerned. The diversity of these military coups, and sharp disagreements over what to call them, points once again to the contested nature of Sudan's national narrative.

The anniversary most cherished by three generations of Sudanese civic nationalists is 21 October: the date on which non-violent protests forced the resignation of General Abboud. The 'October Revolution' is seen as Sudan's 'real' nationalist moment.[45] Speaking to a rally on that anniversary in 2019, the then transitional prime minister, Abdalla Hamdok, told the crowds that the date represented 'a qualitative starting point in the field of the Sudanese Popular Revolutions'.[46] The protestors were calling upon the transitional government to sweep aside the remnants of the al-Bashir regime, just as their grandparents had demanded the removal of a regime that was too redolent of imperial rule. The 1964 uprising wrote the script for the 1985 uprising that overthrew President Jafa'ar Nimeiri. And the 1964 and 1985 uprisings were in turn an important reference point for all the movements of protest against al-Bashir's regime, including the failed 2013 uprising.

To that date is added 17 January, the date of the first street protest under the leadership of the SPA in 2019. The day also commemorated the death of Mustafa Sid Ahmed, popular musician and staunch critic of the Islamist regime, who died in exile in 1996. Also on that day in 2013, Mahmoud Abd al-Aziz, icon of opposition to al-Bashir's ironically named 'Salvation' regime and mouthpiece of the generation born under it, died at the age of 40. That day was also when the protests reached a point from which, in retrospect, there could be no turning back.

The Tide of People's Power

The demonstrations continued to grow on their own in the first weeks of January. The marches were scrupulously non-violent. On 17 January 2019, NISS agents unleashed a campaign of thuggery—the biggest show of intimidation to date. As with so many events in the dying months of al-Bashir's rule, it is not clear who gave the order and why. Did the security chiefs truly fear that a revolution was in the air? Were they playing an inside game (for example, being the one to show resolve, or causing a mini-crisis to put the blame on a rival) to gain factional advantage inside al-Bashir's court? Did they plan to isolate and co-opt the organisers? In retrospect, these questions don't matter much: political agency had passed to the women and men on the street. This hadn't happened for 35 years, perhaps even longer. Politicians—tired old veterans, ambitious courtiers, scheming revolutionaries—were not in charge.

That day, Mubarak, the SPA spokeswoman, watched police grab at protestors like they were animals and smash their heads in. 'The beatings that I saw that day was something that I will never forget,' Samahir recalled. 'They did not differentiate between boys and girls, old and young.'[47] Khartoum was boiling with confusion and death and rage. Worshippers leaving a mosque were teargassed. The chants of 'Down! Down! Enough!' rang through Khartoum.

Dr Babiker Abd al-Hamid Salama, who lived in Burri, died that day. The resistance committee in Buri was one of the most active and, perhaps more than anywhere else, people in the neighbourhood had opened their gates to the young protestors on the street, helping them in their game of hide-and-seek with the security forces. Dr Babiker was on the streets, providing emergency care for injured protestors in the streets near his home, and he asked security officers for permission to transport them to hospital. They shot him dead.

Another man, Moawia Osman, was also shot dead in Burri. The community in Burri turned this killing into a symbol of their confrontation, mobilising the city's middle class.

Funerals of slain protestors are a common flashpoint for escalating popular uprisings. Both the simple fact of the gathering and the issue it represents, indeed personifies, are an accelerant to protest. The event organises itself. As was demonstrated at a comparable crucial moment in the 1964 uprising—the funeral procession for the martyred student Ahmad al-Qurayshi—it is almost impossible for the authorities to ban a funeral and very hard to limit who shows up and how they behave. They cannot co-opt it and if they repress it they complicate their quandary. The Sudanese government got it exactly wrong: they allowed the funeral to go ahead and deployed nervous armed policemen. Around 5,000 people attended Moawia's funeral and threw stones at the police, who responded by shooting at the crowd with live ammunition.[48] Although there were no reported casualties, the bloodless tactics of attacking a funeral was shocking. Videos of brutality were shared on WhatsApp and social media. The stakes were rising. The event solidified the commitment of core SPA members and helped bring Sudanese who were on the fence about the protests over to the side of revolutionaries.

Women made up a visible number of the protestors and led chants in the marches. They had been restricted and repressed by the Islamists. Public order codes kept women at home, or in school or college, or in office employment. Their brothers were expected to go for military service and earn an income. Ironically, this meant that a generation of young women were better educated than their male peers, but also shut out of economic opportunity and political participation. The earlier generations of political leaders were overwhelmingly male, and unsurprisingly the armed groups were almost exclusively led by men. The third generation of heterodox activists did, however, comprise many women, even though the top leadership of the SPA was predominantly male. Aware that they needed to create a domestic and international impression of female leadership inside the SPA, the organisation deliberately sought out female spokespeople who spoke Arabic and English.

As marches continued in February, the regime's security began to flush out the SPA ranks. NISS agents targeted the Communist Party. Slowly NISS closed in on the SPA leadership and in February finally arrested al-Assam and Yousif, its most prominent public members. While they were in prison, the head of NISS, Salah 'Gosh', paid them a visit. Those whom Gosh talked with said that the spy chief first tried to see if he could co-opt the leaders and smother the protests. But Gosh discovered that the leaderless movement could not be bought off so easily. The movement was too decentralised and had taken on a life of its own. These SPA and political leaders say that Gosh changed course and they speculated that the spy chief was trying to create alliances in the event that al-Bashir fell, an eventuality he might also discreetly try to bring about. 'He was basically selling himself as an alternative to Bashir,' said a protest leader.

Gosh was trapped in his own way of thinking: men of his generation would calculate the odds and the rewards and would act rationally according to that logic. For such a master of the political marketplace, it was simply unthinkable that a mass of people would follow a different logic—the logic we here call 'civicness'. He was caught by surprise. So, too, were foreign diplomats and African leaders. They, too, expected political business as usual. Members of the SPA recall how the United States and other Western nations didn't only remain on the sidelines during the revolution, but actively discouraged the protestors. Yousif later recalled how an official from the US embassy in Khartoum, Wallace Bain, tried to convince him to end the protests because they were not large enough.[49] A senior US official in the American special envoy's office at the time, Brian Shukan, celebrated Sudanese independence day with Mohamed Atta, then the top Sudanese official in Washington DC but also, and more to the point, a former director of NISS. Outside the event some 100 protestors demonstrated against Atta and the government. 'Stop shooting peaceful protesters in Sudan,' one sign read. In his stint as security chief it was Atta who commanded the forces that broke up the 2013 protests that killed 200 people. The American position was a disturbing signal for Sudanese activists.[50] At the time, the US was in the midst of normalising relations with Sudan and taking the country off Washington's state sponsor of terror list.[51]

NISS was gathering better intelligence on the SPA and was analysing its structure and organisation. But the SPA also had its own intelligence on what was happening within the citadel. Al-Bashir, his security cabal and his cronies were ageing. Junior members of the regime were also greying, and in some cases their own children were among the protestors. One major general told of his daughter coming home after joining marchers who congregated within sight of her father's office. 'Don't shoot us, dad,' she said. The capillaries of the revolution penetrated the social circle of the regime, and that included officers in the army. The SPA didn't expect to persuade the top army leadership, but it could make them think twice by influencing their subordinates and their families. In February, the SPA's social media platforms called on military officers to defect and stand with the people. The SPA had the details of the roster for the deployment of army units and called on the officers on duty to refuse orders.

The SPA leaders knew from Sudan's history—as well as experience elsewhere—that the crucial inflection point would come when the military abandoned the regime. Choosing when to press this decision was both delicate and high stakes. The date they chose was 6 April, the anniversary of the 1985 revolution against Nimeiri when General Abd al-Rahman Siwar al-Dahab announced the army's decision to 'side with the people'. Escalating the protest on that day sent a signal of how the Sudanese should expect the uprising to end—with the army joining the revolution to popular acclaim. In 1985, the protestors had marched on the Republican Palace, and the army could, in principle, stand back. This time the protestors needed to face down the army itself. In 1985, President Nimeiri was out of town (he flew to Washington DC). In 2019, President al-Bashir was at home, within the walls of the military compound itself. The SPA called for a million-person march in front of the army headquarters. 'The street work was done and work within the communities was done,' said Sara Abd al-Jalil, a spokeswoman for the SPA.

Samahir, another SPA spokeswoman, went to Khartoum Two on 6 April. Like Burri, it is an old inner suburb, close to the military headquarters. It has towering green trees that provide shade at the central market. The marches were supposed to begin at one o'clock in the afternoon but Samahir only saw barren streets. The neighbourhood was waiting for a specific signal: the third time someone yelled 'Freedom, peace and justice.' When protestors flushed from their homes, Samahir travelled with them to the military headquarters.

The 6 April march didn't dislodge al-Bashir, but the SPA intensified the pressure with a new tactic, similar to the Tahrir Square occupation in Cairo in 2011. The idea was to surround the centre of power: the military headquarters and al-Bashir's home. Meanwhile, the Republican Palace on the Blue Nile—both the colonial-era building and the new Chinese extravaganza—were quiet. Demonstrators coming from Omdurman passed it by on the road to confront the real power in the land.

The large space in front of the military headquarters became a city within a city, a non-stop celebration of a vision of a transformed Sudan. Hundreds of thousands of demonstrators transformed a square mile of streets and buildings into a permanent sit-in to show their democratic commitment. There is speculation that NISS officers stood aside and let the protestors congregate, when they could have sealed off the approaches; or, quite possibly, the security leaders were too preoccupied with their own politicking that they failed to appreciate they had definitively lost control. Imagine a giant festival plopped down in the middle of a city, with streets cordoned off, glowing lights, and hollering at all hours. Later, yellow signs were placed at the entrances that apologised for the extra traffic caused by the sit-in. 'Sorry for the delay,' they read. 'Uprooting a regime.'

They succeeded. They removed al-Bashir. It was a beautiful revolution, a near-perfect non-violent show of people's power, universally resonant and uniquely Sudanese. It also contained within it the hierarchies and tensions of the country's troubled geography, history and unresolved questions of identity.

2

REAPING THE WHIRLWIND
THE FALL OF AL-BASHIR

For 29 years, President Omar al-Bashir defied predictions of his imminent fall. He faced determined efforts by internal rivals and external foes to bring down his regime or remove him personally. Even the president's closest aides were baffled by his political longevity.[1] They speculated about why al-Bashir seemed immune from normal political logic. One focused on his encyclopaedic knowledge of people as individual persons. The president knew the members of the army's officer corps, the provincial aristocracy (the so-called 'Native Administration'), and the Khartoum political class one by one; he remembered their names and the names of their family members; he was uncommonly convivial and a generous and amusing host; and, perhaps most crucially, he guarded his reputation for not crossing the line of ordering their deaths.

Another of his aides insisted that al-Bashir lacked the flaw so common to dictators: hubris. The president was keenly aware of the limits of his power and learned to husband it with care. Indeed, the fact that he had so many narrow escapes meant that he never became too comfortable or too ready to believe that he possessed special powers. He did not set out to mould Sudan in his image, and insofar as the regime came to resemble him, it was through a slow and incremental mutual adaptation between ruler, ruling apparatus, and the turbulent tide of events. Over the years, too, al-Bashir's close entourage became skilled at managing his propensity to impulsiveness and anger. For example, they chose carefully how to break the news to him that the Prosecutor of the International Criminal Court was going to seek an arrest warrant against him for crimes committed in Darfur—for two days after he learned this he was raging and unapproachable.

All agreed on a third explanation: al-Bashir was lucky.

On 10 April 2019, al-Bashir ran out of luck. He was removed, swiftly and bloodlessly, by all his senior lieutenants acting in unison. The coup was led by a man of, until that moment, unquestioned loyalty: First Lieutenant General Ahmad Awad Ibn Auf, Minister of Defence and (for the previous seven weeks) First Vice President. Acting as Chairman of the Higher Security Council, Ibn Auf convened a meeting with all the senior military, security and police officials. Of these men, just two could have vetoed the coup. Both held the rank of lieutenant general although neither had formal military training. The director of NISS, Salah Abdalla Gosh, was renowned for ambition and conspiracy. Feared by all and trusted by none, he had come tantalisingly close to snatching the prize at least twice before. Had al-Bashir wanted a capable and ruthless heir apparent, he needed to look no further than Gosh, but the president recoiled from taking the step that might have given him the best chance of securing his legacy. Al-Bashir was probably afraid of what Gosh might do to his former master after he had left office. The second potential veto-holder was Mohamed 'Hemedti' Hamdan Dagolo, a Darfurian militia commander who had risen from modest origins to become commander of the Rapid Support Forces (RSF), the paramilitary force that had grown to rival the Sudan Armed Forces (SAF) in combat capability. Nicknamed 'Hemedti'—the endearing 'little Mohamed' that a mother uses for her child on account of his youthful demeanour—the Darfurian militiaman and trader was a newcomer to the security cabal. Making a play on his nickname, al-Bashir was reported to call him *himayti*, 'my protector'. The president was using the autocrat's handbook and entrusting his political security to a man who came to Khartoum without a support network there and who did not fit the profile of any Sudanese coup-maker. But Gosh and Hemedti assented to the coup, making it a collusive takeover.

The trigger for the coup that brought down al-Bashir was an action that he took that violated his own code. The reason for this fatal misstep was that he had lost touch with his core constituency among the officer corps. That evening, the formidable walled compound that comprised the SAF headquarters, Ministry of Defence, and al-Bashir's personal residence had been blockaded for four days and nights by Sudan's largest-ever sit-in. The demonstrators were more disciplined and unified than the encircled security apparatus, which was visibly fractious and indecisive.

The security cabal that surrounded al-Bashir had always been torn by rivalries, but over the preceding months their calculus had shifted from the question of who would wield most power within that court, to who would succeed the president when his term in office expired little more than a year hence, scheduled for April 2020. In February, those divisions burst into the open with the declaration of a state of emergency. The backdrop to the emergency powers decree were the resilient mass protests, which had, contrary to expectations, lasted three months without losing energy, and the deepening economic crisis, which was one of the main reasons why hundreds of thousands of Sudanese had taken to the streets. The specific reason for the decree was that al-Bashir's stratagem for staying in power beyond 2020 had failed.

Under the Interim Constitution, adopted in 2005 following the Comprehensive Peace Agreement (CPA), the president was entitled to two five-year terms. The first election under that constitution was held in April 2010, and the second in April 2015. Al-Bashir won both handily, chiefly because the National Congress Party (NCP) so thoroughly corrupted the political playing field that competitors operated at a huge disadvantage. His term limit would therefore expire in April 2020. But, following a well-trodden path of elected authoritarians, the president had begun a process of amending the constitution to allow him to run again. On 22 February, he abandoned that effort. The probable reasons were that his closest internal allies and his financial backers in the Middle East told him that he had stayed long enough: they were about to run out of patience. Because al-Bashir was desperately low on the political funds he needed to pay out to keep his subordinates and rivals in line, he submitted. The emergency decree also suspended the NCP, removed the civilian governors of the states (all members of the NCP) and replaced them with military men, and imposed other arbitrary measures such as a ban on demonstrations. He dismissed his vice president, Lieutenant General Bakri Hassan Saleh, a man of ample devotion to his boss but sorely devoid of political skills, and promoted General Ibn Auf in his stead. Most significantly, on that day al-Bashir out-manoeuvred Gosh. The president delayed his own announcement just long enough for Gosh to fall into the trap of making his own premature statement of the state of emergency, thereby sharply illuminating his putschist ambitions.

The decisions of 22 February meant that al-Bashir's tenure in office now had just 14 months to run. One of the features of a political system like Sudan's—centralised and patrimonial, dominated by transactional scheming at the top—is that the last months of a dictator are the most dangerous for him. This may be counter-intuitive but it is explicable. The reason is that any political commitment he undertakes will only be good for that short period. According to the laws of the political market, the value of time-limited contracts is discounted, and therefore the credibility of the chief buyer of allegiances is diminishing. Al-Bashir needed either to designate a successor with undisputed loyalty, pay out higher amounts to the bidders, or turn to repression. The president had no heir apparent. He had no biological children, so a republican dynasty was not an option. Members of the security cabal possessed either loyalty or political skill, not both simultaneously. (Hemedti was to prove the dark horse, underestimated by his peers.) Al-Bashir's money was running out: after his arrest, the leaders of the Transitional Military Council announced that currency worth about US$ 130 million was discovered in his house. As far as the press and the public were concerned, the former president had been caught red-handed. Among the political operators of the Middle East, the surprise was that the cash was so little: the verdict was that his political funds were desperately low. His last option, a turn to violence, entailed enormous risks.

Al-Bashir had 'coup-proofed' his regime, by the well-honed technique of ensuring that no single arm of the military–security establishment could mount a putsch without risking a shootout with the others. The SAF and NISS had more or less balanced each other but, in the 2008–11 period, NISS became dangerously strong, and its capabilities were trimmed back. From 2013 onwards, al-Bashir promoted Hemedti and the RSF as a counterbalance to both SAF and NISS. The only coup that could safely remove the president was one in which all three security arms acted together. That seemed most unlikely.

After February, the jockeying for position among al-Bashir's lieutenants was now in the open. The president had long relied on being every aspiring leader's second-choice candidate. Unless the path to seizing state power was fully assured, the would-be putschist would stick with the status quo. It was much preferable to have al-Bashir in power than any rival contender. The main reason for this was the assurance that al-Bashir might send you into the political wilderness for a while, or even send you to jail, but he wouldn't kill you or hand you over to a foreign power. None of the generals had the same confidence in any other leader—and certainly not in Gosh.

Meanwhile, focused on palace intrigue, the rivals severely underestimated the FFC's cohesion and the people's commitment. They thought they could manipulate the protest movement in support of their own schemes.

Two cracks within the regime became particularly important. One was that NISS did not utilise all its instruments of sowing discord and demoralisation, which had been used so effectively during previous demonstrations in 2013. The SPA and FFC had learned from the mistakes, but it also appears that Gosh was desisting from using his arsenal to full effect because he thought he would be able to capitalise on the protests in pursuit of his own power grab. The most important thing that Gosh did not do was to deploy units to stop the protestors converging on the streets immediately outside military headquarters in April. It is widely believed that NISS officers could have prevented the crowds occupying this strategic spot, but were instructed to stand aside.[2]

The second crack was that the regime's armed units did not use massive force against the protestors. Since the regular army 'sided with the people' during the 1985 uprising, it had not been deployed to suppress urban protests. Senior officers realised that if they gave orders to fire, those orders would not be followed. The people on the street included some sons and daughters, nephews and nieces of the senior ranks in the army, and many more of the children of their colleagues and classmates. Sudanese metropolitan society is close-knit across all political divides, and any battalion commander who ordered his troops to shoot the children of his friends would be ostracised.

If the army wouldn't shoot, would paramilitary and security institutions do so? The security forces had deliberately recruited unscrupulous men from the social margins, and Hemedti's RSF was overwhelmingly from Darfur. Through lack of moral scruple or social ties to urban society, would they be more ruthless? As it turned out, in June, this proved to be the case. But during al-Bashir's last weeks, it seemed that none was ready to sully their reputations with an atrocity on behalf of a ruler who was running down the clock.

Al-Bashir was well aware of the limitations, contrived and imposed, on his key military and security institutions. He spied on the spies and he kept up his tradition of twice-weekly open house for the officer corps. Any commissioned officer in SAF could call on the president on one of those evenings, either just to sit and chat with those who turned up, or with a specific request for personal help from the field marshal himself. Al-Bashir knew the intrigues and was a step ahead of even Gosh. What he didn't know was what anyone under the age of thirty was thinking: his antennae picked up every tremor among the established political class, but not among their children.

The SPA may not have had a comparable organised intelligence system to scrutinise what was happening inside the regime, but it knew enough. The SPA leaders were all in touch with members of the security apparatus through relatives and schoolfriends. The huge numbers of security and military personnel had become a liability for the regime. The divisions and hesitations within the security cabal were on full display. Units made forays into the crowd and opened fire, but other units then took the side of the protestors. The unity and resolve of the demonstrators were strengthened. What could have been a year-long negotiated transition to al-Bashir's constitutional successor was instead becoming a power vacuum. This was the moment at which the African Union and other international actors, which had long sought to engineer peaceful political change in Sudan, could have played an active role in managing the president's graceful departure. But they sat on the sidelines, expecting the demonstrations to blow over.

On the evening of 10 April, al-Bashir decisively lost control. According to the story that then circulated, he ordered that the sit-in be dispersed by force and prepared a *fatwa* from his main Salafi cleric, Abdel Hai Yousif, who also served as lead for the regime's Islamic Fiqh council, to the effect that it was permissible to kill 30% of the demonstrators to preserve order. If even partly true,[3] what this implied for the heads of the security apparatus was clear: al-Bashir was going down in a bloodbath and was going to take them all down with him. He was flagrantly violating the norm against elite murder. Killing thousands in faraway Darfur or southern Sudan was permissible according to this elite code; slaughter of the children of the elite in the centre of Khartoum was not. And the regime was already transgressing this boundary, killing prominent members of the neighbourhood resistance committees, including doctors and professionals with high standing among their communities.

General Ibn Auf immediately convened a meeting of the Higher Security Committee, which included the chiefs of staff of SAF, the director of NISS, the commander of RSF, and the police chief. A general commented afterwards that the spirit of the meeting was, 'If we don't have him for dinner he will have us for breakfast.' Ibn Auf insisted that the coup be a collective takeover and that he lead it. That would minimise the risk of violence among the rivalrous security institutions. It would also postpone for 24 hours the reckoning over the key question of who would take over: the generals naively assumed that once al-Bashir had gone, the sit-in would disperse. Ibn Auf has not spoken about his intentions. In the event it allowed him to serve as head of state for a day, giving him the protection afforded to a former president as well as a casting vote in determining the succession. Ibn Auf duly made the announcement, and while the demonstrators celebrated—and refused to yield—the security chiefs embroiled themselves in a conspicuously shambolic process of deciding what to do next. The most important decision was that Gosh was out and Hemedti was in, though for reasons of rank and decorum the RSF commander would serve as deputy to General Abdel Fattah al-Burhan, so that SAF retained formal seniority. The most probable explanation for this was that Ibn Auf trusted Hemedti, with whom he was in contact through his relative and the third man in the RSF, al-Sadiq Sayyid,[4] more than he trusted Gosh. Gosh had hoped to stake a place for himself within the new order, but removed himself under pressure from both the street and his opponents in the Saudi government.[5]

This narrative of the 'real politics' drama makes sense against the backdrop of the structural shifts that brought a functional centralised kleptocracy to its knees. There are two elements to this: money and guns.

Sudan's Turbulent Political Marketplace

The 'political marketplace' refers to a contemporary version of a transactional political system. It is one in which power (political office, political services and political allegiances) is a commodity that can be traded on a monetised basis, and the formal institutions of government are subordinate to the bargaining among the elite over their immediate transactions. The key operational concepts of the political marketplace include the 'political budget', which is the funds available for the politician to dispense to buy political commodities, and the 'price of loyalty', which is the going rate for such purchases.[6]

Sudan transformed from an institutional state to a political marketplace in a series of jerky steps in the 1970s and 1980s. During the debt-funded boom of the 1970s, corruption ran rampant and the Islamists re-entered politics using the leverage of Islamic finance. In the 1980s, deep economic crisis led to a situation in which the government was unable to fund its basic operating budget, so that government basically collapsed in many rural areas, such as Darfur and most of southern Sudan. President Jafa'ar Nimeiri undertook one of the world's earliest large-scale privatisation programmes, eagerly pursuing the recommendations of the World Bank and IMF beyond even the prescriptions of those famously orthodox financial institutions. He saw more astutely than the Washington economists did that selling state assets to crony capitalists was a way of transitioning to a system of patrimonial governance—institutionalising kleptocracy or putting corruption to work politically.

Nimeiri ran out of money to grease the wheels of his patrimonial system. By the end of 1984, the sums needed to bail out his political budget had simply become too large for his patrons in Washington DC.[7] The Treasury refused to pay. But the State Department valued Sudan more highly than the Treasury, and the Administration wavered. Nimeiri flew to the US and met with President Ronald Reagan, who was persuaded to bail him out. Too late: the cheque was in the mail and Nimeiri was in the air returning home when the trade union leaders in the popular uprising took over the control tower at Khartoum Airport and closed Sudanese airspace. Nimeiri landed in Cairo, and General Siwar al-Dahab announced that the army had sided with the people.

Nimeiri's strategy of cannibalising the state for personal and factional survival involved bringing the army into commerce. Although his proposed Military Economic Board (modelled on Egypt) was vetoed by the World Bank, nonetheless the imbrication of military officers and trade became well established. As the war in southern Sudan re-ignited, and the fiscal means for financing a conventional counter-insurgency did not exist, Nimeiri began subcontracting military operations to militia. Under his successors, the 'militia policy' of 'counter-insurgency on the cheap' dismantled the army's monopoly on legitimate violence. The Islamists seized on this: they distrusted the army and wanted to develop their own ideologically aligned military force. The fact that the Islamist and Ansar fighters of the National Front, who had fought Nimeiri in 1976, had been carelessly demobilised (and not properly disarmed) and were among those most readily mobilised to lead militia units against the SPLA in the borderlands of southern Kordofan and southern Darfur meant that the militia policy readily became a Trojan Horse for Islamist paramilitary training.[8]

In February 1986, two months before Sudan held its first free and fair elections for 18 years, the IMF handed the government a cruel reward: suspension from the Fund for failing to pay the arrears on its debts to the IMF and the World Bank. Sudan's nascent democracy was straitjacketed with a tight discipline that was markedly different to the laxity with which Washington DC had treated its preceding autocracy. Sadiq al-Mahdi won the 1986 general elections and spent the following three years in frenzied indecision on the key issues of the day: Islamic law, peace with the SPLA, and enacting the economic reforms demanded by Sudan's creditors. He failed to square these circles, spending money that he did not have in an attempt to satisfy the appetites of his constituents and his rivals. Sadiq had to run begging to Arab countries to raise funds for counter-offensives when the SPLA attacked in Blue Nile, threatening the Roseires Dam. His otherwise inexplicable deference to the Islamists is best explained by the fact that Islamic banks—which were run with explicit political agendas—still had money in hand even when the coffers of the Central Bank of Sudan (CBOS) were empty. When the political financial system finally seized up in early 1989, Sadiq appeared to invite a military takeover, as if to admit that he couldn't run the country. If that was what he wanted, Sadiq would have been better advised to follow his predecessor in 1958 and choose his general. The Islamist cell that took power jailed him at once.

After taking power in the 1989 coup, the military–Islamist duopoly of al-Bashir and Sheikh Hassan al-Turabi violently repressed opposition, banning the trade unions and professional associations and imprisoning and torturing their leaders, purging the officer corps of non-Islamists, while also undermining the economic basis of the sectarian parties and the highest ranks of the provincial aristocracy. Meanwhile they corralled Islamist volunteers into the ranks of *Mujahideen*, sending them into battle with prayers but minimal training; their numerous martyrs were celebrated as having ascended to Paradise and their numbers replenished through forced conscription. With this combination of fervour and force, the military–Islamists thereby succeeded in keeping down the price of war and of politics. This was necessary because they had little money: Sudan was under international sanctions and no licit businesses were ready to invest. At one point in the mid-1990s, government funds available were less than US$100 million per month, and the CBOS ran a cash budget, counting the money available at the end of the month and paying out according to priorities—essential salaries first. Any semblance of institutional government was limited to an area within a day's drive of Khartoum, the so-called 'Hamdi Triangle', after the minister of finance, Abdel Rahim Hamdi, whose ultra-radical austerity measures had brought a measure of rock-bottom stability to the economy.[9] Meanwhile, in order to run the country on such a tight budget, the regime established an elaborate network of parallel financing. Number two in the Islamic Movement, Ali Osman Taha, was appointed minister of social affairs. In standard political hierarchy this would have been a marginal position, but in this case the regime needed to construct an Islamic apparatus of societal governance that did not rely on the non-existent regular tax revenue. Among other things, this included embracing transnational Islamic charities (which also functioned as commercial businesses, government service providers, security companies and terrorist networks) to establish a parallel state structure.[10] Counter-insurgency in southern Sudan was monetised; paramilitaries proliferated, replacing the wastefully martyred *Mujahideen* of the Popular Defence Forces (PDF). Overall, this was an innovative system of disassembled governance, and it also created fertile conditions for a thoroughly marketised political arena.[11]

Sudan's oil had been discovered in the 1970s, inconveniently (for Nimeiri) located predominantly in southern Sudan. The first oil wells, operated by Chevron, were months away from production when the SPLA attacked and forced them to close. For more than a decade, the infrastructure rusted while the concessions were sold and resold at ever more discounted prices. No major oil company would invest in a country with such a bad reputation: a sponsor of terrorism, unable to service its debts, embroiled in an unending civil war.[12] But China did.[13] The first oil flowed in August 1999. The twin heads of the regime, al-Bashir and al-Turabi, were at that moment locked in a power struggle over who would dominate the other. The winner would not just control the formal apparatus of government—a state machinery that for a decade had been so decrepit as to be virtually worthless—but also oil revenues that would expand the national budget tenfold in the coming five years.

Al-Bashir won. He decisively gained the upper hand in December 1999 by declaring a state of emergency and stripping the Islamist sheikh of his power as speaker of the National Assembly and by suspending the constitution. His path had been laid a year earlier when ten leading Islamists published an open letter criticising al-Turabi. When al-Bashir struck, other Islamists—most crucially Taha—came over to his side.[14] With him came the men who ran many of the Islamist institutions, such as the huge Al-Dawa al-Islamiyya philanthropic business conglomerate. But victory was not certain; Islamists of uncertain loyalties continued in positions throughout state, party and security institutions, and the power struggle played out over the next decade. In Khartoum and the cities of the near periphery of the Hamdi Triangle, the chief instrument was money. Al-Bashir and Taha used the proceeds of the boom to build a new constituency, putting hundreds of thousands on the state payroll and rewarding many more with contracts, large and small, for items ranging from mega dams on the Nile to furniture importation or local manufacturing. In some respects this resembled conventional illiberal statebuilding, but the fractured and unsettled structure of power did not permit Sudan to follow the consolidated trajectory of (say) Egypt. Instead it was a politically functional kleptocracy, recycling revenues into political quiescence that would continue for decades until, like a Ponzi scheme, it collapsed.[15]

A secondary effect of the boom was the growth of a national business sector less dependent on access to political power: not all Sudanese capitalism is of the crony variety. Some of these businesses, notably the DAL group, both supported democratic ideals and also practised them. For example, they adopted more gender-equal hiring and training policies as well as corporate social responsibility programmes. In 2019, some businesses, including DAL, provided in-kind support for the protestors such as food and drink, although it was national charities together with diaspora crowd-source funding that were the mainstay in financing the uprising.[16]

In Darfur, the fight over the legacy of the Islamist project turned very bloody: a generation of Darfurians who had been drawn to the Islamist cause was already discontented and became more so at the egregious imbalance in the allocation of government posts and development projects. The manifesto of Darfurian Islamists was the 'Black Book' detailing this imbalance. It became the call to arms for the Justice and Equality Movement (JEM), which joined hands with secular radical Darfurians (under the Sudan Liberation Movement and Army, SLM/A) to launch an insurrection in 2003.

For the al-Bashir–Taha duopoly, the peace agreement with the SPLA and its leader, John Garang, was primarily a means of restoring international legitimacy. During the 1990s, despairing of achieving a peace agreement under international or African mediation that would allow the Islamist movement to pursue its divisive agenda, the regime developed what it called 'peace from within', which was essentially a series of security pacts with discontented southern Sudanese commanders who had split from the SPLA (or in some cases, never joined) because of the ruthless militarised centralism of the SPLA commander-in-chief, Garang. No sooner had al-Bashir removed al-Turabi, than Libya and Egypt stepped in with a reconciliation initiative that would have rewarded al-Bashir for his improved standing among his fellow Arab heads of state, providing for a political settlement with the conservative northern leadership and an accommodation with Garang. Such a peace process would have run into vigorous opposition from the southern Sudanese rank and file (because it ruled out self-determination) and progress was dependent on the haphazard political attention of Cairo and Tripoli as well as the preference of all Sudanese opposition leaders for hanging on in the hope that a better opportunity lay around the corner. After the terrorist attacks of September 11, al-Bashir was justifiably terrified that Sudan was on the US hit list. Gaining international legitimacy was suddenly a top priority, and the route to that was through a peace deal with the SPLA brokered by the Americans, who had fortuitously just appointed a Special Envoy with the mandate of exploring that possibility. For al-Bashir and Taha, this had the disadvantage that the 'troika' of the US, Britain and Norway insisted that the mediation be conducted through the northeast African regional organisation, the Intergovernmental Authority on Development (IGAD). In an uncharacteristic fit of idealism, IGAD had in 1994 drafted a Declaration of Principles for resolving the Sudanese war that included democracy and self-determination. Assured that Garang was a committed unionist and that democracy would always be secondary to peace and Western interests, the regime now took the IGAD–troika peace process seriously.

The Comprehensive Peace Agreement was signed in January 2005. But no sooner had Garang been sworn in as First Vice President six months later, than the Ugandan helicopter in which he was travelling crashed into a mountainside. His successor, Salva Kiir Mayardit, was a separatist, and used the oil revenues allocated to southern Sudan to build a political–military constituency of southern secessionists, sufficiently unified by sentiment and payouts that even the best-honed NISS divide-and-rule stratagems were insufficient to crack southern unity. Southern Sudanese voted overwhelmingly for separation in the referendum held on 9 January 2011, and the Republic of South Sudan was born six months later.

During the 1999–2011 period, Sudan's political economy consolidated around a rentier crony capitalist system, reliant on oil revenues (see Table 2.1). It was an oil-rentier state with its own particular characteristics. At the centre it functioned as a centralised kleptocracy, with patronage funds flowing through well-defined channels; in the 'far peripheries' (southern Sudan, Darfur and the 'two areas' of South Kordofan and Blue Nile) as a poorly regulated political marketplace with low barriers to entry for aspiring political–military entrepreneurs. At times, in Darfur it resembled a conflict gig economy, with armed units up for hire on a case-by-case basis. Key to the regime's consolidation was the incorporation of the 'near peripheries' into the reach of the central patronage system. Large numbers of people began to share the material benefits of the oil boom, in the form of salaried employment, and a boom in construction and in the trade in consumer commodities.[17] The regime's business plan, or production function, was converting oil into political quiescence.

Table 2.1: The Marketisation of Sudanese Politics, 1970s–2018[18]

Period	*Economic characteristics*	*Political finance*	*Economic beneficiaries*	*Political beneficiaries*
1972–77	Debt-led boom	State borrowing	Crony capitalists	Modern forces
1978–83	Crisis	Privatisation, Islamic banks	Informal sector, finance	Islamists
1983–99	Severe crisis	Islamic banks, pillage	Informal sector, security sector	Islamists and paramilitaries
2000–11	Oil-led boom	Oil and associated contracting	Security actors and crony capitalists	State, army and ruling party
2012–18	Crisis	Gold, state mercenarism	Paramilitaries, smugglers	Paramilitaries, Arab states, and their clients

The secession of the South made the oil-rentier model unsustainable.[19] From late 2011, the Sudanese economy slid into a deepening crisis, which not only inflicted great hardship on the Sudanese people but also entailed a traumatic shift in the structure of the country's political economy to more diversified rentierism, based principally on gold and mercenarism.

The crisis began with the post-secession arrangements for payments for oil. Just before secession, the IMF calculated that Sudan would face a budgetary gap of just over $9 billion during the three and a half years it would take for the country to make the necessary economic adjustments. Under the facilitation of the African Union High-Level Implementation Panel (AUHIP), Sudan and South Sudan agreed that this cost would be divided into three equal parts. Sudan should implement austerity measures to enable it to make its contribution: South Sudan would provide $3.014 billion in 'transitional financial arrangements' (TFA), and the two governments would make a joint approach to international donors for financial aid. None of this worked as planned.

No agreement was reached during month-long negotiations held in Addis Ababa in June 2011. The South Sudanese prevaricated in the expectation that they would be able to cut a better deal once they were an independent sovereign state. The northerners prevaricated because they didn't want to face the need for radical austerity measures and could not organise an internal agreement over who would suffer the painful cuts. As a result, South Sudan obtained independence in July 2011 without agreement on the terms on which South Sudanese oil would be pumped to market through (northern) Sudan and on the terms of the TFA. For the following five months, while on-and-off talks were held, South Sudanese oil was pumped and sold, and the Sudanese received no payment of any kind. This was particularly difficult for the CBOS because it relied almost entirely on oil for foreign currency.

In December that year, Sudan began diverting South Sudanese oil to its refineries for its domestic use and to ships that it had chartered itself. The oil on those tankers would have been declared illegal, but there is an international market for illegal oil, and the NCP businessmen were quite prepared to undertake such black-market trading. In response, South Sudan closed down its entire oil production in January 2012. This was akin to activating an economic doomsday machine, a race towards mutually assured financial Armageddon. The calculation in Juba was that both countries would suffer but that Sudan would collapse first: South Sudan had stashed away some reserves and the SPLA was (they said) ready go back to the days of fighting without pay in the bush. The calculation in Khartoum was that it would hurt Sudan but kill South Sudan. In the short term, the northerners estimated right—South Sudan collapsed first—but the shock waves from the oil shutdown were the first tremor that finally brought the regime in Khartoum to its knees.

The two countries went to war in April 2012. The spark was a conflict on the border near Sudan's major remaining oilfield at Heglig, an area to which South Sudan had laid a claim. The Heglig area, known to southerners as Panthou, had not been one of the areas under discussion by the ad hoc Technical Boundary Committee in the years between the CPA and independence; the territorial claim was chiefly a pretext for a war that hard-line generals on both sides believed was inevitable. It was necessary, the South Sudanese believed, because their country would not be truly independent if it were still the junior partner in a political relationship with Khartoum. Kiir had publicly declared his support for the concept that, after separation, South Sudan and Sudan would be 'two viable states at peace with one another,' but others in Juba did not think the conflict was over. Meanwhile, many in the SAF command believed war was necessary because there was still unfinished business from the CPA and the separation, such as disputed areas along the border (notably the Abyei district) and continuing South Sudanese support for SPLA divisions that had returned to rebellion in the Nuba Mountains and Blue Nile.

South Sudan had joined the club of nations in July 2011, but its leaders somehow believed that they didn't need to play by its rules. They were shocked when their military occupation of Heglig in April 2012 was met, first, by an African Union communiqué demanding withdrawal and a peaceful settlement, and a few days later by a resolution by the UN Security Council that made the same demands, word for word.[20] American officials who had treated SPLM leaders as cherished friends suddenly were not returning phone calls from Juba. Security Council Resolution 2046 not only set a tight timeline (three months) for settling the issues between South Sudan and Sudan but—for the first time—treated the two countries on equal terms. Too ingrained in their paranoid habits and infighting, the leaders in Khartoum failed to seize this diplomatic opportunity and continued playing their game of grinding out every smallest concession from South Sudan, wearing out the African Union mediators in the process.

The border war was settled, along with a deal for reopening South Sudanese oil production, the terms of use of the pipeline, and the TFA, at a late-night session of the African Union in August 2012 and was confirmed at a summit meeting between al-Bashir and Kiir in Addis Ababa a month later. However, production only restarted in April 2013, at a fraction of its previous level, and did not recover to pre-conflict levels by the time civil war erupted in South Sudan at the end of that year. No joint approach was made to donors. Just before the referendum, President Barack Obama had dispatched

Senator John Kerry on a mission to Khartoum, promising that if Khartoum allowed the vote to proceed smoothly, the US would initiate legislation to lift sanctions on Sudan. The regime's officials received Kerry courteously (he could not meet with al-Bashir because the US had a policy of not meeting with a man accused of international crimes) but were sceptical that he would deliver. Sudanese caution was warranted: Kerry could not muster enough support in Congress, and there were consequently no efforts to lift financial sanctions on Sudan (they only began to be lifted in January 2017 in the very last days of the Obama presidency) or for Sudan to enter into debt forgiveness processes. Possibly, an appeal from South Sudan might have made the difference in the brief euphoria after South Sudanese independence. Perhaps, a joint mission with a chastened South Sudanese delegation after the Heglig war might have convinced the US that there was a genuine commitment to the principle of 'two viable states,' and that it was worth making an effort to support them both. In the event, Sudan quickly fell behind on its interest payments to the IMF and the World Bank, making it ineligible for further loans.

After the Addis Ababa summit agreement, neither al-Bashir nor Kiir was able to implement the deal they had made. Some South Sudanese political leaders—notably Paul Malong, at that time governor of Northern Bahr al Ghazal—were unhappy at the compromises made and they demanded that those terms be renegotiated. For example, he objected to the location of the 'security line' between south and north that required the SPLA to withdraw from the banks of the Bahr al-Arab/Kiir river that divided his state from neighbouring Darfur. The SAF generals also found excuses for procrastinating in reopening the pipeline, hoping that a few additional months without oil revenues would be enough to kill the Juba government, whereas it would only harm Khartoum. In their analysis of South Sudan, at least, they were proven correct.

Al-Bashir was desperate for South Sudan to reopen its oil production and export. This happened gradually and provided some revenue to the Sudanese treasury, including fees for the use of the pipeline and TFA payments. The agreement was renegotiated in late 2014 after its first phase concluded: the new deal was struck directly between al-Bashir and Kiir without AU or World Bank intermediaries and the details were not made public, indicating a likelihood of off-the-books payments. One of the downsides of this private negotiation was that the AUHIP, which had been the champion of the 'joint approach' to the international donors, no longer played that role, and advocacy for a more forgiving attitude by the creditors and international financial institutions faded away. Moreover, the reduced production in South Sudan and the low price of oil meant that these payments were relatively limited. The production from Sudan's own oilfield in Heglig barely covered domestic consumption. Oil-based centralised rentierism was finished.

Meanwhile, the regime in Khartoum predictably procrastinated on its domestic austerity measures. Only in August and September 2013 did it belatedly reduce subsidies and cut spending. This was (as they had feared) the trigger for street demonstrations, the first major anti-regime protests of the new era.

One reason for the apparent complacency of the powerbrokers in Khartoum was that they believed they had been astonishingly lucky, again. A large seam of gold was discovered in Darfur in 2012.[21] It appeared a godsend and soon became the country's number one source of hard currency, earning about $2.5 billion per year, about 40% of Sudan's exports. Sudan was already a gold producer, but the mines at Jebel Amir in Northern Darfur represented a breakthrough, both in the quantities that could be mined and in the expectation that more was to be found. There was a gold rush. In 2013, Sudan earned more from its growing gold exports than from its diminished oil exports.

Gold soon proved to be a curse. Sudan's gold is overwhelmingly in seams near the surface. Some 90% of it is mined in about 800 artisanal mines by an estimated 200,000 miners.[22] A map of gold mines is more or less the inverse of the 'Hamdi Triangle': they cover all the peripheries. The richest seams were discovered in Darfur in areas controlled by Arab militia, notably Jebel Amir. The initial winner in the contest to control Jebel Amir was Musa Hilal, commander of the Border Intelligence Brigade (formerly *Janjaweed*) who drove out the local Beni Hussein community in a battle in which more than 800 died.[23] Hilal warned the central government to stay away. According to the UN Panel of Experts, Hilal earned $28 million annually from taxies and levies on prospectors, $17 million from mines he owned, and $9 million through illegal exports.[24] The total income to Arab paramilitaries was estimated at $123 million. Over the following years, Khartoum armed Hilal's rival, General Hemedti, and formalised his paramilitaries as the RSF. In November 2017, Hemedti's RSF defeated Hilal's Border Guards, capturing Hilal and his senior commanders, and taking over Jebel Amir and other mines.[25]

In addition, the Arab paramilitaries gained a very substantial income from smuggling tens of thousands of vehicles to and from Libya and Chad and trafficking migrants across the Sahara. The RSF was deployed to control smuggling and illicit migration, and like any canny gamekeeper on a distant corner of the estate, also made a killing from smuggling and from smugglers' bribes.[26] The RSF was entrusted with disarmament campaigns in Darfur, which served as a means of accumulating weapons and vehicles and taking control over key checkpoints and contraband routes.[27] Hemedti thus became the country's number one gold trader, smuggler and border guard, and the RSF became the de facto military rulers of northern Darfur.

Elsewhere in Sudan, notably in the northern region, gold mining attracted large numbers of prospectors. Tensions with local people arose over attempts by the government to transfer artisanal concessions to foreign companies,[28] and over the despoliation of the local ecology through pollution with mercury and arsenic.

The other major impact of gold was the macroeconomic strategy adopted to minimise smuggling. Artisanal gold is notoriously easy to smuggle: a small nugget can be pocketed or hidden in a car and taken over vast distances. The government needed to pay a premium in order to incentivise traders to sell through official channels. The policy adopted was to require traders to sell the gold to CBOS, which then served as the exclusive exporter of gold. A study of the macroeconomics of gold in Sudan, by Ibrahim Elbadawi—subsequently the post-revolution minister of finance—and Kabbashi Suliman[29] observed: 'The fact that the CBOS, not the Ministry of Finance and National Economy, is the government agent in this market suggests that domestic credit creation is likely to be the main source of financing the gold purchases.'[30] The IMF found that resulting CBOS foreign exchange losses amounted to 2.9% of GDP annually in the period 2012–17. Elbadawi and Suliman concluded: 'the combination of increasing monetization of the fiscal deficit and purchases of gold through money printing by the CBOS have not only been the main source of short-term macroeconomic instability but has also undermined the competitiveness and diversification of exports in the medium to longer runs and worsened the external debt problem.'[31]

This inflationary strategy also had a major socio-economic impact. First, it was a forced transfer of material wealth, reducing the real incomes of those on fixed salaries (such as civil servants) and increasing those in the gold mining and trading economy and others who had access to hard currency. Second, the resulting hyperinflation caused far-reaching economic distress, including inability to afford basic foodstuffs. The main social groups that lost out were those that had gained in the oil boom and 'payroll peace' of the previous decade, and which had also been the largest constituency of supporters for the NCP during the 2010 election. Geographically this group is concentrated in the 'near periphery', in towns such as Atbara and Gedaref along with some 'far periphery' towns such as Damazin. Protests began there and spread quickly to the capital.[32] The immediate spark for the demonstrations that began in December 2018 was continuing rises in the prices of essentials, so that there was a shortage of bread.[33] From the start the protestors' slogans targeted kleptocracy: 'Down with the rule of thieves!'[34] Focused on their own need for political funds, al-Bashir and his circle had broken that tenuous social contract with the constituency that had stabilised their government.

Sudan also tried to revive its old strategy of agriculture-based investment and growth. It made some progress. Most of this consisted of land in the near periphery leased to Arab investors, often dispossessing local farmers and herders. Moreover, relatively little of the land leased was subsequently developed, partly because of the extent to which local officials demanded bribes. In 2009, Qatar leased 250,000 hectares, but after numerous difficulties with the local authorities, disruption caused by angry locals and constant breakdowns in supply chains, it did not develop the land because it feared that the unanticipated costs of doing business would make the farms unprofitable.[35] The system of licensed corruption was gradually becoming self-defeating. Land-leasing also generated considerable local tensions.[36]

The domestic business sector remained dominated by a hybrid of the Islamist corporations established in the 1977–99 period and the oil- and construction-related firms that developed after 1999, which, however, were becoming increasingly squeezed. Sudanese businesses not associated with the crony capitalist networks also struggled as the economy declined and then plunged into free fall. Meanwhile, new businesses emerged out of the booming gold sector. The RSF's 'Special Operations Wing', headed by close relatives of General Hemedti, established the Al-Junaid Corporation, which includes companies engaged in mining, housing, road construction, transportation and a host of other activities.[37]

Gold provided an illusory fix to Sudan's economy and al-Bashir's kleptocracy. It postponed the real financial crunch, which hit in 2016. Despite the rehabilitation of the oil wells in Heglig, despite the hard currency from gold sales, the economy went off the cliff that year. According to World Bank data[38] GDP per capita plunged 31% that year, and it kept on falling.

For al-Bashir, economic development and stability were always less important than the funds he could extract for his political needs. Political finance reflects a country's political economy, though inexactly—some of the mainstays of the economy, such as small-scale agriculture, don't contribute to politicians' budgets, while relatively small transactions from foreign sponsors or banks can have a major impact in the political marketplace. Oil had been the ideal spigot for political funding: it was centralised and could be managed through a few large transactions, and it generated employment and other benefits that kept the NCP constituencies relatively content. The new sources of political finance demanded new skills. And the demand for political payouts—the price of loyalty—stayed high even while the political funds available were shrinking. The system needed radical recalibration.

The number one beneficiary of the new sources of political finance was General Hemedti and the RSF. Among the people of Khartoum and central Sudan, the stereotype of the RSF fighter is that he is a poorly educated ruffian, speaking an unfamiliar dialect of Arabic, with gold in his pocket. The principal losers in the new dispensation were the millions of Sudanese in the capital and the towns and cities of the 'near periphery', people largely uninterested in politics who had extended a conditional tolerance towards al-Bashir and the NCP for bringing them a modicum of stability and a hope for a decent life. When these two groups made common cause—albeit for a fleeting moment—al-Bashir's political career was finished. This happened in the second week of April 2019.

Disassembling the National Security Sector

Since the early days of independence, the officers of the Sudan Armed Forces have seen themselves as the custodians of the nation. Despite a tradition of coups d'état and a record of inflicting grievous abuses on the citizens of the peripheries, despite the radicalism of Nimeiri's Revolutionary Command Council and the Islamism of al-Bashir's National Salvation Revolution, a culture of military patriotism springs eternal among the commissioned officers of the SAF. The reality of war-fighting in forbidding terrain on a tight budget, under the eagle eye of a commander-in-chief who is as fearful of the vaulting ambition of his own generals as he is of the battlefield victories of rebels or invaders, has spelled a different reality for the state monopoly of legitimate violence. The SAF has never developed either doctrine or capacity for sustained counter-insurgency. It is probably just too difficult. If colonial powers such as Britain and France, or the US in Afghanistan and Iraq, could not succeed in pacifying territories in which they had massive technical and material advantages, without resorting to intermittent barbarity (if not worse),[39] then there is little chance for the government of a large, diverse and restless African country to succeed where they failed. While the SAF has many tactical successes to its name, it has never consolidated a victory.

Sudanese counter-insurgency has evolved in an ad hoc way, using hired guns and tribal militias, motivated by greed, vendetta or both. The air force is renowned for its inaccuracy, at times reduced to rolling bombs out of the cargo doors of transport aircraft, any precision achieved by luck as much as training. When fighting resumed in southern Sudan in 1983, Nimeiri was anxious to pretend it was anything but a real war. Instead of deploying the army, he used mercenaries and paid southern rebels who disliked the SPLA leadership to fight, presenting the rebellion as a mix of banditry and inter-tribal fighting. A crucial turning point was the adoption of the 'militia strategy' by the post-Nimeiri Transitional Military Council in July 1985. Faced with incursions by the SPLA into northern Sudan, Minister of Defence Fadlallah Burma Nasir mobilised militia from the cattle-herding Arab tribes of southern Kordofan and southern Darfur to serve as irregular forces.[40] Among them were former fighters from the sectarian–Islamist National Front, who had trained in Libya. Known as *murahaleen*, these militia burned, pillaged, raped, slaughtered and starved a swathe of southern Sudan.[41] One of the military officers who helped coordinate them was Brigadier Omar al-Bashir. In February 1989, the army command presented a memorandum calling for peace with the SPLA in preference to fighting a war in a manner that, the generals foresaw, spelled the ruin of the country. They demanded the disbandment of the militias. Instead, Prime Minister Sadiq al-Mahdi proposed formalising them as 'Popular Defence Forces', a proposal acted upon by al-Bashir soon after he seized power. The generals' earlier prediction was farsighted. Pursued with ever greater vigour, the mercenarisation of counter-insurgency in southern Sudan resulted in a fragmented military arena in which unit commanders with little training but bearing the rank of 'general' rented their services to the highest bidder. They fought one another and slaughtered civilians with abandon, all the time blaming the northerners for inflicting this mayhem. And when in 2006, Salva Kiir offered them all large salaries and benefits, plus other unnumbered material rewards, in return for the unstated goal of protecting the forthcoming vote on the independence of South Sudan, they agreed.

The Interim Period that followed the CPA did not see a 'peace dividend' in the form of government and rebels switching spending from war to welfare and development. On the contrary, it was an opportunity for the SPLA to grow in size and remuneration, and for the SAF to re-equip and expand. There was an arms and patronage race between north and south, which devoured the treasuries on both sides.

It was only one month before the referendum in southern Sudan that al-Bashir recognised that he was not going to win. At a meeting of the senior Islamists' *shura* council on 4 December 2010, al-Bashir called a premature close after just one day of what was scheduled as a two-day meeting. It had become clear that the second day was going to consist of heavy criticism of Second Vice President Taha for having negotiated the CPA with the provision for southern self-determination, probably resulting in a hard-line NCP party line rejecting the referendum and its outcome. Al-Bashir made a strong defence of Taha, saying that nothing was forced upon the government of Sudan when it signed the CPA, and that this was all done willingly and in good faith. To pre-empt the crisis, he then ended the *shura*. Advisors to al-Bashir noted that while the party cadres and generals were still in denial about the imminent break-up of the country and somehow still believed that their bribery and intrigue would prevail, the president had conceded that the game was up.

Having sown the winds of pandemonium over many years, the political masters in Khartoum reaped the whirlwind: a unanimous vote for the south to secede.

A month later, on the very eve of the referendum, al-Bashir flew to Juba to speak to the people who would shortly reject the state he represented. He travelled against the advice of his advisors and tore up the drafts they had prepared. Al-Bashir made a rare speech that he had written himself. He spoke about his love for Sudan—north and south—and his passionate commitment to unity but said that if the southern Sudanese were to vote for separation, he would respect their choice, and he made a pledge that Sudan and South Sudan should go forward in friendship. It was an important speech, defusing tension in the south, but it was far too late to have any other impact at all. The media ignored it entirely. No other northern Sudanese leader spoke publicly to echo the president's sentiments. In some respects, al-Bashir was trying in a rather sad way to write his own political obituary.

In Darfur, al-Bashir fought counter-insurgency on much the same principle as southern Sudan: cheap to instigate, impossible to conclude decisively, and with a legacy that could not be managed. The Darfur rebellion was a shock and a challenge in many respects. The vast western province had long endured privation and neglect, and, despite unending complaints, the Darfurians' anger had invariably been turned against one another in a series of inter-communal wars. The SPLA stoked a rebellion in 1991 but a combination of good intelligence work, the efficacy of an Arab militia, and the errors of the insurgents, meant that it was quickly put down. In 2003, however, most of the Islamists in Darfur had abandoned the regime or joined the rebellion, and the regime found itself fighting without good information about its enemy.[42] Many of the first paramilitaries it armed deserted to the rebels. Instead, the regime entrusted counter-insurgency to Arab militia, known locally as *Janjaweed*. These were an amalgam of diehards from the National Front of the 1970s (some of whom had remained within Gaddafi's Saharan legions' camps), Chadian armed groups who had been chased into Darfur in the 1980s, and local Arab militia.[43]

The southern militia were always held at arm's length from the SAF, and the CPA provided for them either to be absorbed into the SPLA or demobilised. (In principle they could also have become part of the SAF, but that was never seriously contemplated.) In Darfur, there were never any comparable options: security autonomy for Darfur was never canvassed as an option, and in any case the *Janjaweed* were overwhelmingly Darfurian. When the first round of major hostilities was over in 2005, and the Sudanese government had contained the military threat of the rebels, the question also arose of what to do with the numerous, well-armed, capable and dangerous *Janjaweed*. The UN Security Council had called for them to be disarmed: a practical impossibility but a signal that they were considered too toxic to be included in any peace agreement. Neglected by Khartoum, some turned to rebellion, others used their weapons to pursue local feuds, so that within a few years intra-Arab conflict in Darfur was the largest cause of fatalities in the region.

As with southern Sudan in the early 2000s, the SAF high command found that their brigades in Darfur were guests of the proxies they had previously armed and directed. Before long, army units could only travel outside the towns with the permission and escort of the most powerful paramilitary force in the particular locality. Different units of 'government' forces frequently fought one another, typically over who would control (and tax) a marketplace or a checkpoint, or were dragged into territorial disputes or feuds among their proxy militia.[44] A catalogue of 'who is killing whom' from 2008 to 2009 shows that Darfur had become 'a war of all against all'.[45] The most comprehensive listing of violent incidents, compiled by the staff of the UN-African Union hybrid peacekeeping operation in Darfur (UNAMID), sought to attribute the identities of perpetrators and victims for 1,909 violent deaths between January 2008 and August 2009 (with another 600 or so not fully confirmed). Of these, the largest number, 614 deaths (32%), were in 'inter-tribal' clashes, almost entirely among Arab groups previously armed by the government, and 243 (13%) were uniformed soldiers, security men, policemen or paramilitaries killed by *other* men in government uniform.[46] This compares with 402 fatalities (21%) in fighting between government and rebels, and 454 civilians killed (24%) by government or rebel forces. Darfurians described it as *fawda*, 'anarchy', an even worse indictment of the government than the massacres of 2003–04.[47]

Among the uniformed servants of the Sudanese state rampaging in Darfur were the SAF, NISS, the PDF (in this case a mixture of the Islamist *Mujahideen* and sundry militia), the police, and other militia that had been ostensibly brought under the SAF, NISS or Ministry of Interior control. Among the militia were the *Janjaweed*, who had been formalised as the Border Intelligence Brigade and the Central Reserve Police. Of these, the biggest by far was the Border Intelligence Brigade, which expanded to include units ranging across each of the three Darfur states. The commander of the southern Darfur unit was a young and capable field commander: Hemedti.

Hemedti is from a small clan of the Mahariya camel-herding Arabs who have traversed the Sudan–Chad border from the days when no such border existed. He has no chiefly lineage; he attended secondary school but there are no reliable reports of whether he completed his school certificate; he became a small-time trader and in 2003 heeded the government's call to arms and joined the militia.

Hemedti rose to senior rank in the *Janjaweed*-Border Intelligence Brigade by dint of his leadership skills.

In 2007, during the height of the Darfurian Arabs' discontent with Khartoum, Hemedti led his fighters into the bush and battled against government forces. Among other things, he shot down a helicopter. Like Musa Hilal five years earlier, he sought an alliance with the ethnic Fur forces of the SLM/A, and, like Hilal, he found their leader, Abd al-Wahid al-Nur, unreliable. A video of Hemedti during those days shows him among his troops, clearly at ease in the harsh conditions, consulting and debating with his men, and vowing to fight al-Bashir 'until judgement day' on account of the president's broken promises.[48] But Hemedti's money was running out and his 4,000-strong force was slowly depleting as his men trickled back to join their families. Unlike non-Arab rebels, he had no option of getting support from Chad or Gaddafi's Libya. Khartoum also wanted him onside for the escalating proxy war with Chad, and allocated funds accordingly. Al-Bashir made him an offer: cash, salary arrears, promotion, and a post in local government for his brother. The time and the terms were right: Hemedti agreed.

Negotiating directly with Khartoum, Hemedti had bypassed his ostensible commander, Musa Hilal. He dealt equally with NISS and the SAF, and also bargained with the other militia in southern Darfur. He expanded his forces and also his businesses, becoming a warlord-like figure dominating Darfur's commercial capital, Nyala. Geography kept him away from armed clashes with Hilal, now his rival. In 2013, when al-Bashir decided he needed an urgent overhaul of the military, including creating a new strike force, he turned to Hemedti and his units. The Rapid Support Forces (RSF) were born.

The security politics of the time requires some explanation. The Heglig war of April 2012 dramatically revealed the shortcomings of the SAF: the SPLA not only overran Sudan's most strategic oil installation in a single day but also crossed into southern Darfur from where they could not be dislodged. The counter-attack that recaptured the oilfield was spearheaded by South Sudanese rebels in the pay of Khartoum, not SAF troops. From start to finish it was a humiliation for the SAF. The vast spending of the previous decade—expansion in payroll, investment in military industries, the construction of a pharaonic headquarters in Khartoum—had been revealed as entirely useless on the battlefield. A major reform of the security sector was needed, and not the liberal peace kind that brought the armed forces under democratic oversight with accountability to civilians. Al-Bashir demanded a different accountability: the irreducible calculus of winning battles. He wanted to promote Hemedti and his brigade.

Until that time, a paramilitary could fall under the command of either the SAF, NISS or the Ministry of the Interior (i.e. be part of the police). The SAF Chief of Staff, Lieutenant General Imad Adawi, objected to taking responsibility for a force he did not believe he could control, and argued that the resources needed to upgrade the military should be allocated directly to the SAF. At that time, NISS was out of favour, its chief Salah Gosh having been recently dismissed (of which more below), and most of its operational units reallocated to serve under the SAF. Reconfiguring Hemedti's troops as policemen was not seriously considered. Instead, al-Bashir established the RSF directly under his own office: a 'super-paramilitary', as it were, whose senior commander was thereby promoted directly to membership of the inner sanctum, the Higher Security Committee. One of those who supported this decision was the former head of military intelligence who had coordinated Hemedti's supplies and operations: General Ibn Auf. The relationship between the two proved vital to Hemedti six years on, when Ibn Auf had, for a fleeting but crucial moment, the power to choose who would be the de facto leader of the post-al-Bashir order.

Al-Bashir always felt more comfortable with rural chiefs and the commanders of field units than with the urbane and sophisticated Khartoum elites. His sense of humour is coarse if not vulgar, his style rustic and earthy. He brandished his stick like a village chief. In that respect, he was always an outsider to the city that he ruled. He sometimes seemed to treat Hemedti like the biological son he never had.

For the leadership of the NCP and SAF, it was an unspoken assumption that a Darfurian could never rule Sudan. The last occasion had been the Mahdi's successor, the Khalifa Abdullahi Torshein al-Ta'aishi, who had ruled the Mahdist state from 1885 to 1898, an era remembered with dread by the people of the Nile.[49] In the eyes of the riverain people—the *awlad al balad*—the Arab Darfurians were uncouth Bedouins, as much feared as the non-Arabs of Sudan's wild west. In the 1960s and 1970s, army officers from Darfur and the Nuba Mountains had been implicated in planning putsches—which the metropolitans ironically referred to as 'racist' coups, evoking those fears.[50] Hemedti's militiamen were involved in violently suppressing the 2013 Khartoum protests, reprising that fearful script. Whether from fearful denialism or racism, metropolitan Sudanese simply refused to believe that Hemedti was national leadership material.

The core of the RSF is drawn from the Abbala (camel-herding) Rizeigat tribe of northern Darfur, especially Hemedti's own Mahariya clan. In addition, SAF officers have been assigned to the force, and it has recruited from elsewhere in Sudan and has absorbed at least one former rebel group, a splinter faction of the Sudan Liberation Army (SLA), led by Mohamedein Ismail Bachar 'Orgajor', an ethnic Zaghawa.[51] Hemedti is ready to incorporate non-Arab fighting units, though only in subordinate positions. At its core, the RSF is a tribe-in-arms, its officers bound by ties of kinship, and its fighters animated by a spirit of Bedouin solidarity—what the great medieval sociologist, Ibn Khaldun, called *asabiya*.[52] But there is little indication that Hemedti is an Arab supremacist and none that he has ever been an Islamist: his only evident ideology is power.

Al-Bashir instructed that training facilities for the RSF should be established in and around Khartoum, giving it a presence in the capital. While the SAF invested in tanks and aircraft, the RSF imported hundreds of land cruisers, making it the most readily deployable force for urban control. Its troops fought in southern Kordofan, where they performed poorly against the hardened Nuba infantry of the SPLA-North, but Hemedti redeemed his reputation by defeating an incursion by JEM from the Central African Republic into the far south of Darfur at Goz Dango in April 2015. The battle was probably less significant than the profile it earned in the official media, desperate as they were for any good news. The choreography of the victory celebrations, as described in a remarkably prescient column by Magdi El-Gizouli, revealed more than the regime intended about how both the basis and the logic of power were changing:[53]

> The RSF entered Nyala in a victory parade to demonstrate the vehicles and weaponry captured from the JEM, now on display in a town square. The governor of the state, Adam Mahmoud Jar al-Nabi, himself an officer of SAF, declared the RSF victory unprecedented in the history of the Sudanese army. The SAF commander in Nyala, a jolly if not clownish chubby figure, stood beside Himeidti [sic] as a minor, cheering his throat sore. It was on the battlefield of Goz Dango though that Himeidti had his finest moment. The president, the NISS director and the defence minister flew in on 28 April to congratulate the RSF soldiers. A confident Himeidti read out a long list of war booty to enthralled soldiers and then stood aside.
>
> Hoisted on the top of a Land Cruiser to speak, the thankful president skipped the introductory niceties to announce that the rewards and incentives for the fighting force were ready to be paid. 'I signed the list of promotions that I received from you without even looking at it,' he told the RSF soldiers adding that every combatant in the battle will be granted Sudan's 'badge of courage'. For a moment there it was not immediately evident who was commanding whom. The president, obviously overwhelmed by the smouldering heat, the mass of soldiers in arms and the stench of the battlefield, grimaced in discomfort. The cheers around him were no more the familiar religious phrases of the PDF era but thoroughly secular war cries of machismo and vengeance. Loyalty on the battlefields of the really existing New Sudan, as the president recognised, was a function of rewards and incentives, a transaction unmediated by the promises of heartbreaking compliant virgins in heaven. No wonder the president's speech was particularly short; it did not feature the customary celebration of sacrifice and martyrdom for the sake of the Almighty. Judging by the slogans the JEM combatants had on their vehicles, they appeared more convinced of carrying out a mission of divine providence than the RSF chaps.

As El-Gizouli remarks, it was the thoroughly secular and material logic of the political marketplace that had triumphed over Islamist devotion, and Hemedti was the master of this now-dominant mode of power. The 'PDF era' was replaced by the emergent 'RSF era'.

Even in South Kordofan, the original crucible of the PDF, the RSF was by 2013 the most prominent of the militia forces involved in the counter-insurgency.[54] The regime's early efforts to remobilise local communities into the PDF had faltered when local 'Native Administration' leaders refused to support its call.[55] Meanwhile, many of the original PDF commanders were disillusioned with the state of the nominally Islamist regime, following al-Turabi's lead in maintaining that the principles they believed had guided the *jihad* of the 1990s had been lost. Most of those who did not join the JEM, headed by former PDF commander Khalil Ibrahim, were now aligning themselves with the reformist Islamist factions, such as the Sa'ihoun, PCP and Reform Now. General Mohammed Jalil Ibrahim, known as the 'Amir al-Dabbabin' because of his ties to the PDF tank unit paramilitaries used in suicide operations to blow up SPLA tanks in the Second Civil War, was among the Sa'ihoun leaders arrested after being linked to the coup plot against al-Bashir in 2012.[56] It was in this context that al-Bashir needed a new 'protector'.

Al-Bashir's victory jig in Nyala was, in retrospect, a harbinger of the whirlwind he would reap. The militia policy had locked the Sudanese state into a ratchet of hiring more and more armed men, and the instruments of counter-insurgency came to become the masters of government. The Sudanese version of security sector 'reform' just did not work. Like the Sorcerer's Apprentice, al-Bashir's mastery of divide-and-rule militarisation was now entrapping him. His attempts to wrestle back control consisted of formalising paramilitaries, providing them with uniforms and salaries and giving officer rank to their leaders, training them and integrating them into military logistics, and bringing them under the command and control of the SAF (usually military intelligence) or NISS, or (in the case of the RSF) the president's office. The theory was that the process of absorbing them would enable the authorities to instil order and discipline, weed out rogue or criminal elements, in due course demobilising and disarming them. This formula could work for small groups of former rebels. For example, after the Eastern Sudan Peace Agreement of October 2006, in which the guerrillas of the Beja Congress were welcomed back to Sudan and integrated into the SAF, the SAF command dispersed them among different units spread across the country, and, after a nominal period of training, sent most of them into civilian life with modest demobilisation packages. But that was an exception. The *Janjaweed* were too many and too canny to allow this to happen—and as the Heglig fiasco showed, the government needed them to fight elsewhere.

Whereas passion and loot had supplemented cash when it was time to incite young men to fight a rebellion, only cash would do to tame them afterwards. But more and more cash was needed to feed their appetites. With each turn of the ratchet, security spending increased. The government stopped publishing figures but by 2018 it was somewhere between one-half and two-thirds of the national budget. Counter-insurgency on the cheap turned out to be unsustainably expensive. The protest movement recognised this and demanded that it stop.

A Transnational Mercenary Arena

There are two other dimensions to Sudan's security arena, and the rise of Hemedti, that are needed to complete the picture. These elements are NISS and Sudan's external security policy. They are bound together in the person of NISS chief, Salah Gosh, whose three-times rise and fall is a remarkable and essential story in its own right. Hemedti's first intersection with these threads of the narrative was the occasion on which he negotiated a deal to return from the bush. One reason why al-Bashir was ready to be generous was that his NISS director wanted Hemedti to return his military vehicles for a new armed operation (and possibly for some of his junior officers to participate as well). This was an attack on Chad, intended to topple President Idriss Déby, who had been supporting the Darfurian opposition.

Sudan's wars have always been transboundary: the war in the south was intermeshed with armed rivalry between Sudan and its neighbours to the east and south (Ethiopia and Uganda, and, after 1991, Eritrea as well); the war in Darfur began with a spillover from the Chad–Libya wars. Sudan has also exported its conflicts, intervening in the conflicts in Eritrea, Ethiopia, Uganda, the Democratic Republic of Congo, the Central African Republic, Chad, and Libya, as well as sponsoring terrorist groups that operated in Egypt, Saudi Arabia, Yemen and throughout East Africa (thus completing the circle of all its neighbours by land and sea). The particular transboundary wars of concern to this account are those in Chad and Libya.

From December 2005, Chad was in a state of proxy war with Sudan, which escalated to an explosive climax in 2008. In the last months of 2007, the head of NISS, Salah Gosh, assembled a coalition of Chadians under the umbrella Union of Forces for Democracy and Development. It was an ad hoc and quarrelsome coalition,[57] with fighters and weaponry drawn from fighting units of both Chadian and Darfurian *Janjaweed*, unified by the momentum of battlefield victories. (This was the background to the deal to bring Hemedti back into the fold.) They stormed 500 miles across Chad and entered N'djamena on 2 February 2008, whereupon the leaders paused to bicker over who would capture the presidential palace, a hesitation just long enough for Déby—hanging on by his fingernails with a French helicopter poised to evacuate him to safety—to regroup and counter-attack. The rebel coalition fell back in disarray. Three months later JEM forces, armed and equipped by Libya and Chad, staged a return strike across the Sudanese desert, reaching the capital's twin city Omdurman and only being repulsed by NISS armoured brigades on the bridges over the Nile. The JEM land cruisers had crossed the desert apparently undetected, the teenage fighters tied to their posts with rope, eating bananas as they sped across the hard sand flats on their way to a city far larger and busier than anything they had seen except on television. En route to Omdurman, JEM raided an SAF base where soldiers were caught unawares, and the SAF was conspicuously tardy in mobilising to repulse the attack: the battle on the bridges was fought and won by NISS tanks and artillery.

The reciprocal raids on the two capital cities showed how Gosh had run an independent foreign policy and built up a military force to rival the SAF. NISS was a state within a state.

The original logic for NISS was a combination of coup-proofing and the Islamists' requirement for controlling their own security agency. The coup-proofing rationale was that, if the military and security institutions were divided, none of them would be powerful or cohesive enough to launch a coup. This was standard practice among autocrats. The Islamist element was special to Sudan (the only obvious parallels are with Iran): it had developed even before the 1989 coup, emerging from the Islamists' adoption of a military track alongside their earlier avowal of a civic, democratic route to power. Islamists were trained as security officers in Libya in the mid-1970s and, over the following decades, the security branch came to dominate the whole movement.[58] By the early 2000s, most senior NCP members were also NISS officers. NISS also went into business. The army did, too, but whereas the SAF businesses were side ventures for making money and also a means of developing a domestic military industrial base (disturbingly successful, as the Sudanese exhibits at the Doha arms fair show), NISS used its commercial activities for surveillance and political control. Telecoms companies in Sudan were owned, wholly or in part, by NISS, or by former security operators in hock to NISS. Salah Gosh himself owned an oil company and had a stake in arms manufacturing.

As well as intelligence-gathering, NISS developed an operational wing. This was a subject of contention during the negotiations with the SPLM, and the text of the CPA indicates a commitment to dismantling NISS's operational capacity and limiting it to obtaining and analysing intelligence, and advising the executive. The National Security Bill was long delayed in the National Assembly, and the draft presented maintained the status quo rather than enacting the promised reform, and in the end the SPLM voted in favour of it. The SPLM had come to appreciate the value of a security agency of this kind, and in due course independent South Sudan set up its own National Security Service (NSS). Juba's NSS is not only modelled on NISS, and staffed by former NISS officers, but since 2016 President Kiir's national security advisor has been none other than Tut Kew Gatluak, the adopted son of al-Bashir. When serving in southern Sudan in the 1980s, the childless brigadier adopted two Nuer boys, one of whom was the child of his housemaid. Tut Kew grew up in al-Bashir's household and received training as a security officer. In 2016, the rapprochement between Khartoum and Juba was both symbolised and cemented by the assignment of Tut Kew to Kiir's office. As an outcome of the August 2018 negotiations in

Khartoum that 'revitalised' the Agreement on the Resolution of the Conflict in South Sudan (R-ARCSS), Tut Kew was also given the position of chairman of the National Pre-Transitional Committee, in effect the interim prime minister until such time as the Transitional Government of National Unity should be formed. As the former SPLM secretary general, Pagan Amum, pointed out, before independence Sudan was organised as 'one country, two systems', but it had now become 'two countries, one system'.

The best man at Tut Kew's wedding was Salah Gosh. That was in 2018, at the time of Gosh's second comeback.

Salah Gosh was an Islamist from his student days in the 1970s, with responsibility for the Muslim Brothers' information strategy at the university and thereafter.[59] After the 1989 coup he was a security operative, infamous for his role in the torture of detainees in Khartoum's 'ghost houses'. He became the deputy director of security operations and had responsibility for overseeing the 'Arab Afghans' who congregated in Sudan in the 1990s, including Osama bin Laden. Following the assassination attempt against Egyptian president Hosni Mubarak in 1995, carried out by jihadis based in Sudan with the support of elements in the Sudanese intelligence apparatus, Gosh was dismissed from NISS, although he denied any role in the conspiracy. He moved to military manufacturing but kept his links with intelligence operatives active, including in the US, Egypt and across the Gulf kingdoms. His astonishing ability to play both sides of the sharpest divide in the region's recent history continues to baffle commentators, as does his ability to bounce back after what would be considered terminal setbacks to less skilled operators. Gosh was reinstated at NISS in the aftermath of September 11, the confidence that the CIA had in him undoubtedly serving as a character reference. At the height of Sudan's ostracism over the Darfur atrocities, just seven months after Secretary of State Colin Powell had publicly determined that Sudanese government forces had perpetrated genocide there, the CIA decided that Gosh was sufficiently valuable to them to fly him to the Washington DC area.[60]

Gosh was, it appeared, untouchable, a man to whom normal rules did not apply. He was a disconcerting person with whom to engage, partly because of his reputation for cruelty and uncanny intelligence—in both senses of the word—and partly because of his lazy eye. He was also disarmingly frank and had the ability to rationalise otherwise opaque strategies. For example, he was an articulate analyst of how the Sudanese political market operated and what determined the going rate for renting a militia. Gosh was also thoughtful about the rationale for not killing terrorists, saying that it rarely brings a political solution any closer—but perhaps also because he knew how to reel in terrorists and reassign them to other tasks.

Whether in his role as a security consultant and political cadre, or his official position at NISS, Gosh appeared to be running his own private external relations policy. This became clearest in the immediate aftermath of the Darfur atrocities, when the war mutated into an interstate war between Sudan and Chad. Gosh's regime-change agenda for Chad was pursued without fully informing al-Bashir. The president thought it was reckless, although, typically, he was ready to wait and see what transpired before passing judgement. However, when the counter-strike reached Omdurman without NISS having either shared intelligence or coordinated the city's defence with the presidential palace and the SAF command, the dangers of Gosh's rogue operations could no longer be ignored. Against the advice of Gosh and other security advisors, al-Bashir directly contacted Déby and agreed a truce. Then he fired Gosh, reducing him to a presidential advisor serving at his master's beck and call. Al-Bashir had meanwhile begun clipping the wings of the NISS operational units, reassigning them to the SAF: the army was back in charge.

In the months between the referendum in southern Sudan (January 2011) and the independence of South Sudan (July), the Sudanese security establishment was in turmoil. Al-Bashir had overruled those who wanted to fight to stop separation. The Arab Spring was in flower: popular protests had overthrown autocrats in Tunisia and Egypt, and Colonel Muammar Gaddafi's regime in Libya was fighting for its life. Sudan's extensive operations in support of the Libyan revolutionaries (and quietly in coordination with NATO) were undertaken not by Gosh but by SAF Military Intelligence.[61] Al-Bashir was despondent, unwell and semi-reclusive; his attempt to clothe the loss of the south in a cloak of noble acceptance had not resonated among the rancorous politicians of northern Sudan. In May, the SAF chiefs of staff visited the president at home and told him that henceforth they would be keeping him informed of their operational decisions, meaning that they would no longer be consulting him beforehand and implying that his decision as Commander-in-Chief would not be paramount. Days later the SAF forcibly occupied Abyei and then ordered that the SPLA units in South Kordofan and Blue Nile be removed by 1 June, in effect declaring war in the 'two areas'.

Gosh meanwhile had promoted himself. While al-Bashir's attention wandered, he inserted himself as chief government negotiator with the SPLM on the terms of separation, usurping the designated candidate (Ghazi Salahuddin). He announced himself as 'security advisor' to the president (in reality he was just 'advisor') and set up a Security Advisory Consultancy, ostensibly for research only, but used its office as the venue for political meetings while putting a range of politicians and security officials on his payroll. Gosh had no official budget for this: the money was either his own, or from an undeclared patron. When al-Bashir asked his office manager for Gosh's file, there was none. In April 2011, as the climax approached on the potential conflict on the border with the south, and Sudanese troops poured into Libya, al-Bashir fired Gosh.

Resentment within the SAF grew. Mid-level officers who were outside al-Bashir's circle felt humiliated. Sudan's international ostracism, especially the US 'state sponsor of terrorism' designation, meant that the officer corps was shut out of the most valued Western training programmes, could not obtain top-of-the-line equipment (in marked contrast to their peers in Egypt and even more so in the Gulf) and could not get assignments to international peacekeeping operations. It was a source of shame that needled the proud military men, and was one of the motivations of a group of army officers exploring a coup against al-Bashir. Those who were briefed on the initial plans were impressed by the widespread political support—Gosh was brought in as the face of the operation. But poor planning and indecision eventually doomed the group: the plot was then exposed and Gosh was arrested.[62] Still, he was not finished: charges were dropped in April 2013 and he was free again. Gosh spent much of the next five years travelling between Khartoum, the Gulf (especially the United Arab Emirates), and the countries of the Horn (especially South Sudan).

The private deals he made are not known. Two subtle but significant acts of political re-positioning are known. One is that he aligned himself with a reformist group within the Islamic Movement known as Sa'ihoun.[63] Both in 2016 and then after November 2018, the Sa'ihoun leader, Fath al-Alim Abd al-Hayy, identified himself with the 'Peace and Reform Initiative' group of reformist Islamists and pragmatically inclined non-Islamists, which was headed by the 1985–86 interim prime minister, al-Jizouli Dafa'allah, the man who had given the last transition its political centre.[64] Gosh and the Islamist reformists were probably hoping for a soft landing for the Islamists. The second public shift is that Gosh drew on his family ties to the Khatmiyya sect, the discreet and pervasive conservative pro-Egyptian network that ties together many members of Sudan's elite. Gosh formally entered into the order in 2017, as al-Bashir's regime was moving on with its strategy of co-opting the sectarian groups to bolster its worsening position. The Khatmiyya are led by the al-Mirghani family, whose senior members have sought, with some success, to godfather conservative transitions in Sudan's modern history. The rank and file of the Khatmiyya didn't welcome Gosh's rapprochement with the al-Mirghani family[65] but for Gosh this was a certification that his Islamist allegiances were, at least, diluted. It also provided a support network in Egypt, especially important for a man whose fingerprints had been all over Sudan's support for jihadists in the 1990s.

With the active backing of the UAE, which was emerging as a key paymaster for al-Bashir, Gosh was reinstated as director of NISS in February 2018. He spent the next year positioning himself as the Gulf states' favoured successor to al-Bashir.

Rewinding the story to the aftermath of Gosh's dismissal in 2011 and the downsizing of NISS, three dynamics are evident. First, al-Bashir suffered from the absence of Gosh's intelligence capabilities: notably, the SAF was caught unawares by the SPLA attack on Heglig. Second, without the counterbalance of NISS, the army was getting too powerful: although the headline of the 2012 coup plot was Gosh's role, in fact the main conspirators were from the SAF, including sympathisers of the Sa'ihoun movement. Third, the departure of Gosh left a gap in Sudan's regional security strategy.

Hemedti moved into the vacuum in al-Bashir's inner circle created by Gosh's removal, and filled it completely and with a totally different style. The first step towards the RSF's emergence as a transnational mercenary force was facilitated by the head of al-Bashir's office, Taha Hussein, a man with a well-known personal animus towards Gosh. With Gosh out of the way, Hussein could now run the same kind of entrepreneurial security policy that had been the NISS chief's trademark. He made two separate deals to deploy Sudanese troops to Yemen.[66] The first offer was made shortly after the Saudi Arabian crown prince, Mohamed bin Salman (known as 'MBS'), started military operations against the Houthis in March 2015. Initially, MBS waved away Sudanese offers of troops on the grounds that the war would soon be over. But the Houthis were not so easily defeated and a few months later Saudi Arabia returned the call. The first contingent of SAF troops arrived in September. The contingent was on a regular rotation. One of the first force commanders was General Abdel Fattah al-Burhan. A few months after that, Hussein crafted a parallel deal involving Hemedti and the RSF. This bypassed the SAF command—the chief of staff learned about it only when it was announced publicly.

Hussein was less crafty than Gosh, and probably greedier. He dealt only with one side in the Gulf divide, ignoring Qatar. He took a hefty personal commission. When al-Bashir learned this, he angrily ordered Hussein's arrest. Having caught wind of this, Hussein was already at the airport about to board a flight to Saudi Arabia and he waved a Saudi passport in the face of the security officers sent to detain him. As a Saudi citizen under the protection of MBS, he escaped. Unlike Gosh, Hussein had neither indispensable skills nor a network of patrons and commercial partners with deep pockets, and he did not stage a comeback. Hemedti, however, survived this scandal.

The SAF and RSF were deployed separately in Yemen. At their peak in 2018–19, the total numbers in the field were variously estimated at between 7,000 and15,000, and they comprised the largest number of ground troops serving with the coalition. Saudi Arabia and the UAE paid for both deployments, although using different means. Payment for the regular SAF contingent went through the Ministry of Defence in Khartoum; funds and commissions for the RSF were (and may still be) handled through a parallel channel, in which Hemedti (and possibly other commanders) receive the fighters' salaries in hard currency, and they pay their troops in Sudanese pounds, providing them with substantial personal profit. Additionally, Saudi and Emirati recruiters co-operated with RSF commanders to hire individual militiamen from Darfur, paying them the equivalent of $55,000 up front for five years' service.[67] Mercenarism became a vast money earner for Darfurians.[68]

Alongside the RSF's border control operations (and associated smuggling) and its business empire, Hemedti was emerging as a transnational political–military entrepreneur, for whom possession of the institutions of state was a convenience.

Gosh and al-Bashir had tried to balance their ties in the Middle East, dealing equally with the two rival blocs. While Saudi Arabia and the UAE paid for the Yemen deployment and also gave occasional one-off budgetary support payments (for example, in response to Sudan's cutting diplomatic ties with Iran), the Sudanese also kept ties open with the Islamist-sympathising regimes in Qatar and Turkey. Both these countries provided direct investment, such as the Turkish rehabilitation of the port city of Suakin, associated with the construction of a naval facility, and agricultural projects. In principle, Hemedti's secular market politics do not rule out dealing with Qatar and Turkey. He made a different bet: that the anti-Islamist powers in the region were going to be the winners, so he should ally with them instead of attempting to follow al-Bashir and Gosh's strategic balancing act.

The Reckoning

All of al-Bashir's pacts unravelled, one by one. His southern policy, which descended into a marketised militarism, led to the dismemberment of Sudan, a catastrophic loss from which he and his government could never recover. Alone among the NCP and military leadership, al-Bashir seems to have recognised this, and he cut a pathetic figure trying to make the best of it as the referendum approached with its foregone conclusion. His grace in accepting that defeat went unrecognised by South Sudanese, the northern political class, and the international community.

The militia-based counter-insurgency in Darfur created a monstrous instrument that grew to control its creator. Arming and empowering the militia commanders of the far peripheries was a repeated gamble, which paid off at an escalating cost. Ultimately, Hemedti was Brutus to al-Bashir's Caesar: the same qualities that made him an effective and loyal lieutenant made him a lethal danger.

The post-Islamist embrace of the politics of bribery left al-Bashir unable to manage the regime on the dwindling political budget left when he lost the oil windfall. Sudanese who had reluctantly tolerated a government of thieves at a time of relative plenty were no longer ready to do so when the thieves were stealing everything to maintain their rotten order.

A coup-proofing strategy is, by definition, only as good as it lasts. Its fundamental trap is that it privileges allegiance over talent. Those in the leadership who were capable and ambitious, such as Ali Osman Taha and Salah Gosh, could not be loyal indefinitely to a president who offered no solutions to Sudan's crises, only tactical skill in managing the nation's entrapment in disappointment. The loyalists who remained were either incapable or (in the case of Hemedti) underestimated. Al-Bashir's security sector engineering meant that he could be removed only when all the key military–security institutions acted in unison, and like an astrological formula, this alignment was improbable but, over the course of time, inevitable. In due course, al-Bashir found himself in a corner from which all his tactical adroitness offered no escape, and in his desperation he issued an impossibly vile order, thereby creating precisely the scenario in which all members of the security cabal agreed that he had to go.

3

COUNTER-REVOLUTION AND COMPROMISE

Whose Revolution?

There sat General Abdel Fattah al-Burhan, his eyes fixed on the paper in front of him, reading it as fast as he could, spilling out all the sudden new changes. Al-Burhan was a military man and he wore digital camouflage uniform with ribbons and stars. It was 12 April 2019, and if al-Burhan was not nervous then he should have been. The general had spent his entire career as loyal military official with no public profile, and was suddenly and unexpectedly head of state. He knew that the fractious rivalries among the men who were now officially his subordinates were not quelled, and their personal ambitions were ignited by the sudden changes. Al-Burhan knew that there were a few hundred thousand protestors camped out on his doorstep demanding that he step down and dismantle the 'deep state' of which he was a product, albeit more of a military establishment man than a member of the Islamist security–commercial apparatus. Protestors outside his gates and across the country, as well as the US and the African Union, were calling for a swift transition to civilian rule.

Al-Burhan glanced up at the camera so quickly that you could barely see the whites in his eyes before his head snapped back down to read from the script. Burhan was no orator—he was practically shouting his speech at the television, as though he was drilling troops. But what al-Burhan said will be remembered as the moment Sudan's military began a rescue operation to save its political and financial clout. Al-Burhan and the army leaders accepted every demand the protestors had—sometimes even faster than the civilian representatives could put them forward. The junta pledged to nominate a civilian prime minister that opposition parties would name. Al-Burhan pledged to overhaul security organisations. A night-time curfew was lifted (not that it was being observed anyway). Justice would come for protestors who were killed. The concession went so far that members of the new Transitional Military Council (TMC) like Shams al-Din Kabbashi pledged to 'uproot the regime'. The message to the democracy protestors was simple: 'We are on your side.'

For most of the protestors, however, al-Burhan was the face of the 'deep state': the network of security men, army officers and crony merchants who had congregated around al-Bashir and his apparatus. Precisely because the general didn't have a political profile, he was suspected for being the chosen champion of the status quo, who they feared would make cosmetic changes and nothing more.

At the centre of power was the duopoly of al-Burhan and Hemedti. The third potential member of a new security cabal, Salah Gosh, mysteriously absented himself. The two men in charge had different profiles and different styles. Hemedti was conspicuously energetic, al-Burhan reserved. They knew enough about popular uprisings and transitions to democracy to know some of the tactics that would help demobilise the protestors and neutralise the international calls for a swift transition to civilian rule. But they also needed to learn fast on the job, managing tactically from week to week, learning the skills and building their networks. Each was likely driven as much by fear as ambition, neither could be clear about the final destination and, in Sudanese style, each would have anticipated that it would not be a political settlement but rather a political 'unsettlement'[1] on different terms.

Negotiations and Power Struggles

The sit-in around the military headquarters was an exemplar of what the social anthropologist, Victor Turner, called '*communitas*': the spontaneous creation of a community without hierarchy or structure united in a spirit of solidarity and harmony.[2] It is an anti-structure, a shared liminality. Instances of *communitas* can be created by well-crafted ritual, by ideological cults, or, as in the Khartoum case, by moments of collective mobilisation against oppression. Another insight into such moments is that they take the subjectivity of 'bare life'—the reduction of human community to the basic element of sustaining physical existence[3]—and transform it into a force of political affirmation. Thus the experience of the refugee camp becomes the model for the protest camp.[4] *Communitas* of this kind lives on vividly in the memories of those who were lucky enough to have this inspiring experience. But it is, of course, transient, a fleeting vision of social contract. In retrospect, many of the class, race and gender divisions in Sudan were subtly replicated within the camp, and many of the tensions over who counted as an ally, and who did not, were already apparent. Anti-structure cannot prevail and. insofar as it dissolves structures, the hard of heart with an eye for opportunity will take advantage.

The generals were caught by surprise by the strength and tenacity of the civilian uprising. It was something beyond the calculus of their schemings, something that could not be paid for or paid off within the marketplace of loyalties. Al-Burhan and Hemedti tried to let the air out of the democracy movement, slowly, so as to dissipate the revolutionary energy and allow them to consolidate power. And, like other social movements once they topple a dictator, the SPA struggled to convert their mass mobilisation into political representation.

The fall of al-Bashir marked the pinnacle of the SPA, as the leadership of the popular movement. Victory brought crisis. The organisation that had adopted the seemingly-impossible goal of regime change, and succeeded, now had to reset its agenda. There were many possible priorities. They chose to aim at taking down what they called the 'deep state', which they identified as the intricate apparatus of organisations and corporations, charities and networks, that had simultaneously supported the regime and parasitised upon it. It was a logical step, but it required a different political strategy for which the SPA had not prepared itself. This was a version of the challenge that had undone the uprisings in 1964 and 1985 and that echoes how the Arab Spring, the colour revolutions of eastern Europe, and the democracy movements of Indonesia and Myanmar, failed to consolidate power. What happened in each of these cases was that when institutions were dismantled, politics moved into a phase of intense bargaining, and those who were better placed to conduct transactional politics won out. So, too, it was in Khartoum in 2019.

The SPA had a flat leadership structure. Although there was a central committee the real strength of the organisation lay in its grassroots support. When it came to extracting political demands, this lack of hierarchy in the SPA meant that there was no working central committee, let alone singular leader, to make decisions fast and negotiate effectively with the cabal. The SPA had been resilient because it was decentralised and sought consensus during the fight to take down al-Bashir, but that became a liability when he was gone. It was hard to build consensus around issues, which meant that decision-making was slow, if it happened at all. To become a more effective political machine the SPA needed to centralise so that its leaders could have the authority to negotiate over their demands, drive bargains, and move fast as events unfolded.

This problem was compounded by the duplicate leadership. Many of the original leaders of the SPA—the teacher Ahmed Rabie, the young Mohamed Nagi, the senior Mohamed Yousif—had been jailed by al-Bashir. A shadow leadership sprang into place but the relationship between the two groups was not defined. After April, this meant that each could lay claim to the organisation's leadership. Meanwhile activists and professionals from abroad rushed into Sudan, bringing resources and skills, meaning that there was a third group demanding leadership roles. These diaspora advocated the Sudanese cause while setting up intricate transnational funding networks to support the daily actions of resistance on the ground in Sudan. They did it from the international hubs where Sudanese professionals congregated: London, Dubai or Washington. They had prestigious degrees from international universities and experience working for the top companies or non-profit organisations. They rushed to Khartoum to find an entrenched network of revolutionaries hardened by months of protests. Egos clashed among people from these three groups and infighting erupted. There was no single figure with enough stature to enforce unity. The leadership squabbles coincided with the question: what was the group's role now that al-Bashir was gone? As is so often the case for organisations built on short-term goals, the task of a deep political analysis became secondary to the issue of who should do what next, instead of the other way around.

Some in the SPA believed it should take the lead in negotiating with the military and set a political agenda. They argued that it was the country's most popular political body; that it had achieved what nobody else had managed; and that the political parties couldn't be trusted. Others argued that the SPA should be the junior partner of the FFC. 'We are not politicians,' was a common explanation they gave. More accurately, the SPA was not structured as a political body. Indeed its membership overlapped with political parties: some prominent SPA members were senior members of political parties and would face conflicts of interest, even divided loyalties. Entering formal politics would, they argued, betray the SPA's original mandate, which was as important as ever. Hence the SPA decided to be the junior partner of the FFC, passing the negotiating baton to the wider group. It was a critical inflection point.

There was no single face for the revolutionaries either. Some individuals became emblems, such as Alaa Salah, the 'Nubian Queen' or *kandaka*, who was pictured dressed in traditional finery standing on the roof of a car orchestrating the protestors. The SPA was deliberately consensual and non-hierarchical. The political parties of the FFC each had well-known leaders but none could claim pre-eminence. Rather, if there was one person who had the greatest capability to eventually lead the FFC, it was Omar al-Digair. As head of the Khartoum University Student Union, al-Digair had been a major actor in the 1985 Intifada.[5] Subsequently, as leader of the Sudanese Congress Party (SCP), he became a long-time oppositionist during al-Bashir's tenure. However, some core members of the SPA believed that opposition figures like al-Digair were tainted. They argued that they had become an acceptable opposition who did not have a significant ability to corral popular support. Still, al-Digair was quickly arrested in December 2018 after protests began. While in prison, around late February, he was visited by Salah Gosh.[6] It is unclear what they discussed, but al-Digair was released in March and vowed to continue the protests.

Other FFC leaders were also in discreet discussion with the most senior military men and with Sudan's sponsors in the Arab world. One image circulating from the days of the sit-in shows al-Burhan with Ibrahim al-Sheikh, a leader in the SCP. Other pictures surfaced of civilian leaders in amicable conversations with members of the junta. There were rumours of discussions between Gosh and democracy leaders about a collusive takeover, and the security chief was also consolidating his position with the al-Mirghani family and with the authorities in Cairo. Khalid Omar Yousif, deputy head of the SCP, and Mariam al-Sadiq al-Mahdi (National Umma Party) were in Abu Dhabi in April, and Yasir Arman of the SRF was visiting Gulf capitals. Soon after al-Bashir's ouster, Arman publicly endorsed al-Burhan and Hemedti as allies of the 'forces of change' because of their lack of Islamist ties.[7]

But at the moment negotiations began with the Transitional Military Council on 27 April 2019, if there was one man who had the best chance of uniting the FFC it was al-Digair. He had the support of prominent businessmen and members of the Sudan Call alliance.[8] Members of the Sudanese Congress Party, like Khalid Omar Yousif, were placed in key leadership roles in the SPA or FFC. Western officials began to question whether al-Digair could be the acceptable face of the opposition movement. The task for al-Digair was overcoming his lack of legitimacy with SPA protestors and uniting the FFC.

The talks began at a secret location close to the military headquarters. Neither side wanted any attention, and in fact one SPA representative missed the first meeting because he had not been given the address.

The strength of the FFC at the beginning of the negotiations was that its members represented almost the entirety of the political spectrum. That was also its weakness because their interests were so diverse and there was no mechanism to resolve disputes. The opposition members, in the FFC and on its fringes, were free floating. Some individuals had circulated in and out of junior offices as the Islamist-NCP regime had cut deals with selected factions, others had refused to compromise, either from principle or because the offer never came. Some parties were fragments, split off from older parties through factional quarrels of personal ambition, and were little more than one-man shows; others had withered and had been kept alive by the dedication of a small band of ageing veterans nursing their dreams. The Democratic Unionist Party had splintered into seven different factions.[9] One prominent faction, the 'Original Democratic Unionist Party' (*al-Ittihadi al-Asl*) under the head of the Khatmiyya order Muhammad Uthman al-Mirghani, represented those unionists who had been co-opted by the regime in 2011 when al-Mirghani's son Jafa'ar al-Sadiq was appointed a 'presidential assistant', and did not join the FFC on its formation. One faction that did join the FFC, the 'Unionist opposition gathering', was led by figures such as the late Ali Mahmoud Hassanein, a veteran of the 1985 Intifada who led the team of lawyers that brought the lawsuit against the 1989 coup plotters that is still playing out in the courts.[10] Meanwhile rumours that Salah Gosh, whose reported entry into the party was embraced by some leading members and rejected by others, was trying to mediate between members of the Mirghani family and use the 'Original DUP' as a means of staging a political return were strenuously denied by the leadership of this faction.[11]

Some of the civilian parties were centralised and personalised, others scarcely warranted the label 'party' at all, being more akin to a social club or discussion group of perennially disappointed former classmates. What they had in common was that none had held serious power, or had had to make real-time political decisions, for 30 years—sometimes longer. For al-Digair and the FFC, forging a consensus would be almost impossible. They began the negotiation process by assessing their own position. The FFC included many of the armed rebels in Darfur, southern Kordofan and Blue Nile. Their members had not, of course, participated in the non-violent civic protests, and their leaders were either in the field or in neighbouring countries, and not in Khartoum. Although the Declaration of

Freedom and Change put peace near the top of its manifesto, negotiating peace was not at the top of its to-do list.

The revolution had affirmed some core principles for progressive politics. These emerged from the worldview of the new demographic that comprised the street protestors, and the new methods they had used to achieve their success. Hopes were high for their agenda but it was not clear how those demands would be pursued in political negotiations. Notably, the role of women in the organisation and in the mobilisation of the protests was inescapable. Women leaders worked on the development of a gender-equality blueprint for the transitional period which was adopted as a point of consensus. The parties promised to adopt a quota representation system and to pursue the reform of the legal system, which was permeated by purportedly Islamist precepts that were as confusing as they were archaic and inequitable. Just two women were on the FFC negotiating team. Mervat al-Neel represented the progressive civil society strand and Mariam al-Sadiq al-Mahdi (deputising for her father) was the Umma delegate. Gender issues slipped down the priority list as the talks progressed.

Like the SPA, the FFC operated on a consensus basis but had contrived to be even less efficient. Each party in the group had a say in the negotiations and had a seat on committees, but there was no evident structure for how decisions were made. The FFC met in stuffy rooms with broken air conditioners and tried to decide the upper and lower bounds of its negotiating position. The meetings went hours past their scheduled end time. Little was accomplished. The group wanted to have no leader rather than one person whom some disagreed with. Instead, everyone had a say and could essentially filibuster progress. Rivalries that had been cast aside in the quest to remove al-Bashir blistered under pressure. Minor personal or policy differences became major obstacles. The most pressing disagreement was whether to compromise with the junta and form a joint civilian–military government or demand a complete handover of power. With the negotiations looming, the civilian coalition was in a shambles. Al-Digair was running out of time to unite the FFC.

The Communists took the most radical position and said that the military should immediately hand over power to a fully civilian government. It was a stance that was popular at the sit-in: the protestors had discovered their power, were fuelled by idealism, and wanted to consummate their revolution. They had a sense that power was, literally, lying in the street to be picked up by whoever had the audacity to claim it. Occupation of the seat of government is nine-tenths of state authority, and the moment to claim it was 12 April. Others, led by al-Digair, argued that the military had an inescapable role. As head of Khartoum University Student Union in 1985, al-Digair had witnessed the negotiations between the TMC and the National Alliance.[12] A joint government was a more direct and less risky path to power. The FFC negotiators decided to press for a unity government and work out how to partner with the military.

The decision to negotiate was taken too slowly: it signalled that the FFC wasn't unified and it gave the two generals the chance to develop their own strategy and enjoy acting as the *de facto* chief executives. With every passing day, al-Burhan and Hemedti gathered the symbols and instruments of state power, while the revolutionaries argued among themselves. Al-Burhan himself led a team of three generals, flanked by Shams al-Din al-Kabbashi, the spokesman for the TMC, and Yasir al-Atta. The civilian leaders subsequently admitted that their negotiating tactics were also inferior. Instead of beginning with an opening gambit and bargaining down towards their bottom line, the negotiators began their talks with the military by presenting their minimum acceptable offer, which was an equal number of civilian and military figures sitting on a 'sovereign council' to rule the country for a transition period. That negotiating position was not public, and the demonstrators at the sit-in believed a fully civilian government was within their reach. Each night at the sit-in, protestors gathered at night around a hill outside the army headquarters and raised their phones to create a blanket of lights in the night sky—hope piercing darkness. But inside the talks the generals immediately sensed the divisions among the civilians and exploited them. Time was on the side of the military: they just needed to play the politics of delay and their hand would get stronger: they had a country to run and wanted to be seen doing it. Meanwhile, FFC negotiators began to accuse each other of leaking their tactics to the military.

The FFC broke off the talks on 21 April owing to disagreements over the substance of who would compromise on what. They resumed on 13 May and broke off two days later after skirmishes between protestors and soldiers on the boundaries of the sit-in. Meanwhile, informal discussions continued, and a military officer suggested to al-Digair that he should propose an even number of soldiers and civilians on a 'sovereign council' to lead the country and that the head of the body should rotate. The idea of a collective presidency is familiar in Sudan: variants on this had existed in each transitional and democratic period since the 1950s, although the historical sovereignty councils were purely civilian in character. It served as a way of diluting the real and symbolic power of any individual head of state. The proposed Sovereign Council was a version of this.

There is a dispute about what happened next. Some negotiators say that al-Digair then proposed the idea back to military leaders without telling other FFC leaders when negotiations restarted. The civilian coalition was furious. But al-Digair and a member of his party said the offer had been approved by the FFC civilian negotiators. No matter the truth, it is an example of how easily the civilians were picked apart in talks by military officers who were accustomed to hard bargaining and ruthless decision-making. Still, the two sides reached an impasse. Negotiations broke down. And when word spread that al-Digair proposed rotating civilians and military leaders on the sovereign council, protestors at the sit-in were passionate in their disapproval, shouting: 'Go! Go! Enough!' In an attempt to regain the revolutionary momentum, the FFC called for a civil disobedience campaign. But in the eyes of many in the sit-in and the unions, the FFC had lost legitimacy and was bargaining away the revolution for its members' own gain. The civil disobedience call was ignored. The revolution was stalling.

The TMC was behaving more and more like a government. The performance of power was becoming power itself. The police force of Khartoum and other cities had disappeared from the streets because they had not been paid; Hemedti personally took cash to the police commissioner and handed it over and the police returned to their duties. The generals began organising a conference of the leaders of the 'Native Administration'. Hemedti was the pre-eminent figure:

he courted them and touted the conference, promising it would legitimise the status of the chiefs. He personally donated land cruisers to each of the chiefs, and in return they expressed confidence in the TMC. When the conference convened in June, Hemedti had stepped into al-Bashir's shoes as patron of the provincial aristocracy. Hemedti met with teachers on 23 May to pay salary arrears and ensure that they returned to work. Teachers are an important constituency across all parts of the country and, when schools function, it is a sign of normalcy. Electricity workers were another group who returned to work after personal intervention and cash payment by Hemedti. Television showed pictures of RSF officers opening roads and ensuring the delivery of currency to banks.

Inside the negotiations with the FFC, the junta did not have to work hard to regain the upper hand. Whatever their internal frictions, the generals were astute enough to keep a common front when dealing with the civilians. They chipped away at civilian negotiators' credibility by pointing out basic errors they had made, like putting the wrong title of a law in a proposal.[13] But such technical deficiencies were just glitches, albeit embarrassing ones. The core problem was the lack of internal structure or division of authority when it came to the FFC's efforts to bargain with the military. Different groups within the FFC had different goals and divergent tactics, and these came out into the open. Notoriously, different civilian negotiators circulated multiple and conflicting versions of the draft agreement, causing dismay among the general population. Those different agendas were never reconciled, except by dint of pragmatic deal-making, which meant adopting a median position. All the while negotiations dragged out. The April revolution stretched into May. After two weeks of bargaining by press release, the two sides resumed face-to-face talks on 13 May at the military headquarters, and agreed on a three-year transition. But crucial elements were unresolved, especially the composition of the Sovereign Council.

The sit-in remained but the hundreds of thousands-strong celebration was whittled down to the tens of thousands. The longer the talks went on the weaker the civilians became. This had previously been al-Bashir's plan: he would outlast the demonstrators. He had played this game of procrastination during peace talks, too, so much so that his delegates coined (or rather, revived) the word 'tagility'—the talent of delay—to describe it. Sudan's new military rulers had learned this art from the master, and were comfortable with the unsettled status quo. The most important part of the military's plan was to undermine the sit-in. Volunteers patted down everyone who entered the sit-in to make sure they did not have weapons. But al-Burhan and military officers soon said that these makeshift security checkpoints were actually a threat. It was the military's job to handle security, they said, and they would negotiate only if the demonstrators demobilised. At first they did not dispute the sit-in itself but challenged its boundaries, which they said were being expanded to include prostitutes, alcohol sellers and drug dealers. Day by day this boundary was tightened. Soldiers from the RSF began to needle the sit-in, culminating in nights of anarchy when they would outright assault the encampment. One such night was 15 May, when RSF militiamen attacked the volunteers providing security outside the sit-in. Protestors hauled the wounded from the front lines of camp to makeshift hospitals, whose power was cut. Five or six people died. That night demonstrators collected bricks and built a series of barriers to protect the site. The makeshift defences made downtown Khartoum seem like a city under siege with trenches and barricades. The mood of the sit-in changed. What was a festival-like atmosphere turned into something more hard core. The military was testing the protestors' defences both in the negotiation room and in the streets.

Negotiations were again suspended; again they resumed. The FFC organised strikes; the generals threatened to use force to dismantle the entire sit-in. The BBC interviewed soldiers, who said that on 20 May Hemedti ordered the clearance of the sit-in, and told his RSF troops that 'the people have to be made to flee [the sit-in] for this country to move forward and for peace to become a reality we have to deal decisively with all manifestations of chaos'.[14] Embassies in Khartoum received a letter from the Ministry of Foreign Affairs ordering them to stay away from the protest site in the days before any attack. It was a clear warning and an apparent effort to avoid collateral damage. The FFC signalled to its members that dangers were growing.

The generals began by affirming their solidarity with the protestors' aims. They then stalled and gradually reversed course. The idea was to slowly cut away at the gains made by the SPA and the FFC during the revolution. The next stage began when officials announced they wanted to have a majority on the sovereign council. There was no notable outcry from the international community at the military's reversal. The FFC conceded that the initial chair would be a soldier, making al-Burhan the next head of state.

International Policy—or Lack Thereof

For the first decade and a half of this century, Sudan (and South Sudan) consumed an enormous amount of diplomatic attention, possibly as much as the rest of the African continent combined. It was a priority for the UN and the African Union, for the US and the European Union, and for China. It was the site of multiple parallel peacekeeping operations and mediation efforts, along with a full spectrum of peacebuilding initiatives. At times Sudan and South Sudan seemed to resemble a liberal peace theme park, with rides to suit every temperament. And when truly momentous change came to Khartoum, every international player was caught completely by surprise. Not only was the revolution an entirely Sudanese affair but it scarcely elicited a flicker of interest in the world's capitals. It was almost as though diplomats had grown so weary of Sudan that they could not summon up the energy to engage when it actually counted.

The American strategy—or lack thereof—was summarised by the top US official in Khartoum, Steven Koutsis, during a meeting with government officials and experts at the Atlantic Council in Washington DC in late May 2019. Earlier that May, Koutsis had been criticised for attending a prominent *iftar* breakfast along with Hemedti and a representative of the Saudi government.[15] According to six people who attended the Atlantic Council meeting,[16] Koutsis said the US should share the values of Saudi Arabia, Egypt and the UAE. (He might have added Israel, too.) It was a shocking statement for those who were part of a passionate DC circle that had long pushed for democracy in Sudan. Koutsis asked the audience if American interests diverged from these three countries. Johnnie

Carson, a former assistant secretary of state and respected statesman of US policy in Africa, responded to Koutsis: 'Democracy. Human Rights. Good governance. The rule of law.'

Koutsis's statement was an accurate reflection of the Donald Trump administration's policy for large swathes of the Middle East and its adjoining areas, including Sudan. It delegated its powers to its four main friends: Israel plus the 'Arab troika' and backed whatever they chose to do. Over the course of the next two years, this meant that Sudan was backed into a corner and was obliged to recognise the State of Israel in return for the US removing it from the list of state sponsors of terrorism; it also abandoned its balanced position on the Nile waters dispute, aligning with Egypt in opposition to Ethiopia.

Hemedti and al-Burhan were alert to this geopolitical tide. They already had good contacts in Riyadh and Abu Dhabi and were quick to build their links with Cairo. They came away with cash in hand and intelligence cooperation. The FFC leaders were knocking at the gates of Western embassies, where they were warmly received and given promises that proposals for capacity-building projects would be welcomed and the usual suite of democracy and peacebuilding NGOs would in due course come to their assistance.

The African Union has a standing principle that it does not recognise any unconstitutional transfer of power: a country where this happens is automatically suspended from the body. This principle was adjusted during the Arab Spring to accommodate democratic revolutions, and adapted again after a popular uprising in Burkina Faso in 2014 to give interim authorities a deadline to hand over power to civilians. Meeting on 15 April, the AU Peace and Security Council (PSC) followed this precedent and gave the TMC fifteen days to hand over power to a civilian-led government. The Nigerian representative on the PSC was instrumental in pushing this through, arguing that it was both a matter of principle and also that the authority to make this decision rested with the PSC, not with the chairperson of the African Union Commission (Moussa Faki, the former Chadian foreign minister) or the 2019 chair of the African Union Assembly, Egyptian President al-Sisi. The PSC was procedurally and substantively correct, but al-Sisi wasn't happy with this decision—and he didn't like the principle either, after Egypt had itself been suspended following his takeover in 2013. Al-Sisi summoned African leaders to Cairo, where they recommended allowing a ninety-day period for the military to relinquish power. The PSC then met on 1 May and compromised on sixty days. The details of the decision did not matter so much: al-Sisi had sent a clear signal of whose side he was on, and that a compromise would lean towards continued military rule. Hemedti and al-Burhan, increasingly acting as deputy president and president, followed up with visits to Saudi Arabia and the UAE. They weren't exactly state visits, but they met with the most senior officials in those countries.

The 3 June Massacre

As the sun was about to rise on 3 June, thousands of police and RSF paramilitaries gathered outside the sit-in site toting guns and wielding whips. It was the end of Ramadan. The call to prayer belted through the morning sky at 5 a.m. and then the RSF and police opened fire on the sit-in and the crack of gunfire smacked off the buildings and suddenly red stains grew larger and the makeshift brick barricades that volunteers built to defend the sit-in became turnstiles of horror followed by soldiers rushing deeper and deeper into the sit-in to destroy the whole thing. Protestors scattered. Fire and smoke filled the air. Soldiers slinging AK-47 rifles marauded around the freedom that once was to a backdrop of screaming and gunfire. The RSF and police hunted down protestors. Cornered them. Whipped them. The RSF burned tents and torched the carnival of freedom that once was. Activists ran into hospitals for safety. The junta attacked people inside hospitals also. Dead bodies inside the hospitals were covered with Sudanese flags. All the while, the regular army was ordered to stay in its barracks and let Hemedti's men continue their rampage. Accounts of sexual violence were common and horrific. It looked like a deliberate targeting of the women, whose conspicuous role at the forefront of the protests had proved such a practical and symbolic challenge to the men in uniform. Evidence was disposed of. Rocks were tied to dead bodies and thrown into the Nile river so they would sink. Corpses were buried in at least one mass grave. When it was all over—hours later—a cloud of smoke billowed high into the Khartoum sky to represent the hope that was. More than two hundred were dead, hundreds raped or injured, and dozens more were missing.[17] Two years after the revolution concluded, mass graves and dead bodies were still being uncovered, slowly and painfully severing families with 'missing people' hopes.[18]

Non-violent protest is the most powerful means of removing an authoritarian government. It is demonstrably more effective than armed resistance.[19] But no political strategy is costless, infallible, or has a predetermined timeline. The neighbourhood committees and the SPA had perfected the tactics of rigorously non-violent resistance. The massacre was a direct challenge, raising the stakes and giving the SPA and the demonstrators a straightforward choice, namely submit or escalate.

'Violence is red,' writes Donald Donham.[20] An act of large-scale violence, such as a massacre, has the odd effect of slowing down and distorting our sense of time. Killing people in a savage and arbitrary way is a shock to the body politic, a trauma from which it struggles to recover. Such a momentous event must surely have had causes with similarly profound dimensions: long-festering hatreds or deep conspiracies. Sometimes that is the case, sometimes not. Those who document and define the event are not usually the ones who are first on the scene—that's the protagonists and their victims.[21] Nor are they the second—the journalists and those who choose the images to circulate on social media platforms. The writer seeking to chronicle and understand the violence must sift the evidence, trying to recover the indeterminacy and bewilderment of the moment, as well as the order behind it. That is, order in both senses: the instructions given to the men who do the killing and wounding, and the logic of their action. Violence has its own logic. It can be instigated in the service of politics and the market, as an instrument for destroying or creating identities, or law enforcement. It is a currency whose value isn't known until payment is made, a weapon that can control those who believe they are its master.

No ruler, however fearsome he may be, has ever succeeded in ruling through violence and terror alone. As a logic of power, violence works when it is deployed in the service of institutional authority, or charismatic leadership, or systems of reward, such as patrimonial governance and its contemporary version, the political marketplace. When violence as a logic of power is brazen and is not legitimised by other modes of authority, those who wield it are vulnerable. Dictators who have lost their aura of mystique, faced by a crowd that has lost its fear, cannot rule. So it proved in Sudan.

The generals scrambled. They knew how an autocrat was supposed to dissipate popular anger and sow confusion, and they tried. They shut down the internet. They spread alternative stories about what had happened, following the elementary process of simply asking questions to throw doubt on the rather obvious facts. Since nearly the minute after the firing stopped on 3 June, some Sudanese politicians and businessmen who eyed a partnership with Hemedti promoted conspiracy theories about the attack—from the fiction that the warlord was tricked, to the bizarre theory that RSF uniforms were stolen and worn by other people. The generals also tried to shift onto a different political terrain. The next day they announced they would shut down negotiations with the FFC and called for elections in nine months. It was an obvious attempt to divide the civilians, offering a familiar path to power for the conservative sectarians who were best prepared to contest in such an election.

Without their communications platforms, it was harder for the protestors' anger to metastasise inside Sudan. For example, internet activists organised a 'Blue for Sudan' campaign, turning social media profile images the colour blue in honour of Mohamed Matar, a 26-year-old activist who died in the massacre. The pop singer Rihanna joined the online campaign. 'They're shooting people's houses, raping women, burning bodies, throwing them in the Nile like vermin, tormenting people, urinating on them, making them drink sewage water, terrorizing the streets, and stopping Muslims from going to Eid prayer. There is an Internet blackout! Please share. Raise awareness,' the pop star said on Instagram.[22] But outrage boiling over on the web about the massacre was blocked inside Sudan.

The internet shutdown also meant that it was harder for activists to organise a practical response to the break-up of the sit-in. The SPA's main tool of communication was blocked. Each day the junta shut-off slowly suffocated any ability protestors had to regroup. The internet blockade lasted for a month.

To succeed in reversing a popular uprising, a counter-revolution needs to be truly terrifying, to instil such fear that the webs of solidarity are broken. It is for this reason that the episodes that broke civic revolutions in France, Russia and Ethiopia are known as 'terrors', when state violence is exerted without evident limit. The Sudanese generals did not have the will or capacity to inflict this. In other cases, especially where civic resistance has taken to armed rebellion, autocrats have played identity politics and refashioned a struggle between dictator and democrats as an existential fight among sects, tribes or ethno-national groups. The Sudanese generals, their own forces divided by ethno-regional identities and facing a unified resistance, could not play this card. As a political act, the 3 June massacre failed: the revolution was undefeated.

From the start, moreover, the SPA membership had harboured no illusions about a quick or easy struggle. Resistance was what they did, and did well. Their wounds re-energised their movement. The huge number of SPA members who were present at the sit-in, and the unions' membership roster, doubled as a list of survivors. Without needing to debate the matter, its members believed there should be no talks with the military. 'There is nothing to negotiate over,' Samahir Mubarak, the SPA spokeswoman, said a few days after the massacre. The SPA went back to its position of two months earlier: immediate handover of power to civilians. They had one instrument to use in pursuit of that goal: massive popular demonstrations, and they vowed to hold the biggest ever.

The cities-wide web of personal connections forged over the previous six months hummed with energy. Neighbourhood resistance committees coordinated with members of the SPA to plan a march of unprecedented scale. The date was to be 30 June, the thirtieth anniversary of the military–Islamist putsch that citizens had for too long been obliged to celebrate as the 'National Salvation Revolution'. The people would both reclaim the streets and reclaim the day. The organisers aimed for a million. They didn't achieve that number but they showed enough determination and capacity to show the generals—and the world—that the revolutionaries would not forgo their achievement so quickly.

Compromises

Revolutionaries, by definition, do not like to negotiate compromises. They want to sweep away the old order in its entirety. The vibrant *communitas* of the sit-in was not only an act of defiance but was a vision of the transformed Sudan of the future. Some went so far as to argue that Sudan didn't need security forces—they should be abolished, not reformed. From the ashes of the *ancien régime*, a new social contract should spring into life.

Revolutions don't take that course. If the country's political institutions are sufficiently robust to allow for a negotiated compromise, that's the best outcome. If mechanisms for a round table of parties can be willed into existence, that's an option in countries where formal institutions are subordinate to the swirls of transactional politics. International mediators have rarely stepped onto this terrain: they are usually activated when there is a civil war, which for a civic uprising is too late.

In Sudan, the internationals acted much faster. An ad hoc array that included the African Union and the Intergovernmental Authority on Development (IGAD), the US and the UK, and Saudi Arabia and the UAE, all played a role in reaching a negotiated compromise between the military and the civilians, or to be precise, the TMC and the FFC. The efforts had begun in May, they were energised by the June massacre and the astonishing resilience of the democracy movement, and culminated in the signing of the Constitutional Declaration in August. The headline story is that the internationals, having slept through the revolution until after the removal of al-Bashir, belatedly awoke but then acted rapidly and effectively, forestalling a crisis that otherwise threatened to escalate into a still-more-bloody confrontation and a new, deeper round of protracted crises. And indeed, if we contemplate the alternatives to agreement, that story is correct. The peacemaking worked.

It is not, of course, as simple as that. Every peace agreement is a political act that is rooted in both reciprocal concessions by the parties and in a simplified ordering of the political contest—some groups and issues are made secondary or excluded altogether. In any complex conflict, mediators will try to identify the primary problem conflict and then make the rest secondary. This meant that the negotiations over 2001–04 that led to the CPA were primarily between the Sudanese government and the SPLM/A, focused on the relationship between north and south, with the issues of the 'three areas' (Abyei, the Nuba Mountains and Blue Nile) and democratisation reduced to secondary questions, and Darfur and eastern Sudan excluded altogether. The analytics of the mediation fused with the interests of the parties to create a path.[23] Such processes of conflict resolution have been critiqued because the warring parties, with their territorial claims and ethnic constituencies, are elevated over the claims and constituencies of unarmed, civic actors, which in turn creates a perverse incentive for excluded groups to turn to violence to stake a claim in the peace.

The negotiations to resolve the confrontation in Khartoum shared the feature of distilling a complex conflict down to its most immediately salient element and making this the defining issue in a comprehensive settlement. The parties at the table were the TMC and the FFC and the aim was power-sharing on the path to a comprehensive settlement. The structural difference from all previous internationally facilitated peace agreements in Sudan was that it prioritised the urban, civic conflict and made the armed conflicts in the provinces into the secondary question, inverting the customary hierarchy. For good or ill, the mediators, as well as the TMC and the FFC, decided against an all-inclusive process that would have brought the armed groups to the negotiating table as well. That can be criticised as passing up a historic moment at which civic groups and armed groups could have sat together as equals in the negotiations, with the chance of reaching a truly inclusive comprehensive agreement. It can be defended on the grounds that multi party talks are slow and cumbersome and if those talks had dragged on for months, even years, then the TMC would have consolidated power in the interim and the opening for a new political order would have been missed.

What is certain is that the negotiations during July—from the million-person march to the Constitutional Declaration—were the focus of intense bargaining, and the decisions made in those critical weeks shaped the future of the country.

The timing of the June crackdown, days after al-Burhan and Hemedti's visits to the Arab capitals, sent the message that Sudan's sponsors backed the military. The Arab troika may or may not have meant it that way. However, the Saudis and Emiratis were taken aback by the vigour of the resistance.

The African Union stuck to its principles. Three days after the massacre, the PSC met and voted immediately to suspend Sudan, and to keep in place its deadline of the end of the month for the military to hand over to a civilian government. It was a minor but significant victory for the AU's norms against the transactional politics of the Arab autocrats. It also had the consequence that the AU Commission chairperson, Moussa Faki, was obliged to submit a formal report to the PSC on whether Sudan had met the preconditions to be readmitted, and to do so by the end of the month. Faki appointed his long-time advisor, Mohamed al-Hassan Ould Labat, to serve as his envoy. Labat's style was discreet to the point of secrecy: he did not share his proposals with anyone else.

Then the Ethiopian prime minister, Abiy Ahmed, decided to take a personal initiative. He increasingly saw himself as a peacemaker and was confident that his personal charisma and encouragement would get the two sides to agree. A devout Pentecostalist, he was continually enjoining Ethiopians to express love for one another and to overcome their differences through the power of prayer and personal friendship. His approach was the opposite of Labat's: high profile and impulsive. Visiting Khartoum on 20 June, he passed the message that the Sudanese should embrace one another, and left a personal envoy, Mahmoud Dirir, to follow up. A few days later, the IGAD Council of Ministers affirmed its support for Dirir and thereby made it an IGAD initiative—to the irritation of Abiy, who wanted it to remain his own initiative. For him, peace is a matter of personal relationships, not structures. In fact, in an unprecedented turn of events, the Sudanese TMC had to summon the two African envoys to ask them to coordinate their activities.

The two African envoys did not link up with the long-standing efforts to resolve the long-running conflicts in Darfur and the 'two areas' of the Nuba Mountains and Blue Nile, even though these also fell within the AU remit. Ten years earlier, the PSC had mandated the AU High-Level Implementation Panel for Sudan and South Sudan (AUHIP), chaired by the former South African president, Thabo Mbeki, to facilitate a peace process for these conflicts. These efforts had stalled over the previous few years, due to government obstruction and the rebels' disinterest in dealing with a regime that was both weak and not serious about peace. Nonetheless, the opportunity for a joint initiative was there for the taking—but it was not taken.

The African envoys in Khartoum did one important thing: they took the document on which the TMC and FFC had been working before negotiations were suspended, made some minor adjustments, and presented it as a compromise proposal. It was a minimal effort—but it turned out to be a vital one.

The Western powers deplored the massacre but they shared an assumption with the generals and the Arab troika, that the ferocity of the crackdown would put an end to organised democracy activism. When they were proven wrong, they began to step up their interest. Their problem was that they had no workable mechanism in support of a conflict resolution initiative: in principle they supported the UN, which in turn supported the AU, but the AU envoys had not requested their engagement beyond a pro forma backing for the African effort. Instead, Washington DC and London pulled a different set of levers. The mechanism they chose was the informal quartet of powers that had come together to coordinate over the Yemen war and associated security threats: the US, the UK, Saudi Arabia and the UAE. In July they switched the agenda to Sudan. Evidently, the Arab states had miscalculated the strength of the protest. Also, it appeared, they had also been working on the false assumption that democracy was a window through which Islamists would enter government. In Sudan's case, this was of course the opposite: the uprising was almost entirely anti-Islamist. This was just one error that showed the failure of communication, let alone understanding, between these governments and the Sudanese democracy movement. On the other hand, the American and British embassies were regularly receiving visitors from the SPA and FFC, but they had limited contact with the military. The US didn't even have a military attaché, because there was no full diplomatic recognition. At the quartet meeting, the four governments decided to coordinate and push for the two Sudanese sides to resume talks and reach a compromise. The African envoys were also in town. They had neither leverage nor a mediation plan but they possessed two things the quartet lacked: a mandate from an international organisation and a written document, which was a straightforward middle way between the positions of the junta and the FFC before the massacre. The quartet could do the heavy lifting and the Africans could serve as the public face for the result. The division of roles suited everyone involved in the backroom bargaining—whether it served the goal of democracy was another matter.

It is a standard starting point for conflict resolution that the mediators do not choose the parties or the issues. It is not the whole story—the mediators structure and guide the process in many ways, some subtle, some overt—but in an instance where outsiders step in to help resolve an urgent conflict, it is largely the case. The FFC and the TMC had initiated the talks in April and had determined their structure and agenda, and this had not changed during the tumultuous month of June.

The generals in power were clear what they wanted: to stay in power. The democrats were not so clear. Some insisted that the revolution's goal was to sweep the army out of power completely, others thought it was necessary to reach a compromise. 'You can't wish away the military,' tweeted Irfan Siddiq, the British ambassador.[24] Mohamed Yousif of the SPA complained that Western nations 'are putting pressure on us to be flexible and to be more accepting to compromise. But the military council is just an extension of Bashir's regime'.[25]

The FFC negotiators were convinced, however, that striking a deal with the junta was their only option. They feared that trying to push for an exclusively civilian government would risk a civil war. Some on the civilian side were much more accommodating of the soldiers. Sadiq al-Mahdi openly praised Hemedti and the TMC, and called on the other civilian groups to abandon their plans to force the military to step aside by engaging in a general strike.[26]

This was an ideological chasm that sparked strong opinions from each side. The FFC was slowly ripping apart; dissent came into the open. The gap between the street and the negotiators widened.

Despite claims that around 60% of protestors were women there were almost none in leadership positions of the SPA and FFC.[27] The lack of female leaders in Sudan's democratic movement is about more than token equality: 'The lack of diversity makes the negotiating team extremely close-minded and they can't come up with the results that represent the revolutionary forces,' said Hala al-Karib, the regional director of the Strategic Initiative for Women in the Horn of Africa.[28] 'Most of the political parties who are currently negotiating on behalf of the Sudanese people did not invest on addressing the challenges of women, so women are not interested in joining.' Furthermore, even in the best-case scenario, in which women issues had been centred and their representatives consulted, the women's empowerment agenda in the declaration was limited. Its focus was on undoing the discriminatory legal framework of the Islamist regime as enshrined in the Family Law code and increasing women's representation in government. These were important but did not address the deep-seated socio-economic forces that condemn most Sudanese women to lives of poverty and precarity.[29] The FFC negotiators did not raise the issue of whether legal reforms and the 40% representation in government and in leadership roles could address these structural inequalities. Two years later, al-Karib had the opportunity to address the United Nations, and pointedly said: 'women wonder if they are better off than they were under al-Bashir's oppressive regime'.[30]

The armed groups were left out of the process entirely. They were promised that peace would be a priority but their concerns were addressed only in chapter 15 of the sixteen-chapter Constitutional Declaration. It was more than a slight: it was a sharp reminder of the ways in which civilian regimes had reproduced Sudan's geographic and racial hierarchies no less than military ones. The TMC had no need to play divide and rule with the opposition: the opposition leaders were playing into their hands.

By the middle of July military and FFC negotiators settled on a framework deal to make a coalition government. Drawing on the African Union formula, the draft Constitutional Declaration had an even number of civilian and military representatives on a Sovereign Council—a collective presidency in the tradition of Sudan's earlier parliamentary regimes. A figure from each side would take turns leading the country for 18 months. A civilian prime minister would be appointed. When the council's terms of reference were first made public to the people, they gave an honorary role for the military wing, with no executive powers. In fact, the deal promised an even split in the highest offices between the civilians and military. A transitional legislature was planned, with members of the FFC and other political parties joining in. The top opposition negotiators thought it was the best deal they could get.

The preamble to the Constitutional Declaration makes a nod to women, youth, and the martyrs of the struggle, but makes no mention of the armed groups and the immense human losses suffered in the long wars in the peripheries.

The deal 'does not satisfy all of the objectives the Sudanese people wanted to realize in their revolution, but it is a premise for their goals to be recognized through a process,' said Amjad Farid, a leader inside the SPA.[31] 'We have no choice,' one negotiator said. But other members were frustrated. That same negotiator's wife berated him for working with the murderous junta. The SPA representative 'is not listening to his team, thus not linked to what is going (on) at the ground,' a top official from the organisation said.[32] Inside the SPA there was a major dispute over signing the agreement, with a large constituency arguing that its leaders had no authority to sign the deal with the military. 'We still have not achieved what we are fighting for,' said Sara Abd al-Jalil, another spokeswoman for the SPA. 'Omar al-Bashir is not there, but the regime itself is still there. Objective one has not been achieved. Objective two has not been achieved, which is a civilian government. It's like having a diversion in the middle of your journey.'[33]

It would be easy to accuse the leaders of the civilian parties of colluding in a sell-out. Three considerations make this an over-hasty or simplified conclusion.

The first of these is that there was so much uncertainty about what was happening and about what might happen next. No one could ever be sure whether the uprising would culminate in a peaceable denouement or a massacre. Cordial communication between revolutionaries and their adversaries is in fact an important, if under-recognised, element in the success of non-violent revolutions. Mahatma Gandhi's letters to the British Viceroy, and Nelson Mandela's clandestine discussions with the apartheid regime, are cases in point.[34]

Second, the success of any transition from authoritarianism to democracy depends on the reformers' strategic approach to dismantling the institutions of repressive governance. It is tempting to demand that everything be swept away in one grand gesture, and abolishing institutions that have harboured gross corruption or been instruments of repression wins immediate applause. But it is easier to dismantle than to build: what follows may not be a new democratic social contract willed into being by civic-minded people, but a turbulent and violent political market in which power goes to the most ruthless and capable political entrepreneur.

The risk of a negotiated transition is that the revolutionaries, with their limited assets and skills in the transactional political market, are outmanoeuvred and become accomplices in a counter-revolution.

The third consideration goes deepest: what exactly was this revolution, and who owned it? Was it solely a matter of taking down al-Bashir? Was it about transferring power from the military to civilians? If so, which civilians? The question of whether the SPA, the wider civilian coalition, or some other group, should represent civic interest had not been addressed, let alone resolved. Was it a revolution against Islamism and the Islamists? The question of whether all Islamists should be removed from government, or those who had latterly opposed the Salvation Regime, was controversial; so, too, was the extent of de-Islamising public life. To what extent did the revolution align with the long struggles for equality among the diverse peoples of Sudan, ending the racial–geographical and gender hierarchy of power and wealth? And if so, who could represent the peripheries? Should the racial dimension or the centre–periphery dimension be considered primary? This was an especially vexing dimension to the revolution, as General Hemedti was a Darfurian Arab—a man of the peripheries but not from a group that had assumed an 'African' identity; in fact widely seen as its oppressor. And last, was this a revolution of youth against elders?

The revolution was all the above—and the different groups within the FFC coalition all had different priorities. Each actor's agenda aligned with their analyses of the Sudanese crisis, though which came first—the political interests or the framework for analysing the problem—was not clear.

When the Constitutional Declaration was finally signed on 17 August, the new structure of government was apparent. Ahmed Rabie, whose brave protest in 2012 was arguably the starting point of the protest movement, signed the deal on behalf of civilians. Signing for the TMC was not al-Burhan, its leader, but Hemedti, arguably the real powerbroker. After Hemedti signed the declaration he held it aloft—an agreement promising cooperation, justice and progress. Yet in an omen of things to come, Hemedti waved the agreement over his head—upside-down.

As the Sudanese like to say, when God created their country, he laughed.

4

POLITICAL BUSINESS AS USUAL

In August 2019, Sudan was suspended between revolution and counter-revolution. The compromise was a cohabitation between civilians wanting to transform Sudan and generals for whom a democratic façade was the key to legitimising their continued exercise of real power. The hardest tasks, of rehabilitating the formal economy and institutions, were given to a cabinet of apolitical technocrats, while the wheeler-dealers continued to cut their bargains in the back room. The cabinet had authority over the national budget—in massive deficit—while the military cabal controlled the political budget, managing the cash in hand.

The civilian cabinet that took office was a bet in several ways, most crucially that the country's economic crisis could be stabilised before the masses of ordinary Sudanese who had joined the protests became disenchanted with democracy on an empty stomach. For that gamble to succeed, Sudan needed an international economic bailout and a peace agreement that brought the provincial rebels into government. It needed both to move fast. The recovery required that the economic parasitism of the crony capitalists and mafia mercenary bosses be dismantled or bypassed, though whether that should precede or follow international economic normalisation was not clear. In a conversation with one of the authors of this book in July

2019, Abdalla Hamdok estimated that the government had about six months to bring the economic crisis under control before it lost the political initiative.

The transitional government took office on 19 August. The prime minister and cabinet were chosen by the FFC and endorsed by the popular movement precisely because they were not professional politicians. They were thrust into the eye of the storm, supposedly a place of calm, but also where they could scarcely move without being overwhelmed by the political hurricane swirling around them. There is no 'technocratic' agenda that is not also political. The institutional apparatus of state, so thoroughly penetrated by factional interests, so thoroughly depleted by decades of austerity and purges followed by the recruitment of loyalists, does not preside over Sudan's politics, conflicts and economy: it is the arena for those struggles.

Putting technocrats in power in deeply troubled countries rarely turns out well. They tend to identify solutions but become frustrated when the 'political will' to implement them cannot be found. Contemporary cases such as Afghanistan bear this out; so, too, does Sudanese history. In 1965, the interim prime minister, Sirr al-Khatim Khalifa, a formally apolitical educationalist, co-operated with a young Sadiq al-Mahdi to replace his initial interim cabinet with one less dominated by the left.[1] In 1985, the former association of the nominally technocratic interim prime minister, al-Jizouli Dafa'allah, with the Muslim Brotherhood was the source of much concern among critics, who saw him as a proxy for the Islamists and the military.[2]

In 2019, in contrast to their modest personal ambitions, the technocrats' agenda was nothing less than transforming Sudan: peace with the armed rebels, economic reform, democratisation, de-Islamisation. They dreamed of a civic and developmental state but they possessed neither the money nor the guns to make it happen. The cabinet of technocrats lasted 18 months, after which they were replaced by a nearly all-inclusive government of politicians.

A Technocratic Experiment

Abdalla Hamdok had retired from the United Nations, where he was deputy executive secretary of the Economic Commission for

Africa in Addis Ababa, Ethiopia. He had no political ambition, and instead talked about taking an academic fellowship to reflect on the economic challenges facing Africa, and continuing to offer informal advice to African Union and UN mediators and governance reform experts. Hamdok also wanted to make a contribution to his country. Like so many professionals of his generation, he had been forced out of the country and had been unable to make use of his expertise in service of Sudan's development and democracy. When his name was first floated as a candidate for the civilian prime minister, Hamdok hesitated: the expectations were so high, the problems so profound, the capacity of the position so limited, that the office was likely to be more of a burden than an opportunity. But he also had a clear vision of what the Sudanese government needed to do: provide an agenda for change.

When Hamdok became prime minister, the uprising accomplished its declared goal of a civilian government—in part. It was a cohabitation with the military, with al-Burhan as the chair of the Sovereign Council—the closest to a president—for the first half of the transition. Hamdok's cabinet adopted a plan with ten priorities, announced by the information minister, Faisal Mohamed Saleh, at a press conference after the first cabinet meeting in September 2019:

> The priorities include stopping the war, building peace, addressing the economic crisis, cancelling freedoms restricting laws, enhancing women's rights, reforming state institutions, setting up balanced external policy, enhancing social care and development, enhancing role of youth, preparing for the constitutional conference and fighting corruption.[3]

The aim was to implement all of these within 200 days. Faithful to that collective decision, Hamdok often repeats that priority list. As every politician knows, ten priorities is at least seven too many. Before he took office, Hamdok identified the three essential actions: fixing the economy, achieving peace with the armed groups in Darfur and the 'two areas' of southern Kordofan and Blue Nile, and reforming the security sector and its sprawling kleptocratic commercial empire.

Underpinning this is a particular vision of how Sudan could transform. Hamdok presents his vision quietly but firmly: it is a deeply held conviction. From his days as a UN economist to his position as prime minister, Hamdok's demeanour, ideals and values have not changed. His voice is so quiet that it approaches a mumble, and then it rises to an audible level while explaining his thesis for Sudan's transition. His moustache will barely move and the blue shade in his eyes will become more prominent—a man articulating the distant shore to which he hopes to guide his country, while navigating the squalls along the way.

His profile as a possible candidate for a senior government job started in 2018 when al-Bashir asked him to return to Sudan and take a senior position. At that time, Hamdok was a career international civil servant. He had a distinguished record at the African Development Bank, International IDEA, and had had two stints at the UN Economic Commission for Africa, the first as director of the department that researched governance and the second as deputy executive director (from 2011 until he retired in 2018). Among other things, he was involved in forging the thinking behind the governance criteria for the New Partnership for Economic Development and convened a high-level group to study illicit financial flows out of the continent, as well as overseeing the routine work of the UN Economic Commission for Africa. Civil service reform. Good governance. Women's economic empowerment. Page by page, the studies he commissioned guided him along a path that prepared Hamdok for his future role. More crucial was his location: in Addis Ababa, Hamdok interacted daily with the Sudanese who visited the city for the unending round of peace talks, and he also became informal advisor to the African Union and United Nations peace envoys.

In September 2018, al-Bashir called. As explained in Chapters 2 and 3, the shock waves of the secession of South Sudan took five years to hit, and Sudan's economy started contracting at a terrifying rate. Inflation shot up. The government had been living in denial about the reforms needed, and in particular had failed to grapple with a national budget based on arithmetic that was now just fantasy. Sudan could not afford to subsidise bread and fuel, it could not afford its enormous civil service payroll, and it could not pay its military—whose budget was no longer published. Yet, al-Bashir also knew that he could not abolish the subsidies or eviscerate the public sector without facing street protests, and nor could he fail to pay the soldiers. His government took half-hearted steps on cutting subsidies.

Al-Bashir had no strategy for resolving his impossible dilemma. But, as always, he had tactics: he wanted a public face for economic reform more acceptable to the Sudanese public and to international donors and creditors. He asked Hamdok to be his finance minister. The little that was known about Hamdok in Sudan at this time revolved around his long-lapsed association with the Sudan Communist Party, something shared with many intellectuals of his generation. The key tenets of the 'Communist' label today are secularism, respect for civil and political rights, and a distrust of the 'deep state'—the predatory and kleptocratic Islamist and security networks that control so much of the Sudanese economy. If it had ever been classically Marxist, Hamdok's economic philosophy had long since moved on, as documented by his international career and his interest in the 'developmental state' model in Asia and certain African countries including Ethiopia under Prime Minister Meles Zenawi. He is fond of citing the 'experience of the Vietnamese Communist party's pragmatism' in their 25-year-long partnership with the supposedly neoliberal World Bank that has built the East Asian economy into an engine of productivity. Still, the Communist association was a political signal for al-Bashir to try to assuage the boisterous Khartoum elite. But Hamdok said no. 'When he refused everyone loved him,' said al-Shafie Khidir, once the Communist Party's secretary general and subsequently an informal advisor to Hamdok and an influential public intellectual among the youth and the political left.

When the TMC and FFC began negotiating in earnest, Hamdok's name emerged as the leading candidate to be the prime minister. To his supporters, he offered a solution to economic woes that had long plagued Sudan. The SPA was an especially strong backer, with some former Communist Party members energetically backing him for the job. His relationships with the UN, the World Bank and foreign ambassadors seemed to promise a golden ticket to remove Sudan from the US state sponsors of terror list and secure overdue debt relief. And perhaps the greatest advantage Hamdok had was that he had no discernible political ambition. He would not try to extend his tenure as the transitional prime minister into indefinite rule. He was an understated technocrat, not an autocrat in waiting.

Hamdok wrestled with the decision of whether to accept the job. He knew that the office could be a façade for the kleptocratic generals—the retailer selling soap and matches in the store front while the mafia bosses laundered their illicit profits in the backroom. As he debated the offer, he privately observed that he had six months to a year to stave off national financial collapse, that would in turn threaten state collapse. 'I thought it would have been better for this change to be led by people inside the country, physically inside the country,' Hamdok recalled in December 2020. 'And some of us in the diaspora supporting.'[4] But he was deeply affected by the young people who died during the revolution. Hamdok simply believed he had a patriotic duty to serve his country. Yet, even after informally accepting the nomination, the second thoughts lingered. Hamdok called close confidants and wondered aloud if he would make a better minister of lesser importance—like international cooperation. He considered backing out. What kept him in the position, in part, was that Hamdok had a theory of change for Sudan and it meshed with the FFC's template.

The great let-down of prime ministers and presidents once they take office is that they find their ability to carry out change is greatly constrained. They are not generals on horseback who come sweeping into a town to unveil a new regime. In the 21st century, heads of state are captains of a ship, trying to adjust the course of a complex political economy a few degrees this way or that while squalls and tides threaten to swamp the vessel. The threat that Hamdok would end up a puppet to a military junta was never clearer when the military made Hamdok homeless on arrival. Al-Burhan refused to give the new prime minister any of al-Bashir's old palaces to stay in when he first landed in Khartoum, an action that sent an unmistakable signal over who controlled Khartoum's governmental real estate. The generals also didn't give the prime minister a budget to staff his office. Instead, Hamdok initially plotted his prime ministership from a house lent to him by a prominent family in Sudan, as if the head of government had a short-term vacation rental, drawing upon the efforts of volunteer staff and holdovers from the old regime who knew the secrets of bureaucratic influence all too well. From this marble-pillared house, Hamdok began to put his model into action. He put together a team of advisors, many of whom were, like himself, prominent ex-members of the Sudan Communist Party and diaspora technocratic experts. Along with Hamdok himself, figures like Shafie Khidir and Amjad Farid, who had both left the party in mid-2016, were understood by their former comrades to constitute a 'centrist' political faction that was 'pragmatic' about dealing with Hemedti and the military.[5]

No role for women in the leadership was discernible at this stage, and there were some ominous augurs. Some female secretaries and support staff were hired from among the educated younger generation but they left a short while afterwards, complaining of ill-treatment and a misogynist atmosphere from the men controlling the office—ironically, the leftists.

Hamdok took office armed with a tool that he was most familiar with: a model to change Sudan. The account of Hamdok's tenure as prime minister and the fate of Sudan's revolution is the story of the variables in Hamdok's model. These variables are economic stabilisation and development, peace and solving the root causes of conflict, and security sector reform, all of which should make possible legal reform, transitional justice and finally political–constitutional reform. 'I coined this term, "the Sudan model of transition",' Hamdok says, before adding, 'which so many people are not happy with.'[6]

The tragedy of Hamdok's first 18 months in office was that on each of these items on his agenda, the ruthless practitioners of transactional politics, with cash in one hand and a gun in the other, prevailed.

Peace

The first test of the new government was peace. The Constitutional Declaration gave a six-month window for a peace deal to be signed with the many rebel groups in Sudan. 'Unless we address this war issue and establish sustainable peace, we are not going to make progress on any other thing,' Hamdok explained.[7] 'All this talk about development and democracy itself will be shaky. All these issues are interlinked. Peace is key.'

Excluding the armed groups from the negotiations leading to the Constitutional Declaration had itself been a step backwards: the rebel leaders were distrustful of both the FFC and the TMC. By separating the two tracks of negotiations, the political leaders also tacitly accepted a standard model for the peace talks. This formula consists of the government sitting across the table from representatives of armed groups, and working on a tripartite agenda: ceasefire and security arrangements; power-sharing; and wealth-sharing. Tacked on at the end are questions of transitional justice and democratisation, but agreement on the main three issues usually precludes any serious efforts at either criminal accountability or political accountability, because the premise of the deal is that the parties at the table are going to be the winners in the end. This model was enshrined in the 2005 CPA and was reproduced in every negotiation subsequently, including those in South Sudan to try to resolve the civil war that broke out in 2013. Such a peace deal boils down to a sharing of the spoils, and often a security pact among those who sign to suppress those who do not sign. It is a 'payroll peace' or a 'rent-sharing deal'. It is workable when the package of jobs, development aid and payoffs is enough to leave everyone satisfied. The CPA was signed when Sudan's oil boom was in full swing and the budget was expanding by 25% every year. Peace agreements for Darfur, Eastern Sudan, the 'two areas' and among the South Sudanese have struggled to end the fighting partly because the rewards of peace have not been big enough.

The armed groups could have broken this mould if they had acted swiftly and in unison. The secretary general of the Sudan Revolutionary Front, Yasir Arman, saw this opportunity when al-Bashir fell. Himself a former communist and long-time senior leader of the SPLM, from northern Sudan, and presidential candidate in 2010, he was a rarity among the leadership of the provincial insurgents: a politician equally at home in both regional rebel politics and Khartoum civic politics. Arman spent six weeks feverishly travelling to meet with the dispersed leadership of the SRF and trying to forge unity of purpose with the rebels who were not part of the SRF—the Sudan Liberation Movement of Abd al-Wahid al-Nur and the SPLM–North of Abd al-Aziz al-Hilu—as well as gauging the intent of the FFC leadership in Khartoum. The rebel leaders were cautious, suspicious not only of the capacity and agenda of the FFC but also of one another. By the time Arman arrived in Khartoum at the end of May, the political dynamics had shifted. Instead of helping lead a broad alliance of the urban democracy movement and the fighting groups, he was sheltering for safety during the massacre of 3 June and was then deported by the military to Juba.[8] Thereafter, the moment for creativity and innovation had passed. Just as the negotiations between the civilians and the generals were organised on a power-sharing formula so, too, the peace talks would revert to the standard format. The question was quietly changing from, 'How will Sudan be run?' to 'Who will run it?'

In Khartoum, the immediate question was: Who would lead the talks with armed groups? Whoever headed the delegation would be able to have a controlling influence over the allocation of jobs and money. The generals saw this and seized the chance. The TMC had already finalised the proposal for the Supreme Peace Council, headed by al-Burhan, and he appointed a negotiating team led by Hemedti. Military officers have a standard justification for taking charge of this: the security arrangements are the most onerous agenda item and this should be shouldered by them. Civilians are easily intimidated by this, and those unfamiliar with peace negotiations tend to think of ceasefires and security arrangements as technical issues rather than political ones, and to believe that 'peace' on its own is a sufficient prize. Hamdok did not share this *naïveté*. Nonetheless the peace agenda was rapidly taken out of his hands.

The peace talks got off to a slow start in part because the armed groups were in disarray. One faction of the SRF was headed by Minni Minawi, the only major rebel leader to sign the 2006 Darfur Peace Agreement with the former regime and now also the most amenable to negotiating with Hemedti and the RSF. In part, Minawi's negotiating posture was informed by his dubious command of his own soldiers. Many had been drawn to fight in Libya by offers of money or by coercion and it is likely that he had as many fighters outside Sudan as inside it. Some were on the same UAE payroll as RSF contingents that had fought in Yemen—in effect they had already made a deal with Hemedti. Chief among the other Darfurian factions was the Sudan Liberation Movement, led by Minawi's old rival, Abd al-Wahid al-Nur, whose forces controlled the heights of the Jebel Marra Mountains and who retained a strong following in Darfur's vast displaced camps. In Blue Nile and southern Kordofan, the SPLM–N had split into two factions. One was headed by Abd al-Aziz al-Hilu, who commanded a sizeable force and controlled and administered hilly terrain in the Nuba Mountains. He had a political programme founded on secularism and self-determination for the Nuba people. Al-Hilu also had a reputation for being incorruptible, a rare man of principle, and therefore someone unlikely to make the political trades necessary for a quick deal. The other grouping of the SPLM–N was headed by Arman and Malik Agar, who commanded few troops but held the political capital of capable leadership during the CPA Interim Period. The last major group was Darfur-based JEM, which on account of its ties to Qatar and Libya was still a political and military force to be reckoned with. The JEM leader, Jibril Ibrahim, younger brother of the movement's founder, who was killed in 2011, kept his ties to the Islamist movement in Sudan as well, and later, on arrival in Khartoum, signalled this by visiting the house of the late Islamist sheikh, Hasan al-Turabi.

South Sudan was chosen to mediate the talks, primarily because it was already hosting the armed groups. The venue in Juba was more than neighbourly convenience. The head of the South Sudanese mediation team was Tut Gatluak, presidential advisor on national security, and the adopted son of al-Bashir. His role pointed to the peace talks reverting to political business as usual. So it transpired.

Early on, Khartoum was represented by both civilian and military delegates. It was the civilians who responded positively to the Darfurian rebels' proposal that al-Bashir be handed over to the International Criminal Court for prosecution. The generals did not reverse that decision—they had plenty of ways of killing off this kind of step by slow-walking and introducing complications—but they did not want this kind of decision repeated. With the discreet assistance of Gatluak, the government negotiation team exercised closer control. Hemedti rarely visited Juba himself. Instead, a team of military advisors negotiated for him. He knew how to strike bargains with the practitioners of mercenary politics in Darfur's turbulent political market, such as Minawi and JEM's Ibrahim. Meanwhile, others in the Juba talks saw that Hamdok was absent. He did not have his own advisor at the talks in Juba, and some in Juba questioned whether he was regularly updated on the talks. Civilian delegates in Juba were kept on the margins. 'We feel like we are battling each other for information every day,' an aide to a minister said. 'To get anything done we have to go to Burhan.'[9]

The technocrats in cabinet tended to see peace as an abstraction and a general, collective good. The minister of justice, Nasr al-Din Abd al-Bari, liked to quote John Locke and John Rawls. The deputy minister of foreign affairs, Omer Ismail, had long been an activist for human rights, who campaigned for an all-inclusive grassroots peace in Darfur. The generals, on the other hand, saw peace negotiations as politics pursued by other means. For them, 'peace' was not an end to violence, but was when violence no longer mattered politically. To be more precise, the logic of a peace agreement in a political marketplace is that it is a bargain among the practitioners of violence not to use violence against one another. Instead, the violence of a peace is the violence used to enforce the bargain. This could be fighting against those who have not signed the deal, or forcible disarmament of militia groups that are now considered unlawfully armed. Clashes that break out may be dismissed as inter-communal violence rather than an organised political opposition, needing local reconciliation combined with police action.

A decade before the revolution, Sudan's international headlines had screamed 'Darfur!' It was the location of—depending on one's perspective—a state-sponsored campaign of genocide, a brutal inter-ethnic war and humanitarian crisis, or a breakdown in provincial governance resulting in anarchy, which in the Arab tradition is as much a dereliction of government as the most draconian repression. No peace agreement signed by factional leaders could resolve these problems. Such a deal could, at best, be a starting point for addressing them.

Continuing Violence in Darfur

The civic revolution in Khartoum meant little for many ordinary people in Darfur. Violence and dispossession remained an everyday lived reality, and it always had the potential to escalate. The emergence of Hemedti as a protagonist in the revolution and the counter-revolution was received with, at best, ambivalence and, at worst, outright fear. The RSF was seen as the direct descendant of the *Janjaweed*, who had come to rule the region and now, it seemed, the country as a whole.

All Sudan's peripheries were combustible, and Darfur was particularly so. After a young ethnic Masalit man killed an Arab Mahameed herder in al-Geneina in Western Darfur in December 2019, militiamen rode on RSF vehicles into the town and attacked the non-Arab community. The locals called them '*janjaweed*'. Victims were wrapped in white sheets, some with blood seeping through. Displacement camps were reportedly attacked and modest houses burned, their thatched roofs rapidly turning into blazing torches. Around 80 people were killed and nearly 200 were injured. Even the al-Geneina Teaching Hospital was raided by the Arab militiamen.[10] It was the worst violence that Darfur had seen in years. 'Sunday's events brought to mind the acts of genocide and ethnic cleansing,' said a statement from the Masalit sultanate.[11] 'The Western Darfur government did not do anything to protect the unarmed displaced, but rather left them to the brutality of militiamen.'[12] For all the promises of peace and security in Darfur that the RSF and the SAF made after the revolution, the attacks in al-Geneina were an indication that nothing had fundamentally changed.

At the height of the Darfur war in 2004–05, Darfur had been the focus of intense UN scrutiny. The UN Security Council had called for the *Janjaweed* to be disarmed. It had authorised an African Union ceasefire monitoring mission. It had referred the case to the International Criminal Court. It had demanded that the AU mission be upgraded to a UN peacekeeping operation—'rehatted' in the parlance as the troops on the ground would have changed their green AU helmets for blue UN ones. After al-Bashir defied this demand, and expelled the outspoken special representative of the secretary general, Jan Pronk, the UN found a compromise: a hybrid UN–AU mission known as UNAMID, the United Nations–African Union Mission in Darfur. By this time (2008–09) the mandate and composition of the peace mission was determined more by the posturing of the Security Council and its key members, and the bureaucratic logic of a UN system consumed by questions of numbers of personnel, operational procedures and logistics, than it was by any political analysis of what was actually happening in Darfur. The result was an enormous and enormously expensive mission that allowed Western countries to say 'Mission accomplished.' According to any metrics of effectiveness, UNAMID was inefficient: fighting continued, displaced people could not return to their homes, and civilians still lived in fear. At its height, with 26,000 uniformed personnel—briefly surpassing Congo as the largest mission in the world—it did of course have some impact. Patrols helped protect camps for displaced people. Civil affairs officers became skilled at defusing local disputes. But the Sudanese government wanted it gone and the UN and its paymasters became tired of the expense. In 2018, the first agreements were made for scaling down and closing UNAMID. The resigned, pragmatic expectation on all sides was that Darfur had become a troubled periphery plagued by low-intensity conflicts that time would solve.

The revolution didn't change this. UNAMID was scaling back and the RSF was taking over its bases, on occasion eliciting formal objections from the UN. When Hamdok took office, the UN system was so far down this road that it couldn't be turned around without gargantuan effort, and the new government had other priorities. But Hamdok wanted UN assistance for Sudan: he wanted expertise, resources, and the kind of international engagement that would legitimise and strengthen the transition. As a UN man himself, he had goodwill and friends, but even he overestimated how quickly the organisation would respond.

As the blood had barely been cleaned up from the RSF-aided attacks in al-Geneina and thousands of shawled women and children trundled across the barren Sudanese desert to Chad for safety, Hamdok proposed a new political mission in Sudan. According to mandate and public statements, the UN was supposed to help draft the constitution, conduct elections, and help displaced people return home. And, of course, the UN is nothing if not technocratic: it would be a boost to the legitimacy of the technocratic cabinet. The timing was, however, unfortunate. The multi-dimensional peace operation in Darfur, with a mandate to protect civilians, had languished for a decade, and precisely at the moment when it could have been most useful, it was winding down. No one seriously thought that UNAMID could have prevented conflict erupting in al-Geneina, but its patrols could have dampened its escalation and protected displaced people. Even the presence of international monitors has a well-attested role in reducing atrocities.

Peacekeeping operations are most effective in support of a peace agreement. They work on the basis of consent and impartiality; they can be a neutral umpire for the disputes that arise during a ceasefire, the return of fighters from abroad, the encampment or integration of fighting forces; they are a forum to which the parties to the agreement can bring their complaints and see their grievances reported. In almost any other circumstances, the Juba talks would have included plans for an international peace mission to provide monitoring and assistance. As it turned out, the agenda of the Juba talks and the outcome—known as the Juba Peace Agreement (JPA), dubbed a historical peace agreement and signed on 31 August 2020 by Hamdok in the presence of al-Burhan and the Sudan Revolutionary Front—were ambitious in every respect except this one.

The outcome of the JPA was a version of payroll peace on steroids. They hashed out an agreement so that 25% of the seats on the Sovereign Council were allocated to the SRF as well as posts in regional administrations and the cabinet. It added up to an extravagant wish list of jobs and resources for the SRF leaders who signed up. For Minawi the incentive was an outsize share of seats in the Transitional National Assembly and salaries for his commanders and men. For Agar, who had commanded just a few hundred fighters, it was also a chance to gain a stake in the assembly and a budget to contribute troops to the security arrangements—which in reality meant recruiting new men to fill the quota. Hemedti also saw the RSF budget increased massively.

The Juba Peace Agreement achieved what neither the interim government of 1964 nor that of 1985 could: bringing the majority of the regional rebel movements to Khartoum and forging a transitional peace deal. However, the deal put transactional politics before radical redress of regional inequalities. Central to the real politics of the Juba deal was expanding the country's already over-inflated security forces by putting numerous fighters—many of them returning from Libya or South Sudan—on the armed forces roster. Little noticed, this provision also underscored what had already become evident, which was that the security sector reform agenda was off-limits to the civilians. The agreement committed the government to an ambitious programme of rehabilitation of the afflicted areas. The total bill added up to $7.55 billion. Hamdok was handed the role of finding this huge amount. And the factions that actually controlled territory as well as armed men—the SLM of al-Nur and the SPLM–N of al-Hilu—did not sign. Meanwhile, PDF militias, who unlike the RSF had fallen foul of the transitional arrangement, began to remobilise in South Kordofan due to anger at the exclusion of the Misseriya from the Juba talks.[13]

The Juba Peace Agreement brought two major security risks. One was that the exclusion of the two most important rebel groups would lead to an escalation rather than a diminution of fighting. The excluded groups might stage attacks to make their presence felt, or the combined forces of those who signed the deal might try to enforce the new order on them or, more likely, on groups with wavering allegiances. Given the concern of the civilians, especially Hamdok, for the al-Nur and al-Hilu groups, these dangers were lessened, but not eliminated. The second risk was more serious. The agreement entailed the return of substantial numbers of fighters from Libya and South Sudan. The SLA-Minawi and JEM had fighters in Libya and all had forces in South Sudan. The return home of these groups was a potential flashpoint for outbreaks of violence. It is precisely to contain such a danger that a UN force could have been critical. But UNAMID was departing.

Al-Bashir had long insisted that the Sudanese government could provide security for its people. The TMC said the same. Hamdok fell into line. 'Sudan is responsible for protecting its own people,' he reasoned to the UN and foreign diplomats.[14]

Human rights advocates and some diplomats believed that Hamdok secretly wanted a mission with peacekeepers and would have supported this plan. But Hamdok denies this. His close links with the UN had already made him the object of suspicion by the generals so he needed to be especially careful in advocating any UN role in security. The line he took was that Sudan should shift from being a country on which the UN could impose its plans (using the enforcement authority contained in the UN Charter's Chapter VII) to being a fully willing partner with UN plans (under Chapter VI). The latter does not exclude peacekeepers. 'I wanted to get our country out of the problems of Chapter VII and go into [Chapter] VI which will give us dignity', he later said.[15]

The UK and Germany created a draft plan at the UN Security Council for a new mission that almost perfectly mirrored what Hamdok wanted. In their proposal the two countries slipped in the deployment of up to 2,500 international police and one battalion of a 'quick reaction force' of between 500 and 800 troops that could protect civilians who came under attack. The plan was circulated widely but not within Sudan's government. The first time that the prime minister heard about the British and German plan was not through formal diplomatic channels: the proposal was leaked to a journalist. Hamdok had no option. He said: 'This was never going to be a peace mission—it is a technical mission.'[16]

Thus was the United Nations Integrated Transition Assistance Mission in Sudan (UNITAMS) born. Easily overlooked in the history of the UN will be how its character and purpose changed during the process of its inception. Its aims were noble but its execution was neither fast nor politically astute. Not only did it face the suspicions of the Sudanese military along with civil servants in the government, holdovers from the former regime who were expert at strangling UN activities, but the UN agencies themselves saw this as an opportunity to get their hands on resources. At a time of budgetary stringency within the UN, a new mission in Sudan was an opportunity that the UN's own bureaucrats pursued with skill and determination. It was more of a feeding trough in which standardised activities could be programmed and budgeted than a strategic political advisory service. Lost in this was a critical assessment of Sudan's priority needs. Thus, when the government released a protection of civilians strategy, a sweeping document stacked with recycled commitments from previous years, members of the planning team from New York acted as if the riddle of war in Sudan had been solved.

Ultimately, the end of UNAMID and the creation of UNITAMS meant that Hamdok achieved neither goal. He didn't have a high-level political lobby when he needed it most, and the scramble for resources among the UN agencies didn't meet Sudan's increasingly desperate need for aid. Worse still, the withdrawal of peacekeepers from Darfur just as the Juba Peace Agreement was signed meant that the generals would be implementing the security arrangements in Darfur with much reduced international scrutiny. The modest protection that UNAMID had provided was being withdrawn when the vulnerable people of Darfur needed it most.

Perhaps most unfortunately, the agreement lays the foundation for a new chapter of conflict in Darfur. The Juba Peace Agreement calls for the return of displaced civilians to their home. But the returns, mostly of the Masalit and non-Arab tribes, would cause a secondary displacement of Arab communities occupying those territories. The wave of conflict in 2021 is partly a result of these land disputes. By September 2021, armed conflict had displaced 418,000 people.[17] This is a higher rate for forced displacement for any year since at least 2009, when regular tracking began.[18] There is little prospect that Hamdok, the civilian cabinet or the security forces wanted to seriously address the conflict in Darfur. After renewed conflict in al-Geneina in April, the response from Khartoum was silence. There is no evidence Hamdok made a public statement about the attacks. Political parties were almost universally silent about the violence. The security forces responded with a fundraising ruse to the international community—promising that with more training and money they could send a joint security force into the city to protect civilians. That many soldiers on the force have bee
civilians for decades did not seem to matter

In liberal democratic theory, the prosp
provide incentives for the political elite to re
problems of Darfur—after all, the region co
winner of a general election. In Sudan's elite

has never gone further than scheming for how to buy the allegiance of the provincial leadership who will, it is assumed, broker the necessary votes or supply the required militia. With Hemedti and Minawi, both entrepreneurs in the political marketplace, as the dominant figures in Darfur, there is little sign of change.

The Economy

If there was a singular mission for which Hamdok's government was set up it was fixing a broken economy. This had to be pursued at home and abroad. Domestically, the challenge was to take control of the Central Bank of Sudan—and with it monetary policy—and reduce the subsidies on bread and fuel that dominated the government's non-security spending, while also devaluing the Sudanese pound to bring the official exchange rate in line with the free market rate. The bargain was that short-term pain from the overdue austerity measures would be softened by public welfare and would translate into economic growth.

Hamdok built a strong team of reform-minded officials headed by his minister of finance, Ibrahim Elbadawi, a World Bank economist. They believed that they had been given a mandate to fix the economy and that this should begin with balancing the budget.[19] 'The subsidy is very high. It is close to 40% of our budget. It is a drain,' Hamdok said.[20] Technocratic governments are swept into power on the assumption that they will make hard decisions that politicians are not willing to make, as if governing is something that consists of getting the formulae for an equation right. The subsidy debate was the second key test of Hamdok's agenda for change. This contest took place on a field the prime minister had defined as his own. And, as much as the Juba peace deal set the stage for Hamdok's relationship with the military, the subsidy debate was the first indication of the civilian coalition's capacity to respond to popular demands while also acting decisively.

Sudan's entanglement with subsidies started after the 1969 [illegible]oup, when the radical regime of Nimeiri began to fix prices as a [illegible] to manage the restive urban constituencies.[21] Within a decade [illegible]ic of cheap essentials was both driving a massive change in consumption—favouring imported wheat over homegrown sorghum—and also becoming a growing burden on the budget. It was an addiction that Sudan has not succeeded in shaking off.[22] It was a bet that meant as long as the government provided cheap bread to urban consumers then it could withstand political shockwaves across the rest of the country. The oil subsidy was later added to make electricity cheaper and commercial farming more profitable. The twin subsidies resulted in a decades-long dance of stressed finance ministers, who wanted to slash the assistance after crunching their budget numbers, and politicians, who wanted to keep their constituents happy. At times, the dance was thrown off balance. Nimeiri correctly predicted, in 1985, that slashing the subsidies would bring down his government. Two years later, Sadiq al-Mahdi refused to take the same step even though it was the one remaining reform needed to unlock debt rescheduling and international aid.

By the end of al-Bashir's era, in 2019, the subsidy cost hundreds of millions of dollars from the budget every month in money that the government simply did not have.[23] The bread lines snaked a little longer. Lines of men in clean white jellabiyas queued outside tattered bakeries in Khartoum for hours. Electrical grid operators had to place swathes of the city on hours-long blackouts each night so that from the sky it looked like a winking city—lights flashing and then fading into darkness across the metropolis. There simply wasn't enough fuel. Tractors stood idle in the breadbasket state of Gedarif. As it has done throughout Sudan's history, the military swallowed up a disproportionate share of the public budget, but this didn't seem to matter that much as the government searched for money.

Hamdok's years working for the United Nations meant that he was well aware of the economic black hole that was the country's fuel subsidy. In its 2019 report the World Bank reiterated the orthodoxy.[24] Sudanese pay less for their electricity compared to every sub-Saharan African nation, but they use it far more than their regional peers. Each year the fuel costs would grow by about 50% so its share of the budget would balloon exponentially until country simply couldn't pay the bills. By 2019 the fuel subsid 10% of GDP.[25] 'Given the ongoing economic crisis and the heavily constrained access to external financing, there is a the GoS cannot sustain the current subsidy level for fuel and capital investment. This will create fuel shortages,' the World Bank report said, 'frequent and long load shedding.'[26] The conventional critique of subsidy lifting was the harsh impact on the poor, especially low-income urban wage earners. The World Bank and IMF proposed that these impacts be cushioned by a version of universal basic income known as the Family Support Programme, which would provide US$ 5 per person per month to 80% of the population. Foreign donors indicated they would pay for it. Sudan 'can implement a reform package that will gradually increase the tariff and strengthen the social security net for those affected'.[27]

For Hamdok and Elbadawi, the adjustment was essential, not least because the other element in the package was debt relief, which needed the IMF and World Bank to sign off on Sudan's performance. Since the 1970s, Sudan had been accumulating debts it could not pay. Between 1977 and 1985, the country set a world record of eight successive debt reschedulings and in 1986 it was the first to be suspended from the IMF because of overdue arrears on its payments to the IMF. Sudan was then the first-ever country to have a 'shadow programme' with the World Bank and the IMF, in which technocrats in Khartoum and Washington DC found ways of cooperating even though the rules of the Bretton Woods institutions formally debarred dealings between them and a country that had broken the financial rules. What this meant was that Sudan's debt mounted year by year, and it missed out on the great millennium debt forgiveness write-off: the Jubilee Campaign and the Heavily Indebted Poor Countries Initiative (HIPC Initiative) that converted unpaid, discounted external debts into social programme funding for those countries to help them meet the UN's Millennium Development Goals. To get back into the creditors' good books, Sudan first needed to find about $4 billion in cash to pay off accumulated arrears to the IMF and World Bank, after which the creditors could meet and reschedule the total sovereign debt of more than $60 billion, after which Sudan would be able to get fresh loans on favourable terms. The only countries that could help Sudan pull this off were the US, China, and the cash-rich Gulf states. China had lost interest in Sudan when it lost its oil. The US, Saudi Arabia and the UAE wanted something in return.

Washington DC held a trump card in its hand. Sudan had to vault another hurdle: it was listed as a state sponsor of terror (SST). This was imposed in 1993 after the first terrorist attack on the World Trade Center in New York, a plot traced back to jihadis resident in Khartoum under the protection of al-Bashir and al-Turabi. Osama bin Laden was among those enjoying Sudanese official hospitality and, even though he left the country in 1996, responsibility for the 1998 al-Qaeda attacks on the US embassies in Kenya and Tanzania that killed more than 200 people, and on the USS Cole in Yemen that killed 17, was traced back to Sudan.

Hamdok's first visit abroad as prime minister was to the UN General Assembly in September 2019. There, he was feted by the assembled heads of state and other dignitaries: Sudan was back as a fully credited member of the international community. All promised to help. The devil was in the detail. On that visit, Hamdok did not spend time in Washington DC exploring the complexities of what would be needed to unlock the SST delisting, and it would prove a much more troublesome obstacle than he anticipated. While Sudan remained on the SST list, any entity doing business in Sudan needed a special licence from the US Treasury, or they would fall foul of the PATRIOT Act and risk prosecution. Debt rescheduling and normalisation of financial relations with the rest of the world needed Washington DC to act first—and neither members of Congress nor the Trump Administration were ready to do this on request.

In the meantime, Hamdok and Elbadawi were on their own. They decided to go for the most dramatic option, proposing to remove the energy subsidy in one fell swoop. This was a dramatic step, beyond what the international financial institutions had demanded. In fact, the IMF cautioned against it. Predictably, led by the communists, the FFC was opposed. The communist, Siddiq Yousif, argued that ending the subsidy would leave people destitute. 'If he removed the measures, the streets would turn against him,' said Mohammad Yousif of the SPA.[28] That studies showed that urban factory owners and businesses were the biggest beneficiaries of the subsidy because they used the most electricity did not much sway their beliefs. Why Hamdok and Elbadawi took the line they did is a puzzle: predictably, it led to a confrontation with the political parties in the FFC, for which they were not prepared.

For all the military's might during the transitional period, Hamdok saw how there were moments when the political parties successfully banded together. Particularly after the demonstrations of 30 June 2020, the unified FFC objected to a total military takeover, thanks to the power of tens of thousands of protestors. Hamdok theorised that if the FFC parties could work together and make decisions then they could overcome even the most hard-nosed junta.[29] 'We have well entrenched, resilient political parties that make it different from the other [Arab Spring] nations,' he explained. 'And I think more than that we have this public opinion, public movement which is there to guard it ... this will help us keep the flame.'[30]

All this stood before Hamdok as his government announced the removal of subsidies on 27 December 2019, just before the budget was finalised. The Ba'athist and the Communist parties rushed into a meeting with Hamdok's government and plainly stated that they were against the plan. 'The lifting of the subsidies contradicts the agenda of the revolution, which calls for supporting the people's purchasing power, tackling youth unemployment and improving access to health insurance and economic services,' Kamal Karrar, a member of the FFC's economic committee, told the journalist Mohammed Amin.[31] Joining the political parties was the SPA. Hamdok's government gave in: they announced a delay in the subsidy removal until a planned conference occurred around March 2020 to set the country's economic agenda. It was a very serious setback for Hamdok. 'Having left the country after so many years I had thought that the economic thinking and practices had evolved like everywhere else in the world,' he admitted in hindsight.[32] Parties in the FFC 'went back to their [previous] orientation, there was very sharp polarization and almost a sloganist embrace of policies without clearly articulating an alternative vision.'

The decision to create a conference foreshadowed Hamdok's governing style. Committees and conferences were a classic tool of Sudanese politics, a means of managing difficult problems partly by means of postponing the hard decisions. To the prime minister's supporters it was a consensus-based approach that aimed to unify rather than divide. Hamdok recognised that he had limited powers and needed to use what influence he had very carefully. But, to his critics, backing down to the FFC on an issue so clear as the need to reduce subsidies revealed a prime minister who was simply averse to leading. He was now getting criticised from all sides. 'Every single decision making process you will find Hamdok is absent. He is not there,' said a onetime advisor to the prime minister.[33]

Meanwhile, Hamdok was struggling with the SST agenda in Washington DC. He returned to the US in December 2019, this time not to the warm embrace of the UN General Assembly but rather to the hard grind of working the levers of the Trump Administration and Capitol Hill. Since the outgoing Obama administration had begun a process of removing sanctions, the main thing that had been revealed was how difficult it would be to complete that process. It certainly wasn't going to happen by the end of the year, as the incoming civilians had hoped in their optimism.

The difference between the halls of the UN and the corridors of the US government was that Sudan was automatically on the UN agenda and it was straightforward to win a standing ovation and promises that international donors would come together to pledge support for Sudan. By contrast, in Washington DC the Sudanese were hardly on the radar at all. There was an odd consensus of lethargy between the holdover career diplomats and the higher-level transactional Trump appointees. Having helped engineer the resolution of the confrontation between the civilians and the generals, the administration officials were sceptical that the transitional government would deliver. As if expecting it to fail, they wanted to keep their arsenal of punitive measures in place so that they could incentivise the reform measures they themselves wanted. Congressional staffers and State Department officials simply did not know if Sudan's transition was real.[34] They were unwilling to give substantial financial assistance without proof that Hamdok could govern. For Hamdok, on the other hand, it was as though he was a boxer sent into the ring with one hand tied behind his back, with the promise that if he won the bout then they would untie his hand. His reforms would not succeed without financial support and could only overcome the standoff of indecision if he could push Sudan up Washington's agenda.

Hamdok made a pitch for Sudan's importance. He told Robbie Gramer of *Foreign Policy* magazine about the US business opportunities present. 'Sudan is an oil-rich country. For us, to open the country for investment, we cannot do that under the SST [list],' he said.[35] And to the *Wall Street Journal,* Hamdok dangled an increased counter-terrorism partnership with the US. 'When it comes to combating terrorism, we would like to benefit from US experience, not only of training but intelligence sharing, gathering, equipment, training,' Hamdok said. 'We have Boko Haram on our west, al-Shabaab further east. We have al Qaeda and ISIS in the north and the sides.' But the Americans already knew all this: US corporations had been lobbied to lift sanctions some years earlier and the CIA had been cooperating with NISS for 20 years, to the extent of bringing Salah Gosh to its headquarters at Langley, Virginia. Ever since August 2001 when George W. Bush appointed a special envoy to test whether Sudan had good faith in wanting peace in southern Sudan, the US had put forward conditions for normalising relations: co-operate with the CIA, make peace with the SPLA, allow the UN into Darfur, enable the south to hold its referendum and secede. From the Sudanese perspective, each time they had delivered, and the US had not. Now the Sudanese had done on their own what four successive US administrations had failed to do—remove al-Bashir—and once again a Sudanese mission to Washington was greeted with a cynical shrug.

To be removed from the SST list it wasn't enough to stop sponsoring terror. Congressional officials said that Sudan needed to reach a settlement with families who had suffered from terrorist attacks two decades prior. Sudan agreed to a package of $335 million. But two Democrat senators—Chuck Schumer (New York) and Bob Menendez (New Jersey)—blocked the measure, partly because they wanted to keep open the prospects of the relatives of victims of 9/11 mounting a case. The families of those killed on that day could not sue the obvious state culprits—Saudi Arabia or Afghanistan—and even though everyone knew that Sudan couldn't pay and wasn't implicated in the planning of the attacks, the senators did not want to abandon the demand for a full accounting for who was responsible.

To the Sudanese, this was a double standard twice over. Sudan was being singled out even though others were more culpable, and its once-in-a-generation chance for democracy was being held hostage for crimes for which the new government had absolutely no responsibility. Grudgingly, Hamdok promised to pay. 'In some respects, the visit was a success. Hamdok was enthusiastically received in both his public and private engagements—a packed agenda,' wrote Richard Downie of the Center for Strategic and International Studies. 'Yet in spite of these achievements, the prime minister has little to show for his diplomatic efforts.'[36] It was a typically hedged assessment, that was shared by officials in the US government.

Appealing to democracy and the norms of international cooperation did not cut much ice in Trump's White House. Its transactional ethos demanded a quid pro quo, even from a weak country in a parlous situation that could truly offer only a break from its history of being a problem. At this point, America's Middle Eastern strategy stepped in. The relevant part was that the US aimed to make Arab countries see Israel as their ally and Iran as their enemy. The quartet of Israel, Egypt, Saudi Arabia and the UAE were the arbiters of US policy towards northeast Africa, including Sudan, and the brokers of those countries' relations with Washington DC.

In 2011, Ethiopia began building a huge dam on the Nile to generate electricity for its economic development. The Grand Ethiopian Renaissance Dam (GERD) would also benefit Sudan: it would control flooding, enable more water to be used for irrigation, and provide cheap electricity, too. Sudan had therefore been a partner in the Ethiopian strategy of building an African coalition of countries in the Nile basin that could isolate Egypt and revisit the colonial-era treaties that gave Egypt a veto on upstream countries' water use. That carefully constructed edifice came apart in October 2019 when the Ethiopian prime minister, Abiy Ahmed—young, energetic, reformist and wholly unschooled in foreign relations and strategic affairs—overrode the reservations of his foreign ministry and declared he would go for direct talks with Cairo mediated by the US Treasury.

Hamdok was visiting Addis Ababa the month when Abiy was awarded the Nobel Peace Prize. The contrasting styles of the two reformist prime ministers was on display. While Hamdok was studious and institutionally focused, Abiy was transactional and charismatic. He reportedly felt that the Nobel Prize signalled that his personal mission of saving his country and the region had been endorsed by the highest earthly authority. Ten days later, Abiy flew to the Russia–Africa summit in Sochi and met personally with President Abd al-Fattah al-Sisi of Egypt, apparently convinced that his magic touch would succeed where a generation of his country's diplomacy had failed. Discovering that Abiy had left for Sochi alone, Ethiopian foreign minister, Gedu Andargachew, desperately scrambled to find a commercial flight to join the meeting. Too late: by the time Gedu arrived, al-Sisi had made sure that Abiy was fully locked in the cage into which he had so blithely wandered. US treasury secretary, Steven Mnuchin, convened the talks in Washington DC and invited Sudan as the third riparian state. There was a new political reality in the region and Sudan had to adjust. Hamdok knew from the outset that the cards were stacked in favour of al-Sisi, a man Donald Trump had called his 'favorite dictator'. But he also knew there was no option but to hew closely to the US–Egyptian line—not especially favourable to Sudan, but definitely a major setback for Ethiopia. Abiy discovered this later: when popular pressure in Ethiopia forced him to stall on agreeing to the proposals, the US promptly suspended a package of financial assistance.

The harder part of the quid pro quo was Israel, and specifically the dynamics unlocked by the negotiations between Israel, the UAE and the US that culminated in the Abraham Accords of August 2020. Sudan had long been a faithful adherent to the Arab League policy of refusing to normalise relations with Israel until the Palestinians gave a green light. The Arab League summit meeting at which this decision had been made was held in Khartoum in 1967. Although Sudan had dealt clandestinely with Israel since then, most infamously in 1984–85 when Nimeiri allowed the country to be a staging post for the secret airlift of Ethiopian Jews to Israel, it had not wavered on its public stand. Hamdok took the line that, just as an elected government had taken the decision to refuse recognition for Israel in 1967, so too it was only an elected government that could reverse that decision. This prevarication was also tactical. He knew that the civilian coalition would divide on the issue and it wasn't a dispute he wanted.

General al-Burhan had no such scruples. For several years, the intermediary between Washington, Israel and the Arab countries on the normalisation question was the UAE. It was positioning itself to recognise Israel but wanted to be part of a bigger shift across the Arab world, both so that the rulers could cover themselves against a domestic outcry and also to secure the Emirates' position as the key broker in the region. Candidates included Morocco (in return for the US recognising its territorial claim on the Western Sahara), Bahrain—and Sudan. In the Sudanese case the quid pro quo would be removal from the SST list. At a meeting in Kampala in Uganda, arranged by the UAE, al-Burhan met with Israeli prime minister, Benjamin Netanyahu. It went well. Hamdok learned about it only when it was about to happen. When US secretary of state, Mike Pompeo, briefly visited Khartoum on his tour of the Middle East in August 2020, top of his agenda was the question: when will you recognise Israel? The trip was in many ways a disaster. The tight US security detail guarding Pompeo manhandled senior officials in the civilian cabinet, which left them fuming. During a photo opportunity a dispute broke out between the two countries' press secretaries. Hamdok repeated his position that normalising relations was not within the mandate of the transitional government. Al-Burhan went ahead anyway—he had a sharp sense that the last-minute dash by Jared Kushner, son-in-law of President Trump, to get Arab states to recognise Israel, opened a small window of opportunity that should not be let pass. Al-Burhan was probably right. Only a transactional politician with disregard for constitutional procedures at home and abroad, such as Trump, could cut the Gordian Knot of the SST listing. Hamdok still hesitated. He is a proud man, and the Americans' back-handed deal-making angered him. It unveiled that, for all the effort his government had put into re-calibrating its relationship with the West and the rhetoric of democracy the Americans proclaimed, Sudan ended up being a pawn for a doomed re-election campaign. Grudgingly, in October 2020, Hamdok eventually accepted the deal. Sudan was de-listed in December 2020 and Mnuchin delivered on the extra part of the deal, which was funds to help pay off Sudan's arrears to the IMF and World Bank.[37] The long-overdue recognition that Sudan was not a haven for terrorists, tentatively initiated in the dying days of the Obama presidency, was consummated in the last hours of the Trump administration. For the incoming Biden administration, it was a knotty problem that they were happy to see out of the way.

Corruption and Control

It is a truism of transitions that to dismantle is not to build. Every disruption to the formal institutions of power is both an opportunity for progressive change but also an opening for those specialists in transactional politics to ply their cynical trade. Unencumbered by the need to consult and abide by process and law, soldiers and merchants typically move quicker than democrats. In Sudan, every delay in normalising the economy, every crisis, and every hesitation by the democrats and the technocrats, gave the generals and their cronies a chance to sink their teeth deeper into the country's commerce. The 'rule of thieves' did not end in April 2019, or indeed in August.[38] The regime was able to track down and confiscate the assets of al-Bashir and his closest associates,[39] but, behind the curtain, the most senior generals were ensuring that their own grip on the economy was consolidated, not weakened. Hemedti, who had built his commercial empire in the shadows, also moved promptly to legitimise his businesses. He formally handed over his gold mines to the government and relinquished his influence at the Central Bank,[40] but compensated with his diversifying portfolio in other sectors of the economy. Hamdok protested against the army's continuing involvement in business, but he could do little to stop it.[41]

In fact, the anti-corruption agenda was manipulated from the outset. In the early months of 2020, just six months after the new transitional government was sworn in, Moamar Musa, a politically active member of the Future Trend Party, aged 25, was detained. He was arrested alongside Michael Butrus, another young activist, and remained in prison for a year without charge, a reminder of the injustices of the former regime. Worse, the criminal code used to detain him indefinitely was the reviled 2001 anti-terror law that the al-Bashir regime had used against dissent.[42] While the procedures used against Moamar were familiar, the context was different. The young activist was apprehended on the premises of the Removal of Tamkeen Committee taking photos of its members' cars and other assets to publish on social media.[43] The footage was intended as part of a popular anti-corruption campaign whose objective was to expose the transitional government's mishandling of the issue, of which failure to regain control of public funds, including parallel military and militia budgets, was key. While the transitional government was announcing the dismantling of the Islamist institutions and businesses, activists such as Moamar were keenly aware that the official efforts were not all that they seemed.

The new anti-corruption laws were named for their target, the *tamkeen* project of the Islamists, a term variously translated as 'hegemony' and 'empowerment'. The new flagship legislation was officially the Law for Dismantling the June 30 1989 Regime, Removal of Empowerment and Corruption, and Recovering Public Funds, and was commonly known as the 'Removal of Tamkeen Law' (*Qanun Izalat al-Tamkeen*). It was proposed by the civilians in the transitional government and backed by the Sovereign Council. Its express process was to reverse the Islamists' penetration of social institutions, corporations and government departments whereby they had sought to consolidate their power after 1989. They had purged non-Islamists and replaced them with loyal affiliates, in part with the intent of so entrenching themselves that their political infrastructure could survive a coup or uprising.[44] The law creates a 'Removal of Tamkeen Committee' and stipulates that it possesses unlimited authority to extract and confiscate what they deem 'public funds' from privately owned sources, and dissolve the institutions of NCP, affiliates and subsidiaries including the unions which they deem a front to the previous regime's unlawful activities. Anyone opposed to this is open to prosecution, as in the case of Moamar and Michael and subsequently Aisha al-Majidi.[45]

Without any active legislative body to provide oversight, the executive and the members of the Removal of Tamkeen Committee have a free hand in using the law punitively in the name of national interest and the greater good. The nebulous nature of the Removal of Tamkeen Law and the overall legislative framework under which it operates makes it impossible to disentangle, leaving activists incapable of challenging its proceedings or demanding reform.

Anti-corruption efforts always require great transparency if they are not to be co-opted into new and more sophisticated forms of control. In this case, a particular concern for activists was how the committee's jurisdiction overlaps with the new Informatics and Cyber Law. For several years, most political mobilisation has taken place online. Campaigns, documentation and other forms of association shape vigorous political discussion. But there is also online predatory behaviour and misinformation. Getting the balance right is remarkably difficult even for the most sophisticated political systems. Abusing the powers of regulation and surveillance is a temptation to all. Sudanese activists are worried that cyber laws will be used to control and suppress popular demands for reform. For example, in 2021 what was said to be a leaked memorandum from the attorney general's office appeared online, in which the Informatics and Cyber Law authorities requested the ministry of telecommunications to reveal the names, contact details and other information associated with online and social media accounts at the forefront of the post-revolution political coverage.[46] Known and trusted platforms such as Darfur News and Radio Dabanga, whose presence was part of the pre-revolution civic movement, were included. Also, the ministry of information and culture contracted a foreign cyber firm to close down a number of online platforms they claimed had a negative influence on public opinion, arguing that they might pose a risk to the transition.[47] There were protests in July 2021 as the government closed down more than 30 online websites.[48] These actions were preceded by an onslaught against NCP-associated businesses and charities, including their broadcasting services, either through direct confiscation or by drying up their sources of funding, but the transitional government's media regulation activities have now gone beyond simply removing the remnants of the old regime. The instruments for state control over the means of communication are gradually being put in place.

The Democratic Agenda

From its first day in office, the transitional government was in a precarious position. The cabinet—even the prime minister, who was about to become an international celebrity—sat atop a state structure that they did not control. Any action the cabinet took needed the cooperation of bureaucrats in ministries who, if they were not themselves NCP sympathisers, had become so schooled in pleasing their masters and so habituated to thwarting any initiatives that came from outside that they were a force for stasis. Even more significantly, the civilians were the guests of the generals, who had both guns and money. The army and the RSF were busy taking over the semi-secret mechanisms of control inherited from NISS, including the security agency's shadowy business empire, while they still controlled their own networks of companies. Most dangerously, they could use violence, openly or deniably, to get their way.

In the months between April and July 2019, most of the democratic leaders dismissed Hemedti as an upstart hoodlum who had no place within the community of the state. Not so Hamdok, who was quick to recognise both Hemedti's formidable political skills and the brutal reality that the young paramilitary leader and entrepreneur needed to be accommodated. The question of how the RSF and the SAF would work together was also critically important. The SAF leadership, including al-Burhan, were viscerally distrustful of the paramilitaries, whom they saw as a direct threat to their status and power. Hemedti was aware of this: many Khartoum residents saw in him the spectre of a takeover by wild Bedouins or a return to the dreaded rule of the Darfuris under the Khalifa Abdullahi from 1885 to 1898. Many in the army leadership and even among the wider political establishment would have welcomed a decisive military move by al-Burhan against the RSF and its leader, even if that meant putting democracy on hold, or worse. Hemedti could rely only on his own fighters for his personal security and could not gain legitimacy in Khartoum or internationally: he needed to cohabit with the civilians.

The tensions between al-Burhan and Hemedti, between the SAF and the RSF, created an important but delicate space for Hamdok to manoeuvre. He couldn't play the two generals against each other, but he needed to be sure that he triangulated between them.

Hamdok's awkward position was evident when he visited Washington DC in December 2019. Peppered with questions about the RSF commander and his role in the 3 June massacre, Hamdok did the best he could to avoid public contradiction. 'When you look at the way how the revolution evolved, the Rapid Support Forces, the RSF, played an important role,' Hamdok said to Robbie Gramer of *Foreign Policy*. Gramer responded by pointing out that Hemedti and the RSF were accused of massacring scores of civilians on that day.[49] Privately, as expressed to several diplomats and others, Hamdok would come believe that it was not the right time for transitional justice in Sudan. It was against the principles of the revolution and contradicted his original vision in office. He knew that justice would be controversial and could derail the transition: 'The way you resolve this is not legal. It is essentially a political process that requires deeper thinking and understanding that means going through the whole area of transitional justice,' Hamdok said at the end of 2020. 'It has requirements for both sides. The ability and the courage to accept responsibility of certain acts. But also the ability and the courage to reciprocate that. Are we there? Today I don't think we are there.'[50]

But Hamdok was always hesitant to express this publicly and also did not prioritise justice for the 3 June massacre. 'That is an issue for an investigation,' Hamdok said, promising that the results would be finalized in 'three to six months'.[51] That deadline quietly expired without progress.

The problem was, of course, that a finding that implicated the military would imperil the co-habitation. There was good reason why the inquiry into who was responsible for the 3 June massacre would languish, why the finest talents for 'tajility'[52] would be needed. Nearly two years on, hundreds of videos had still not been analysed by the committee to investigate the bloodshed. The supposed reason for this, as the head of the investigative committee, Nabil Adib, explained, was a lack of technical expertise. This was not very convincing as news organisations were able to compile and analyse video footage far more quickly. The committee also seemed to entertain some implausible conspiracy theories. For example, Adib speculated that the Al Jazeera news channel's videos of the RSF and SAF forces perpetrating atrocities may be a ploy to cover up the role of Islamists—a version of events widely discredited.[53] Adib is not naïve: 'Whatever we decide will destabilize the country,' he said.

In January 2020 it became clear just how insecure Hamdok's political position was. A group of security officials, upset after their units had been disbanded, engaged in a day-long street battle with the military, sending the capital into chaos. The quiet hum of coup rumours against the prime minister that typically filled the backdrop of political gossip in Sudan reached a roar. And, most disturbingly, Hamdok himself became a target. A roadside bomb detonated near his car. It was an assassination attempt, albeit a clumsy one. Hamdok later put his life into the context of the transition. 'This is a revolution, we lost some of the most talented young people during the uprising and I cannot say that I am any more valuable than those people,' he later said.[54] It was among Hamdok's finest moments in office. While others might have used the assassination attempt to grab the mantle of power, Hamdok's reserved response kept the revolution on course. 'What happened today will not stand in the way of our transition, instead it is an additional push to the wheel of change in Sudan,' he said.[55]

The wheels of change were turning altogether too slowly for the revolutionaries' taste. As the one-year anniversary of the removal of al-Bashir approached in April 2020, civic mobilisation had reverted to resistance mode. The Constitutional Declaration included a transitional legislative assembly that would give a formal role to the parties in the FFC. The cabinet had, however, postponed actually forming it, so that the armed groups would be able to have their representatives there from the beginning—they did not want to preside over a two-track process of democratisation. One drawback of this was that it meant that key reforms were pursued by ad hoc methods without sufficient legal oversight. Another drawback was that it kept the parties in the FFC out of any formal structure, leaving them to play politics in their familiar informal oppositional style. That meant they could obstruct only, and they managed to get the national economic conference postponed. They went on to conspire against members of the cabinet.

In May 2020 the National Umma Party, the Ba'athists, the Sudanese Congress Party and a faction of the Unionist Party created a coalition with the goal of removing members of Hamdok's cabinet, particularly the finance minister, Elbadawi, who was a fierce advocate of the subsidy reform. One member of the group said that they would not rule out trying to remove Hamdok himself. In these hushed discussions in party headquarters over sweetened coffee, the makeshift coalition found that attempts to remove the prime minister were pointless. They had no agreement on a candidate to replace Hamdok nor any clear agenda for what to do if they succeeded. The personal ambitions of each party leader in the coalition cancelled one another out and meant that retaining Hamdok was everyone's second choice.

The tool at the FFC's disposal was mass mobilisation and especially the resistance committees. However, the political parties and the SPA took these for granted. What had held the civic opposition together was the energy generated by the grassroots. The ostensible leaders of this mass movement did not resolve their differences, and neither did they put in place structures to allow them to act in a disciplined and decisive way. No longer channelling the passion and principle of the protestors, their unity evaporated. In the spring, the SPA held another election after an influx of new unions joined. Top leaders in the association—most prominently the former council leader and DUP man, Mohamed Nagi al-Assam—were voted out by a bloc of communist supporters, and the new leadership withdrew the organisation from the FFC.[56] The consensus that had held the SPA and FFC together had fractured.

The divisions within the SPA arise from disputes about the nature of revolutionary praxis within the Sudanese left. The vocabulary and political infighting appears anachronistic, belonging to a half-remembered era of Marxist–Leninist struggles. But this tradition lives on in the Sudan Communist Party, its following small in number but still pivotal in national politics. Following the doctors' strike in 2016, members of the doctors' branch of the party resigned en masse, maintaining that its leadership had obstructed its campaign and caricatured their movement as bourgeois.[57] Some of these doctors, including Amjad Farid, went on to play a prominent role in the SPA's mobilisation of medical cadres in 2019, and Farid himself became Hamdok's deputy chief of staff. Yet many of Sudan's Marxists remained sceptical as to the potential for the professional class, including the doctors, to move beyond their class interests and engineer truly genuine revolutionary change. The history of the Sudan Communist Party is defined by conflicts between 'revolutionary democrats', who advocate pragmatic alliances with the military and professional interests, and those purists who maintain that long-term structural and economic change must precede revolution, maintaining that 'precipitate action' simply empowers 'petty bourgeois' opportunists.[58] In the 1960s, with socialist revolution a real prospect, this division was about more than doctrine: it was about the crucial choice facing a movement on the threshold of state power. Fifty years on, non-communists were baffled about some party members' doggedness in holding to a revolutionary vision that had no resonance anywhere else in the contemporary world. However, purist communists insisted that people's power showed that nothing was impossible. After the signing of the Constitutional Declaration, leftists in the SPA sought to isolate members like Ahmad Rabie, who co-signed the document alongside Hemedti, and Farid.[59] The subsequent takeover of the SPA by the communists (and some of the leftists within other parties) showed the continuing power of those opposed to the 'opportunist' and 'pragmatic' faction, which had become closely associated with the transitional government.

The leftist takeover of the SPA also sundered its nascent relationship with the private sector. Sudanese business leaders had been among those who backed the protests and courted the SPA after its success, offering it premises to use as offices in Garden City and inviting the SPA to lavish lunches with the diplomatic corps. This also gave the SPA access to the media, including the Sudan News Agency (SUNA). When the communists took the reins, this abruptly ended.

The real power of the SPA lay in its link to the resistance committees. This was where the new leadership placed its faith. Resistance committees continue to hold the mantle of the uprising, many adhering to its purist and even utopian vision. Some of these had been created as the first protests intensified, and the model spread during the revolution. Their membership and style varied.[60] Some were educated and well resourced, connected to the diaspora and now embraced by international support groups that arrived to run workshops on non-violent tactics. Others were less formal, less educated and less networked. The committees were nominally unconnected to each other but bound by the same spirit of civic solidarity. Their offices were pop-up cafes nestled under thick trees and their fuel was tea with extra spoonsful of sugar. Inside Khartoum alone there were an estimated 700 neighbourhood resistance committees, with around 3,000 across the country. Even among themselves, the resistance committees rejected a hierarchy but they were admired by the public, who saw them as the true torch carriers of the revolutionary spirit. Meetings with the resistance committees from Khartoum revealed how they were unified in their distrust of politics, although disunited on the issues of the day, whether that be normalisation with Israel or the devaluation of the Sudanese pound.[61]

The SPA had inspired the resistance committees but the realities of the transition had disappointed them. They described how opposition parties in Khartoum left them hopeless that government was a way to pursue change. Their members believed that their biggest tool to correct the course of Sudan's revolution was protesting, sticking with the formula that they had perfected. Had they linked up and formed a political party themselves, they would likely command a huge electoral following, but then they would need to engage with precisely those political questions on which they could not find agreement. As with Sudan's previous uprisings, and indeed in common with those animated by the principles of civicness, the rank and file of the democracy movement wanted to transform politics without becoming politicians themselves. Meanwhile, the technocratic cabinet did not seize on the resistance committees as a constituency to be consulted and mobilised, leaving them either on their own or to drift into the arms of political parties accustomed to constituency politics. The technocrats were losing legitimacy, and the resistance committees were heading back to the street, marking 30 June 2020 as a date to push change forward.

Red, green, white and black Sudanese flags waved in the sky as demonstrators marched around the sand-blasted streets of Khartoum in the crippling heat. It was billed as a 'million-man' march but perhaps tens of thousands of people were flushed out by the country's resistance committees, who wanted faster reforms. 'The army is ruling the country, not civilians. You see that they are leading the peace process in Juba, they are leading the economy and the market through the companies of the army, they are controlling security,' Amjad al-Zain told the journalist Mohamed Amin.[62] 'We haven't achieved the goals of the revolution and this is why we are protesting again.'

Hamdok's office was always tense on protest days. The prime minister's normally highly-strung staff scurried in and out of the wood-panelled offices with an extra dose of jitters during marches. It was in part a fear that the protests would eventually take their aim at Hamdok. After the march, the prime minister met with some of the members of the resistance committee, in his spacious office, who presented a list of demands. The young protestors called for the appointment of civilian governors, demanded a reshuffling of the civilian cabinet and the replacement of the Sudan police chief. Hamdok met all their demands. What the FFC had tried to do for months unsuccessfully the protestors did in a matter of days: they forced the removal of the finance minister, Elbadawi, along with other ministers for 'non-performance'. The radicals in the SPA had their scalp, but they didn't have an alternative policy: the policies envisaged by Elbadawi were implemented in early 2021.

Crisis after Crisis

Sudan's economic plight was worsened by two shocks in 2020, neither of them anticipated. The first was the Covid-19 pandemic. This was a triple blow: the disease; the lockdown and recession in global trade; and what the emergency meant for the political control of the economy. The coronavirus spread first in the national capital. Between April and September 2020 an estimated 16,000 people died from the disease in Khartoum alone,[63] including most prominently the former prime minister, Sadiq al Mahdi.

The virus was immediately followed by the economic shock of the lockdown implemented in an attempt to contain its spread, along with the sudden downturn in the world economy. Like the population of most poor countries, many of Sudan's people lived from week-to-week if not day-to-day, and simply had no livelihood in the case of a general lockdown. Sudan also suffered because of the massive contraction in world trade and the loss of remittances from Sudanese working abroad. The economy simply stalled. The country entered a gradual lockdown that first limited night-time activity and travel between states, then entailed a shutdown of all air travel, finally becoming a full lockdown.

Following the twin shocks was the political blow. The standard response to an epidemic of infectious disease is to declare 'war' on the virus, which entails imposing a state of emergency with military-style curfews and other restrictions on civil liberties, as well as putting security agencies in charge of essential supplies. This kind of response is usually ineffective as a public health measure, principally because the measures undermine trust between the people and the authorities; post-epidemic assessments conclude that a community-orientated approach should have been followed from the outset. However, such is the grip of the military model for 'fighting' infectious disease that the top-down, coercive model is almost always tried first.[64] So it was in the case of Sudan. The authoritarian reflexes of the military set the tone. For example, despite a formidable mobilisation of civilian medical expertise, the army called the shots. Military intelligence consistently blocked access for humanitarian supplies to travel into and across Sudan. Covid swabs in Darfur were untested for days because the only national laboratory was in Khartoum and the kits were not given permission to fly. Government offices, still filled with holdovers from the al-Bashir era, also obstructed foreign support. When the UN put out a tepid statement in an attempt to get humanitarian access, officials in the foreign ministry called the heads of agencies into a meeting and scolded them. The UN resident coordinator, Gwi-Yeop Son, was threatened with expulsion.

The pandemic tightened the military's grip on the transition. The plunging economy came to cripple the prime minister's plans. To ensure that food continued and electricity kept humming, Hamdok and the civilian government were forced to scramble for cash that they simply didn't have. Sudan's economic output was estimated to drop by more than 8% in 2021 because of the Covid-19 crisis.[65] It was a devastating outlook because it meant that the bargain of the revolution—that life would be better after al-Bashir fell—could not be delivered.

Desperate, Hamdok and the transitional government joined the rush of African countries clamouring for money wherever they could. Western donors responded by relaxing the terms of debt repayment (no solace for Sudan, which wasn't paying its debts anyway) and by expanding funds for emergency welfare (which were still insufficient for Sudan's needs). What the international financial response to Covid-19 showed was that, when the stakes were high, donors and financial institutions could break the rules. Hamdok and Elbadawi ruefully reflected that no such latitude had been shown when Sudanese democracy was at stake. Now, for the cash-strapped government, it was too little and far too late. Instead, Sudan was forced to beg the UAE and Saudi Arabia for cash assistance. The Emirates delivered more than $100 million that was a life preserver, but with conditions. Hemedti, who had no formal education, became head of the crisis economic committee. Hamdok, who held a PhD in economics, was relegated to serve as his deputy. It was a signal of the further power that Hemedti and the military accrued amid the Covid-19 crisis.

The next shock to Sudan was the border conflict with Ethiopia. The two countries have a long history of reciprocal destabilisation,[66] but during the 2000s the governments made strategic decisions to focus on their common economic interests, especially trade and infrastructure. They mended fences, literally: they decided to find a workable compromise on the border dispute in the area of al-Fashaga, just south of where the Sudanese boundary meets Eritrea and Ethiopia. The border was delineated on a map by agreements in the early colonial days (1902 and 1909), but there were no boundary markers erected on the ground.[67] Farmers from Ethiopia had settled in the frontier area and many of them had begun farming on land that was (on the map) Sudanese, inside the so-called 'al-Fashaga triangle'. It was, in fact, characteristic of many African borders, in which the line on the map did not correspond to how communities on the ground had settled.[68] The African Union Border Programme had developed a manual of best practices for such 'soft borders'[69] and Ethiopia sent a delegation to Khartoum in 2008 to design a compromise along these lines: the two countries would recognise the formal legal boundary but the Ethiopian communities would continue to farm the land inside Sudan, undisturbed, paying their taxes to Ethiopia, sending their children to Ethiopian schools and, crucially, maintaining law and order through Ethiopian police and militia. This agreement was negotiated discreetly, some said secretly.[70]

The border agreement unravelled in 2020, bringing the two countries to the point of war. In advance of joint Ethiopian and Eritrean military operations in Tigray, Ethiopian prime minister, Abiy Ahmed, invited al-Burhan to Addis Ababa. The public agenda of the meeting, held on 1 November that year, was the Nile Waters, but the real reason was to brief the Sudanese leader on the upcoming offensive (al-Burhan tried to dissuade the Ethiopians from acting) and to ask him to send troops to seal the border. Al-Burhan agreed. He had reason to go along with the plan: it would affirm Sudanese sovereignty and it might also open up a very fertile area for Sudanese agriculture. As it happened, much of the farmland close to al-Fashaga had been allocated as retirement benefits to senior SAF officers. The army moved in and cleared out the Ethiopian villagers. They were ethnic Amhara, well-connected to the political establishment in Addis Ababa and were themselves implementing a long-cherished agenda of taking over land on the eastern side of the boundary (within Ethiopia), which they claimed as ancestral Amhara lands that had been unlawfully annexed by Tigray in 1991.

The merits of the dispute over who was entitled to what territory in what had been the northern Gondar province and had become the Western Tigray zone are in dispute,[71] and the Amhara were fired up to defend their land claims. That passion for defending—or acquiring—territory spilled over to al-Fashaga, and the Amhara leaders accused the Sudanese of aggression and escalated the dispute to the national level, much to the dismay of the army chiefs in Addis Ababa, who had their hands full with their own internal civil war and did not want to face a war with Sudan. Politically, however, the escalation was inescapable: it helped divert public attention away from a conflict in Tigray that had not gone according to plan and allowed Abiy to blame foreign meddling.

The Sudanese prime minister was the chair of IGAD, and he called an emergency summit to try to address the conflict in Ethiopia. The leaders met in Djibouti on 20 December 2020, and to Hamdok's dismay the meeting began with a statement by the AU Commission chairperson, Moussa Faki, that went far beyond the expected pro forma welcome and instead redefined the summit's agenda as dealing with South Sudan and Somalia, and accepting at face value the Ethiopian government's narrative on Tigray. In paragraph 10 of its communiqué, the summit recorded only that it 'Received a briefing by H.E. Dr. Abiy Ahmed Ali, Prime Minister of Ethiopia on the operation in the Tigray region, and reaffirmed the primacy of constitutional order, stability and unity of the Federal Democratic Republic of Ethiopia.'[72] Hamdok's attempt to keep a regional multilateral order intact was thwarted and Sudan was pushed more firmly into the Egyptian orbit.

War always benefits generals politically and leads to more military spending. So, too, with this conflict. It brought the civilians and generals in the government together in a common cause, but with the army's role, reputation and budget increased. The generals also embraced Egyptian offers of military and political partnership and they strengthened the countries' mutual defence pact.

For any politician, crises have the useful effect of diverting public attention from longer-term problems, and from those leaders' failure to solve them. So, too, with Hamdok. By the end of 2020, his technocratic project had stalled. The economic crisis had deepened; the postponement of painful reforms had only sharpened the pain that would follow. Promises that foreign countries made to Hamdok about financial assistance failed to materialise. The US effort to de-list Sudan as an SST had succeeded, but only through the kind of mercenary deal-making that was anathema to the prime minister's principles.

A few weeks after the final Juba Peace Agreement was signed, Hamdok sipped tea in his spacious office and contemplated what the peace agreement meant for his transition. Each week in Sudan seemingly brought a new crisis. On that week Hamdok faced another set of protests organised by the resistance committees. The military had re-drafted a portion of the Juba Peace Agreement, which would further undermine the prime minister's authority. It was a crisis—and a very normal week in a turbulent transition. The model Hamdok created for Sudan's transition had been overwhelmed by the pace of events and the demands of skilled and ruthless practitioners of transactional politics. Instead, Hamdok spoke about the state of the transition: 'This is civilian–military partnership. It will always reflect the balance of power.'[73]

5

MORE THAN HISTORY REPEATING ITSELF

Sudan's revolutionaries of 2019 consciously positioned themselves as the heirs of a distinctive national tradition of uprisings. Three times in six decades, the Sudanese people have brought down a dictatorship through non-violent action on the streets of the capital. That is an inspiring and enduring script. There is also the minor key story of the failed uprisings—such as 2013—and mass peaceful mobilisations to challenge the policies of civilian governments. The changes over the decades, however, are as striking as the continuities: the 2019 revolution was much more gendered than its predecessors, with women taking a conspicuous role in leading the protests, and it also had new elements, including diasporic mobilisation and rootedness in neighbourhood organisation, in this case the resistance committees. Each revolution was also incomplete, confronting powerful alliances of conservative forces and the military, struggling to cope with the challenge of diverse identities within Sudan, and constrained by inescapable economic realities. Furthermore, Sudan's democratic revolutions have been out of step with the wider cycles of democratisation in Africa and the Middle East, achieving their victories at inopportune moments in global affairs when the most important international actors have not been sympathetic.

On each of the previous two occasions, in 1964 and 1985, the subsequent transitions generated a form of parliamentary democracy that failed to satisfy the radical appetites of the country's more ambitious ideologues and failed to end the country's civil wars. Transformative aspirations were quickly subdued in the face of a 'conservative transition'[1] led by specific factions within the army as well as the political and professional class. The two revolutions brought to power parliamentary regimes that were ineffective, unstable, and shortlived. A leftist coup in 1969 and an Islamist one in 1989 reproduced the country's cycle of switching between military and civilian rule. Political and professional groups with close ties to institutions inherited from the era of colonial rule—specifically, the military establishment and the University of Khartoum—shaped the decisive political events that would mark the country's future, and the peripheries of the country that had been marginalised under 19th-century Turco–Egyptian and then 20th-century Anglo–Egyptian colonialism continued to be neglected. Parliamentary politics became an arena for squabbling among the metropolitan elite while the country suffered.

In neither case was a parliamentary coalition able to manage, let alone resolve, the issues of equity, inclusion and identity that underlay the civil wars. Sudan's civic revolutions have not settled the ambiguities of the country's nationalism: rather, they have made those contradictions more clearly evident.

Patterns of Civic Revolution

Sudan's three uprisings have much in common, beginning with what they looked like: carnivals of people's power. The Sudanese are proud that they had their own histories of protest prior to, and independent of, the Arab Spring. While the large-volume street protest is the central motif—a challenge to the ruling generals to shoot if they dared—each one innovated a repertoire of forms of protest. Funerals of slain protestors were one specific form, particularly effective in 1964 and reprised since.[2] Processions led by chosen groups were another. In 1985, sweltering in the April heat, judges in their full regalia marched to the Republican Palace to demand that Nimeiri go. In 2019, the role of women was notably prominent. Mass general strikes were particularly effective in both 1964 and 1985. On 5 April 1985 the organisers of the Intifada staged a 'dead city day'—the opposite of a street protest—to avoid a potentially violent confrontation with a pro-regime demonstration, and to show their power to shut down the capital. A more recent variant of this was the 'stay at home day' protests of 2016.[3] In 2019 the principal innovation was the sit-in at army headquarters, which constituted a more successful version of the 'towards the palace until victory' march of 1964, when protestors had marched on the seat of government until a hail of military bullets prevented them entering the building.[4] There were a number of attempts to repeat the march on the palace in 2018–19, before protestors turned their attention towards the military complex.[5]

The obvious template for the occupation of the space surrounding the army headquarters was the Tahrir Square sit-in of 2011 in Cairo. However, the Egyptians may have themselves learned from the Sudanese. Starting in 2005, Sudanese asylum seekers took the social technologies of the refugee camp and transformed them into a celebrated sit-in at the Mustapha Mahmoud protest camp, at a small park one block away from the office of the UN High Commissioner for Refugees in the Muhandiseen quarter of the city, demanding recognition of their rights.[6] In every uprising, singers, poets and artists have been prominent, showing the barren joylessness of the sclerotic soldiers they challenged.

A combination of socio-political elements persists across the three cases. Professional and labour activists co-operated uneasily with civilian political parties. Middle-class actors worked with particular factions in the military to dissolve the old regime. The leading actors identified with a modern and progressive brand of Sudanese nationalism. And last, the initial unity of the revolutionary elements gave way to dispute over the resolution of Sudan's peripheral conflicts and the nature of the Sudanese state.

The October Revolution of 1964 was seen by many of its protagonists as Sudan's true nationalist moment, not only in that it overthrew a military junta with close ties to the institutions and practices of the old colonial regime, but also in that it gave rise to a younger generation of politicians that would shape the politics of the country for the next five decades. Prominent among them was Colonel Jafa'ar Nimeiri, whose Free Officers claimed to be fulfilling the agenda of 1964 when they staged a coup in May 1969. The Communist Party was at its zenith. The Islamists came into their own. A new generation of sectarian leaders, notably Sadiq al-Mahdi, sought to redefine their parties as modern. It is only in the last few years that this generation is handing on the torch to the next. The nationalism of the October generation continued to share many of the pitfalls of the first wave of Sudanese nationalism, being shaped by a vision of 'Arab' identity that excluded many of the most marginalised people of Sudan.

The event that sparked the October Revolution was a student seminar at the University of Khartoum held to discuss the 'Southern Problem', after a rise in public awareness of the regime's ruthless counter-insurgency in the country's most neglected region. The killing of the student, Ahmad al-Qurayshi, on 21 October 1964 during on-campus clashes with the police who arrived to break up the seminar led to a funeral procession the next day that political parties and trade unions seized upon to galvanise a popular uprising, or *thawra*, against Abboud's regime. Two days later professional and labour unions launched a general strike and by 26 October Abboud agreed to dissolve his government.

Yet southern Sudanese remained on the margins of the debate over the 'Southern Problem' that had sparked the uprising. The first civil war in Sudan is often recorded as having begun in 1955, following a mutiny by southern Sudanese members of the Sudan Defence Force who refused to be transferred out of the south by their northern officers upon independence. In practice, it began in earnest with a campaign by the Anya-Nya militia movement, with ties to the officers who mutinied in 1955, to capture the southern town of Wau in January 1964.[7]

In this era it was common to characterise the civil war as an 'African–Arab conflict',[8] or speak of a conflict between a Muslim and Arab north and Christian south. Since the mid-1980s, however, both scholars and revolutionaries have tended to reject this narrow focus on identity and understand conflict as the result of the economic domination of the riverain centre and the marginalisation of the country's eastern, western and southern peripheries.[9] As far back as the 1950s, there were regionalist movements in west and east, such as the Darfur Renaissance Front, that sought to contest the dominance of the central region. This was far from simply an 'African–Arab' conflict: while some riverain Sudanese or *awlad al-bahr* (sons of the river) have embraced Arab identity and claimed Arab ancestry so as to display their elite credentials,[10] at other times they have used the term 'Arab' to evoke the perceived backwardness of pastoralist communities in the west and east. A widely received and discussed article published by al-Nur Hamad in 2016 entitled 'Change and the Shackle of the Pastoralist Mentality', in which the author laments the role of 'an inpouring of Arab pastoralists (*ru'a*)' in the decline of Nubian civilisation, is indicative of this view.[11] Even some riverain Islamists would often use 'Arab' in a negative sense, associating Arab identity with the values of the Arabian peninsula before the rise of Islam.[12]

In 1965, despite a 'Round Table' conference in which the challenges of the southern conflict were extensively discussed, which in fact worked out the draft of the formula for the 1972 Addis Ababa agreement that later ended that civil war, neither the brief interim government nor the parliamentary coalitions that followed was able to bring that war to an end. Instead, the revolution saw power pass into the hands of a new generation of northern elites. In a manner similar to the British divide-and-rule strategy in the wake of the 1924 uprising, through which the colonial government had tribalised the system of governance and marginalised the urban educated classes in favour of neo-traditional elites through a system of 'Native Administration', in the aftermath of the 1964 Revolution, conservative political forces in the north attempted to preserve that same provincial aristocracy in the face of onslaught by urban revolutionaries.

The revolutionaries of October raised the slogan of the 'modern forces', but they largely excluded subsistence farmers and pastoralists from their vision of progress.[13] Development was *for* these people, not *by* them. However, economically neglected pastoralist communities in the north were targeted by the military and conservative nationalists for recruitment into the militias that were used to fight both against rebels in southern Sudan and urban protestors in the north.[14] For example, the Umma Party marched its supporters into Khartoum to sideline the communists in 1965. In response, Abd al-Khaliq Mahjub, the leader of the Sudan Communist Party, coined the term *unf al-badiya*, or 'violence of the desert'.[15] The term *badiya* comes from the same root as the word 'Bedouin'.[16] It is a distinction that resonates in Arab sociological thinking from as far back as Ibn Khaldun, who contrasted the primordial solidarity of the Bedouin, which he called *asabiyya*, with the values of urban civilisation, *hadhari*. It is a distinction and a fear that resurfaced in the current era with the arrival in Khartoum of the Rapid Support Forces, drawn from the nomads of Darfur. For the metropolitan elite, this rang alarm bells.

In the 1960s, debates following the outbreak of war in the south led to the first revolutionary movement, but the revolutionaries could not construct a government capable of addressing the issue. Politics in Khartoum quickly reverted to politicking redolent of a decade earlier. Elections were held after six months. Once the parliamentary regime dominated by the Umma Party had replaced the leftist transitional government it continued the war, perpetrating even worse massacres than the military regime that had initiated the conflict. Ironically, it was not a civilian-led government but another military-dominated regime that brought an end to Sudan's first civil war. As the parliamentary period continued, Sudan's growing Islamist movement attempted to displace the Sudan Communist Party as the hegemon of the modern forces, pressuring the sectarian parties to outlaw communism as an atheistic movement and introduce an Islamic constitution, which further alienated rebels in the predominantly non-Muslim south. A faction of the Sudan Communist Party retaliated by backing another military coup in 1969, leading to the exclusion of both the Islamists and the sectarians from the political arena. Although the military regime turned violently on the Sudan Communist Party in 1971, it was still able to sign the Addis Ababa Agreement with the rebels in 1972, which established an autonomous southern region. Those events marked an ironic reversal of the pattern of violent repression on the periphery, and more delicate management of the urban opposition—a precedent many of the Khartoum parties will be conscious of in the wake of Hemedti and al-Burhan's bargain with the rebels through the Juba Peace Agreement.

The conflicts among the parties and individuals that comprised the brief transitional government of 1964–65 shaped both the parliamentary period that immediately followed and the entire political discourse of the next 50 years. A transitional government dominated by the political left was forced out of power by more conservative and Islamist parties, including the Umma Party and National Unionist Party, each of which had a loyal sectarian constituency. The conservative forces achieved this by insisting on rapid elections, confident that they would dominate the rural votes and consequently form a government. The call for a general election was something the radicals could scarcely veto, even though it meant that the same provisional constitution in force at the time of independence was restituted, unreformed. The sectarian parties subsequently used the post-transitional parliament to outlaw the party that encapsulated the radical urban left at the time of the October Revolution, namely the communists. Nimeiri's coup of 1969 turned the tables on the sectarian parties, but this eventually proved a bittersweet moment for the northern left after Nimeiri turned against the communists in 1971.

Nimeiri eliminated the Sudan Communist Party but sought to create a developmental state using the modern forces. This did not work, because his support base among the riverain elite was too small and bringing southern Sudanese into prominent positions could not fill the gap. His gamble on rapid economic growth didn't pay off. In 1977 Nimeiri reconciled with the sectarian and Islamist forces he had driven out of politics in the first phase of his regime, notably the Islamic Movement of Hasan al-Turabi.

Nimeiri's conservative turn led to three fundamental shifts in how Sudan was governed, which in turn set the scene for the popular uprising of 1985. The first was that Nimeiri mortified urban secularists by taking measures designed to appease the Islamists, introducing a series of arbitrary 'Islamic' codes in 1983 and executing the liberal Islamic intellectual, Mahmud Muhammad Taha, in January

1985. Two months after Taha's execution, Nimeiri turned against his former Islamist allies, leaving him with few supporters outside the army and security services.

The second was that he unravelled his single major achievement, the peace agreement with southern Sudan, prompting disaffected southern army officers to mutiny. Thus was ignited Sudan's second civil war, with the rebels corralled into the SPLA by a radical officer, Colonel John Garang.

The third was the insertion of monetised transactional politics into the system of governance. This was a combination of systematic corruption and the strategic use of finance by the Islamists to take control of key sectors of society—the incubation of Sudan's 'political marketplace'.[17] Among the rationales for the conservative switch was that the government needed to pay its debts and therefore needed to adopt austerity measures such as selling off nationalised corporations and devaluing the currency. Intended to resolve the economic crisis, these measures only made it worse. Emblematic of Nimeiri's failure was his refusal to acknowledge devastating drought and hunger in rural Sudan, and rejection of international aid. His government exported grain even while ordinary townspeople mobilised to help feed the starving who were turning up on their doorsteps.

In this context, a coalition of professionals and trade unionists began organising what they anticipated would be a protracted campaign of civil disobedience. When the first demonstrations broke out in late March and the Doctors' Union initiated a country-wide general strike, the demise of the regime came swiftly. The army, fearing division in its own ranks, turned on Nimeiri, overthrowing him on 6 April while he was attempting to return from a visit to Washington DC. The defence minister, Siwar al-Dahab, then established a Transitional Military Council to oversee a one-year transition to a parliamentary democracy. Quick elections on the basis of the same unreformed provisional constitution that took place in 1985 duly returned a parliament dominated by conservative sectarian parties, in this case with a substantial minority representation of the National Islamic Front. As with its predecessor 20 years earlier, the parliamentary regime neither resolved the conflict in the south nor pursued a radical agenda compatible with the ambitions of the urban revolutionaries.

The Islamists tried democracy and were the third largest party in the post-Intifada parliament, with disproportionate influence due to their strong finances and organisation. Despite the fact that the Islamist agenda stood in the way of settling the war in the south, Prime Minister Sadiq al-Mahdi insisted that the NIF be a coalition partner in government. The NIF leader, al-Turabi, tried and failed to pass a penal code similar to that introduced by Nimeiri in 1983 and suspended after the 1985 Intifada. Popular opinion clearly backed an agenda of peace over one of Islamisation. The second largest sectarian party, the Democratic Unionist Party, swung towards a peace agreement with the SPLA and pushed al-Mahdi to accept. Three days before serious negotiations were due to begin, al-Bashir mounted a coup.

The military coup of 30 June 1989 was backed by al-Turabi's Islamic Movement. It was the Islamists' reaction to the 1985 Intifada: they insisted that their agenda should prevail over peace and democracy. Once al-Turabi had seized power via al-Bashir and the Islamist cell in the military, a raft of Islamist-inspired legislation was indeed passed. Since the biggest threat to the Islamist regime was another urban uprising, all the institutions that had participated in the 1985 Intifada were targeted by the new regime—professional and labour unions were dissolved, while the regular army and police services were marginalised in favour of a panoply of Islamist-dominated militias and security institutions. The regime employed these same units both to crush all subsequent efforts to recreate the 1964 and 1985 uprisings.

Chapter 2 detailed how the al-Bashir regime used multiplying irregular forces to try to suppress insurrections in southern Sudan, the borderlands of northern Sudan such as the Nuba Mountains, and then in Darfur in 2003, and how in each case the militia strategy was ultimately self-defeating. The ultimate political cost of the war in southern Sudan was the Comprehensive Peace Agreement of 2005, which led to the secession of South Sudan. This was a massive blow to the legitimacy of the regime, that had fought so hard and demanded such sacrifice from the Sudanese in the name of preserving the country's unity. It was also an economic calamity, as the government lost most of its oil production and almost all its foreign exchange. Unsurprisingly, the urban population protested. Popular demonstrations in 2013 were the most serious challenge to al-Bashir's rule yet. To suppress them, al-Bashir deployed not only the feared NISS but also pro-regime militias, including the RSF from Darfur. They killed over 200 protestors, more than the number killed by the regime in the 1964 and 1985 movements put together. In spite of mass mobilisation in the poorest areas of Khartoum, the 2013 protests failed to unseat the regime, in part due to the intensity of this repression and in part due to the inability of civil society leaders to co-ordinate effectively with the more localised and decentralised movements of resistance to the regime.[18]

Al-Bashir's use of the RSF in Khartoum was a harbinger of the political perils of militarising the provinces. Over the previous decade, the costs of the Darfur counter-insurgency included fatally wounding al-Bashir's attempt to gain international legitimacy after signing the CPA while the Darfur militia accrued enough power to become a force capable of determining who would rule in Khartoum.

In 1985, the Khartoum protests had been foreshadowed by demonstrations in al-Fashir (Darfur) and in the railway town of Atbara, long a centre of trade union activism. That pattern was followed in the last weeks of 2018, when demonstrations erupted in al-Damazein and Atbara. As in 1985, the momentum was soon taken up by political forces similar to those that engineered the previous transitions. Professional activists co-ordinated strikes, sit-ins and demonstrations, while Sudan's bickering opposition groupings set aside their differences to constitute the FFC. It took the uprising of 2018–19 far longer to unseat al-Bashir's regime than its predecessors. With al-Bashir still refusing to budge in April 2019, the protestors seized upon the anniversary of the military's ouster of Nimeiri on 6 April 1985 to stage a mass sit-in at army headquarters and demand that the generals of 2019 repeat the feat. The leaders of the uprising decided to besiege the huge military complex adjacent to Khartoum's central business area with a round-the-clock civic encampment. To the protestors who had already burned down various party buildings in Sudan's regions associated with the ruling Islamist–military establishment, the petrodollar-funded military compound at the heart of the capital was the principal physical reminder of the security regime that had dismantled civilian rule. As Chapter 2 recounted, the internal calculations of the men in uniform were more complicated than before: the leaders of the institutionally-fractured military–security establishment had either to act in unison or risk fighting one another. At first they prevaricated and then, on the night of 10/11 April, a committee of the heads of the different military–security branches—the Sudan Armed Forces, NISS and the RSF—collectively did the deed.

The Community of the State

The uprisings of 1964 and 1985 left the status of Khartoum and the broader 'riverain centre' intact as the country's political and economic powerhouse. The fate of the third uprising is still in the balance, but it may yet do the same. Part of the reason for this is that each transition has been managed by three core sets of actors that are historically invested in what Abdullahi Gallab terms the 'community of the state': the military, the professional class and the Khartoum-centred political parties, namely the Umma Party and the Unionist Party (in its various incarnations), and their constituencies.[19] This group spans both the 'modern forces'—the graduates, professionals, labour unions and the officer corps of the Sudanese Armed Forces—and also the leaders of the sectarian parties rooted in the provincial aristocracy. Each time, leading factions within this group have diluted the transformative agenda of the men and women who instigated the revolution, to the point at which they might be called 'soft' counter revolutionaries.

In each of the three uprisings, elite professionals acted as organisers of the uprising, and negotiators of the transition. One marked continuity in each of the three uprisings has been the mobilisation of professional activists and organised labour, and the disjuncture between their forms of revolutionary agency. In 1964, 1985 and 2018–19, lawyers, lecturers, and doctors came to the forefront through the Professional Front, Union Alliance and SPA respectively. In 1964, it was the university lecturers who had accompanied al-Qurayshi's funeral bier through the streets of Khartoum who proposed the formation of the Professional Front, and it was the head of the Bar Association, Abdin Ismail, who, from atop the judiciary headquarters on 24 October, declared the general strike that toppled Abboud. Although certain unions had closer links to the Sudan Communist Party than others, the Professional Front was more of a nationalist than a Marxist organisation. The vast majority of its members graduated from the University of Khartoum (previously Gordon Memorial College), the cradle of Sudan's 'developmental state'. Prominent state professionals, including members of the judiciary, were at the forefront of the protests. This was what made it so easy for its members to take over a largely unmodified version of that state during the subsequent transitional, parliamentary and military periods. Most of the major professional activists were also leading figures in the Khartoum-centred political groups, including the communists, the various Arab nationalist factions, the Islamic Movement, and even some of the parties with close ties to the neo-traditional sector such as the Umma Party and National Unionist Party. The Professional Front incorporated Muhammad Ahmad Mahjub, a future prime minister in the Umma Party-dominated parliamentary regime, as well as the 'revolutionary democrats'[20] who would support the military coup of 1969. Even Hasan al-Turabi, the later architect of the Islamist Salvation Regime's rule, played a prominent role as a university lecturer who galvanised the students to confront the Abboud regime in the weeks before the uprising. The Professional Front, socially heterogeneous but ideologically eclectic, spawned the 'October Generation', and the working out of the inner conflicts of that generation would define Sudanese politics for the next 50 years.

The revolutionary movement of October 1964 also gave representatives of organised labour an unprecedented degree of access to state power. While they may not have led the call for a general strike, it was the labour and tenant farmers' unions—through shadow leaderships that emerged following their official dissolution subsequent to Abboud's coup—that made it work on the ground in revolutionary cities such as Atbara, Wad Medani and elsewhere. The Sudan Trade Unions and Workers' Federation, and the Gezira Tenants Association, representing the labourers on Sudan's major export-orientated cotton scheme, each had a representative in the transitional government, which was in power for a brief six months before elections ushered in a parliamentary government under the same interim constitution in place at independence. Organised labour was more empowered during the October Revolution than at any point before or after, but its degree of representation was still limited relative to that of the professional class. In the meeting in which union and political party representatives combined to form the United National Front coalition in the early stages of the revolution, workers were outnumbered by professionals by four to one. The demands of the communists and Arab socialists for sectoral representation of organised labour in the post-transitional parliament were ultimately thwarted by the more conservative parties, and it was only the university-educated elites that received separate representation through the 'graduates seats'[21]—a legacy of the vanguard role of the graduates of Gordon College in leading the nationalist movement, whereby a number of parliamentary seats was set aside for this elite constituency of voters. Although less than the union leaders' demands, a degree of advancement for organised labour was achieved: for instance, as health minister in the transitional government al-Amin Muhammad al-Amin of the Gezira Tenants' Association enthusiastically expanded the range of social services available to workers on the scheme.[22]

In spite of the interim regime's achievements, including the expansion of women's suffrage and the development of public services in central riverain Sudan, the problem with understanding October as a moment of genuine social transformation is that it was mainly those classes that fell within the rubric of the 'modern forces' that benefited from the socio-economic changes that it brought about. Working on a modern, export-orientated cash crop scheme, the farm workers of Gezira were more effectively represented in the tenants' movement than any of the rural farmers elsewhere in Sudan.[23] Urban revolution was ultimately unable to prevent the ongoing marginalisation of the country's western and southern peripheries, which in turn brought about mass rural–urban migration and led to the flourishing of the informal economy in the sprawling peri-urban settlements or *ashwa'iyyat*—literally, 'random areas'—of Sudan's major cities. The term *ashwa'iyyat* also conveyed the perceived illegality of urban zones that were outside the scope of state design, where land was inhabited without authority and purchase deeds. These areas were often targeted by particularly arbitrary forms of state policing.[24] Meanwhile, the politically disenfranchised lumpenproletariat, known as the *shamasa* (literally 'children of the sun'), received no representation from the formal union establishment, but turned out en masse in the street protests of 1985.

Nevertheless, the leadership of the 1985 Intifada remained in the hands of six major professional unions, who allied themselves with the main political parties through the National Alliance, which negotiated the transition with the military. Nimeiri's security services had dominated the labour unions far more successfully than had Abboud's regime, and the main professional activists were more comfortable relying on their own highly inter-networked social base. Workers demonstrated spontaneously, but by the time they had reclaimed their union leaderships and entered the strike alongside the professionals, the Transitional Military Council had taken over. The interim regime soon banned further protests, and set up a cabinet dominated by the more conservative professionals. The more radical unionists then established a separate Union Alliance, which campaigned against, but was unable to prevent, ongoing IMF-prescribed austerity, the retention of bosses who had thrived under Nimeiri, and the failure to reinstate activist workers who had been summarily dismissed by the former regime.[25]

In the 2018–19 protests, professional activists were once again at the forefront. Although the protests emerged more spontaneously than in 1964 and 1985, the SPA proved itself to be the one revolutionary body most capable of co-ordinating mass demonstrations, sit-ins and strikes. Like the professionals of the 1985 Intifada, it had since its formation in 2012 initially campaigned on economic issues, but when the revolutionary opportunity emerged, it shifted towards calling for the downfall of the regime. However, the challenges in the face of a labour–professional alliance were even greater than in 1985. Workers' activism was so effective in 1964 and 1985 because the government relied on the Gezira tenants to generate a cash crop economy, and upon the railway workers to export this produce beyond Sudan's borders.[26] In 1989, however, the government consolidated all the unions into a single government-dominated General Union of Sudanese Workers (*nagabat almonsha'a*, GUSW), and sidelined the old cotton economy in favour of a highly corrupt and privatised oil and (since 2011) gold sector. In the words of El-Gizouli: 'the SPA is somewhat removed from the concerns and challenges of Sudan's many subsistence farmers, small peasantry, agricultural labourers, the many artisan miners scavenging for gold in deserts and valleys far and wide, urban small producers, and the masses of urban poor'.[27] Nevertheless, in recent years, a tea sellers' union has emerged representing the many dispossessed women of the informal economy whose street-side businesses were targeted by the various police units of the former regime.[28] This in itself highlights the contrasting concerns of the different revolutionary classes. While Khartoum's liberal middle classes protested against the regime's infamous public order laws as a tool of moral and social re-engineering, for the working classes and those in the informal economy those laws were primarily a means of extracting bribes from the vulnerable.

The professional movement in 2019 did have the advantage of being more united than was the case earlier, given the absence of Islamists in the organisation this time around; factional conflict would nevertheless break out later in 2020. It had a relatively closer relationship with the rebel movements through individuals such as Muhammad Yousif Mustafa, a university lecturer and son of a Gezira Tenants' activist from the October era, who is also a member of the SPLM-North.[29] This reflects the unprecedented degree of co-ordination between the opposition forces after the Islamist takeover in 1989, when the civilian parties, trade unionists and SPLA collectively formed the National Democratic Alliance, the forerunner to the FFC.

Unlike the Professional Front and the National Alliance in 1964 and 1985, the SPA has not directly involved itself in the transitional government, enabling it to continue acting as a pressure group. In this regard it has played a similar function to the 'Union Alliance' during the 1985 transition, while once again centrist professionals, such as the minister of industry and investment, Ibrahim al-Sheikh, have taken up roles in the cabinet and steered the regime's cautious economic policies.

Another commonality of 1964, 1985 and 2019 is that in each case a faction within the security forces helped to oust the existing military rulers and then attempted to safeguard a conservative transition that marginalised the most radical actors. The internal dynamics of this conservative transition within the military have differed on each occasion, but the obstinacy of the security forces as a collective set of actors, and their desire to bolster their reputation, has not. In 1964, in a decade marked by a vibrant tradition of attempted military coups, it was a faction of middle-ranking officers who engineered a transition that marginalised the junior radicals. The radical younger generation in the army had their aspirations represented by the Free Officer Movement, which emerged in the years leading up to the October Revolution and modelled itself on its namesake movement that had brought down the Egyptian monarchy. During the uprising, Free Officer-affiliated NCOs and junior officers co-ordinated with the opposition and worked to prevent the armed forces from firing on the crowds. The rise of the Free Officers marked an increasing social gulf within the military between the more pro-British senior generation, educated at the elite colonial school, Gordon Memorial College, and close to the notables fostered by the British through the Native Administration, and the more radical youth schooled in the independent *ahliyya* schools during the colonial era. The older generation feared the younger radicals' ties with communist and Arab nationalist political groups. In the event, a faction of middle ranking officers with ties to both the young radicals and old guard was able to negotiate a transition that allowed the leading generals to give up power and—in the long run—escape revolutionary justice. The Free Officers would later maintain that they represented the true radical legacy of October, but they were hardly advocates of civilian multiparty democracy—according to at least one account they were planning their own in-house coup in the weeks before October, and they were also responsible for the coup of 1969 that overthrew the post-October parliamentary system.[30]

One of the reasons that the army was able to usher out its own leadership so quickly in 1964 was that Abboud's regime had not created any parallel security organs to guard against a potential movement from within the military. After the Free Officer putsch of 1969 Jafa'ar Nimeiri was far more careful, respectively creating a National Security Organisation then a State Security Organisation, as well as parallel police units, to act as alternative power centres. These organisations benefited greatly from the economic munificence of the regime, and, although the regular army retained some of its privileges, Nimeiri was unable to shelter it and the police service from the effects of the austerity measures brought about by his overspending and subsequent IMF-backed restructuring in the late 1970s. As a result, both the regular police and regular military showed considerable reluctance to suppress the protests that broke out during the 1985 Intifada, and were able to outnumber and then dissolve the State Security Organisation when it did attempt to take action against the protestors.[31]

Sudanese politics has been chronically unstable with frequent shifts of power between multiple ideological movements and political factions, and as such it proved hard—at least up till 1989—for a single faction to dominate the military.[32] The scramble for politico–military power that accompanied the 1985 Intifada was defined not only by the military–security conflict, but also by the contest among competing Islamist, Ba'athist and Free Officer factions within the armed forces. The Islamists had grown in strength in the military following their reconciliation with Nimeiri in 1977, and were able to purchase the loyalty of senior officers with capital from the emergent Islamic banking system. Meanwhile, a separate Ba'athist cell emerged among officers sent by Nimeiri to support Saddam Hussein's war against Khomeini's Iran, and their conflict with the military Islamists during the Intifada reflected the contentious Arab nationalist versus Islamist politics of the wider region. The 1985 Free Officers remained more committed to the principle of multiparty democracy than the namesake organisation of 1964, although they were accused of subservience to US interests by their opponents in the military. Each of these factions, while competing with each other, exerted upwards pressure on the military leadership and middle-ranking officers to oust the regime, and the military leadership under Abd al-Rahman Siwar al-Dahab, most probably fearing a coup against itself by one of the radical factions, intervened. Siwar al-Dahab himself was a conservative figure with both Islamist sympathies and familial ties to the Khatmiyya Sufi order, which itself has historic links with both the army and the various unionist parties. His detractors identified him as an Islamist satellite in the military and he headed a major Islamist charity after the 1989 coup, but he was also happy at the time to work with the 'sectarian' parties to prevent a leftist or Ba'athist takeover.[33]

One major difference in 2019 was that the Sudan Armed Forces (SAF) had been far more effectively captured by a single ideological faction than was ever the case before, as a result of the Islamist coup of 1989. Al-Bashir purged the officer corps and ruthlessly crushed a Ba'athist counter-coup in 1990, while the Free Officers formed a separate Legitimate Command affiliated with the National Democratic Alliance.[34] He also established a wide array of parallel security agencies, including the NISS, the PDF, and the Popular Police, as well as a host of private militias affiliated with individual politicians, most notably the RSF. As Chapter 2 explored, it is true that the security establishment was 'fractious'[35] at the time of the 2018–19 uprising. This was due to separate factions within the security forces being drawn towards different corners of the political marketplace and towards the regional actors who had penetrated that marketplace, more than it was due to the emergence of any new political vision within the military.

There are numerous parallels between the role of the security actors following the revolutions in 1985 and 2019, but also some significant new developments. The new government has not dissolved the NISS outright, like the Sudan Security Organisation in 1985, but placed it in the hands of an individual who had worked in Sudan's embassies in Saudi and Egypt,[36] and eventually reformed it as a General Intelligence Service, which will in theory restrict itself purely to intelligence-gathering duties.[37] However, just as a number of former State Security Organisation officers joined the NIF in 1985 to enable its rise to power,[38] former NISS officers are now joining the RSF in great numbers.[39] The RSF itself, as represented by Hemedti, is the most novel feature of this current transition as far as the security actors are concerned. There is no precedent in Sudan for a group of paramilitary mercenaries acting as the overseers of a political transition. In the tension between the regular army and the RSF, we might see a partial precedent in the 1985 TMC, when the Ansari Misseriyya general, Fadlallah Burma Nasir, began recruiting militias from nomadic communities in western Sudan to offset the dominance of the regular military by the Ansar's Khatmiyya rivals.[40] Indeed, the relationship between the religious sects and the core military and paramilitary actors has been a feature of each transition.

Another visible continuity linking each of the three uprisings has been the role of the Umma Party, then the National Umma Party in securing a conservative transition.[41] This organisation was first established as just the Umma Party in 1945, under the patronage of the son of the Sudanese Mahdi, Sayyid Abd al-Rahman al-Mahdi. For half a century it was dominated by one persona: Sadiq al-Mahdi, the Mahdi's great-grandson. He remained politically energetic until his death from Covid in November 2020. The party drew its strength both from its affiliation with the Mahdist Ansar movement that had been at the heart of the late 19th-century struggle against British and Egyptian colonialism in the Nile Valley, but also from its relationship with the cotton landlords and Native Administration notables who were co-opted by the British colonial state between 1898 and 1956.[42] It was the first party to campaign in earnest for the country's independence, although ironically this drew it closer to the British colonisers, who saw fostering Sudanese nationalism as a means of preventing a takeover by their rival Egyptian co-dominus. Along with its pro-Egyptian 'unionist' rivals—who have variously manifested themselves as the National Unionist Party, the People's Democratic Party and the Democratic Unionist Party—it went on to dominate the politics of Sudan's three parliamentary eras (1953–58, 1965–69, 1986–89). Its opponents in the 'modern forces' labelled both the unionists and the Umma as 'sectarian', on account of the fact that they were reliant on the political and economic support of religious orders: the Khatmiyya and the Ansar, respectively.

In each of the three uprisings, the Umma Party supported the popular mobilisation against the military regime, but then worked with the military to ensure that the subsequent transition would ensure its interests and not those of its radical and leftist opponents. At a critical point of the 1964 transition, immediately after the dissolution of Abboud's ruling military council, it was two Ansari- and Umma-affiliated generals who approached the political parties gathered at the tomb (*gubba*) of the Mahdi to negotiate the transition to the new order.[43] Those same generals were working to restrict the influence of the Professional Front and its radical Free Officer allies within the military. The Umma Party was unable to prevent the domination of the first transitional regime by affiliates and members of leftist parties, but pushed backed hard against the latter's policies. In particular, it fought against the plans of the first transitional government to dissolve the formalised provincial tribalism known as 'Native Administration'—a core source of the Umma's own support—and to introduce direct representation of the professionals, urban labourers and cotton farmers. It allied itself to other parties, including the Muslim Brotherhood, with the aim of toppling the first transitional cabinet, and ultimately achieved this feat in February 1965 by marching its Ansari followers into Khartoum as the regular army looked on. The subsequent transitional cabinet abandoned the principle of direct class-based representation—a few seats allocated to the educated classes aside—and the Umma Party won the largest share of the vote in the 1965 parliamentary elections, with the National Unionist Party coming in in second place. Once it was in government, the Umma Party abandoned the ongoing trials that the radical professionals had initiated to prosecute the former military junta's crimes in southern Sudan, and, under the Umma-dominated parliamentary regimes, the army perpetrated further massacres in the south.[44] Meanwhile, the Muslim Brothers were able to work with the Umma-dominated parliaments to ban the Sudan Communist Party on the grounds of its purported atheism.[45]

In 1985, the Umma Party once more worked with the military to thwart the aspirations of the more radical actors with which it had aligned itself during the uprising. Both the Umma and the DUP signed a National Charter with the professional groups and the Sudan Communist Party on 5 April, but, then when the TMC ousted Nimeiri the next day, they cancelled meetings with the professional groups to visit the new junta instead and commit to a 12-month transitional period, which was shorter than that agreed upon with the union activists. The rationale for a quick transition was that this would give the best chance for the conservative sectarian parties, with their organic constituencies still intact, to win a majority. The TMC was then able to clamp down on further demonstrations and marginalise leftist groups within the transitional regime. Many of the interim generals had close ties with the DUP, but one individual who was instrumental in developing the Umma Party's relationship with the TMC was Fadlallah Burma Nasir, the Ansari member of the military council. As seen previously, Nasir was instrumental in the establishment of militias in South Kordofan that would morph into the PDF under the post-1989 Islamist regime, which drew on legislation already drawn up by the Umma Party government for its militia policy.[46] Before the Islamists ousted Sadiq al-Mahdi in the 1989 coup, the Umma Party had worked with al-Turabi's National Islamic Front in a coalition that suppressed street protests organised by the urban left.

When the anniversary of the TMC takeover arrived on 6 April 2019, the National Umma Party issued a statement declaring that it was an 'individual duty' (*fard al-ayn*) for each of its members to take to the streets and call for the army to 'side with the people' once more.[47] The reference to the classic jurisprudence of *jihad* built on Sadiq al-Mahdi's own development of a concept of 'civil jihad' after he recognised in the late 1970s that his Ansari fighters could not defeat the regular military by force of arms.[48] Al-Mahdi's political and religious philosophy was capable of inspiring popular mobilisation but here, as previously, his ultimate goal was to strike a deal with the military. Once the military leadership established another TMC on 11 April 2019, the National Umma Party followed its time-honoured script of seeking to prevent further popular mobilisation and increasingly aligned itself with the generals. Even after the 2019 TMC's ruthless dispersal of the sit-in at army headquarters, al-Mahdi continued to praise the role of the junta in enabling the revolution, and, unlike the other civilian groups in the FFC, supported the soldiers remaining in government in the transitional period.[49] He even invited members of the TMC, including Hemedti, to join his party once the transition was over, effectively encouraging them to follow the example set by Fadlallah Burma Nasir.[50] Once more, al-Mahdi, who remained an influential figure, broke with the principle of a lengthy transitional period agreed upon in the initial revolutionary charter and called for early elections, eliciting an angry response from the Sudan Communist Party.[51] After al-Mahdi's passing, Nasir took on the role of interim leader of the Umma Party, and remained a staunch advocate of the political role of the military, calling for the appointment of military governors in 'sensitive' regions.[52]

To summarize: in 1964, 1985 and 2019, specific factions within three highly socially interpenetrated sectors—the professional class, the army, and the sectarian parties—collaborated to ensure a conservative transition. The professional movement itself was ideologically eclectic in 1964 and 1985: while many were sympathetic to the Sudan Communist Party and the rebels, others were closer to the religious parties. In 1964 and 1985, respectively, the Islamist professionals, al-Turabi and al-Jizouli Dafa'allah, brokered transitions with the military and the sectarian parties, which eventually excluded the more radical actors. Al-Turabi's role in October has often been represented as 'counter-revolutionary'.[53] This is true in the sense that the Islamists were viscerally hostile to the political left. But he did not want a return to the *ancien régime* or indeed (at that time) a military authoritarianism, but rather a modernisation in a distinctively Islamist form. In reality October was marked by multiple competing and at times overlapping revolutions all occurring at once: a Leninist socialist revolution led by the vanguardist communists, a Nasserist revolution led by the Arab nationalists, a bourgeois revolution on the French model led the Turabists, and a religious, cultural and legal anti-colonial revolution, also led by the Turabists. Al-Turabi sought in the post-October period to make his Islamism consistent with a particular form of representative democracy that could embrace the 'sectarian' forces but would exclude the revolutionary left, invoking the principle of absolute parliamentary sovereignty in his campaign to ban the Sudan Communist Party due to its purported atheism. His was a parallel revolution opposed to the organised left and liberals, while adopting and refashioning some of their methods and even some of their ideas.[54]

The 1964 and 1985 transitions broke down because of the conflict between the multiple modes of revolution, and the comprehensive failure of each mode of revolution to overcome the gap between centre and periphery. As would later be the case with the FFC and the SPA, the vaguely defined nationalism of the Professional Front enabled it to draw together multiple groups with divergent ideologies; it fell apart during the transitional period when its various constituent factions failed to agree upon what exactly Sudanese nationalism meant. The communists and Nasserists raised the slogan of the 'modern forces' most vociferously, calling for sectoral representation for workers, tenants and professionals in the forthcoming elections and insisting that the 'traditional' sector represented by the Native Administration be dismantled. The Umma Party, which saw the provincial aristocracy as a valuable means to capture tenant labour and mobilise electoral support, reacted aggressively to these demands. The Islamists, meanwhile, despite drawing their own strength from within the 'modern forces', feared that the communists' proposals to reform the electoral system would lead to a leftist takeover, and started to see the 'sectarian' parties as a counterweight to the communists. Islamist- and Umma-affiliated professionals withdrew from the Professional Front, and, in February 1965, the Ansar show of force in Khartoum, with the tacit backing of the Islamic Charter Front, forced the dissolution of the left-leaning first transitional cabinet.

A similar polarisation occurred, at a much earlier stage, in the second transitional period in 1985. Al-Jizouli Dafa'allah had furious debates with leftists and secularists who wanted to reverse the Islamisation of the Sudanese legal system outright, and his ascent as prime minister led to the most radical professionals disassociating themselves from the transitional government. Even though debates over the secular character of the state remain prominent in the current transition, we should be wary of identifying a binary struggle between left and right, religion and secularism, the 'sectarians' and the 'modern forces'. The 'turbulent' and fluid character of Sudanese politics has not always allowed that. The Nasserists and Ba'athists of Sudan themselves drew on the financial and religious support of the Khatmiyya Sufi order, which enabled them to organise as the Popular Democratic Party. The Islamic Charter Front, which backed the Umma campaign against the Sudan Communist Party's electoral plans, went against it in supporting the dissolution of the Native Administration.[55] After the 1969 coup Abd al-Khaliq Mahjub, fearing the rise of adventurist coup-plotters in his own party, would attempt to develop an alliance with Sadiq al-Mahdi as a 'modernist' within the Umma–Ansar hybrid movement.[56] Sudanese politicians have often explored ways of escaping the modern–traditional, Islamic–secular, left–right binaries, although at crucial moments in Sudanese history, including 1964, 1969 and 1985, these binaries have proved difficult to evade.

The revolutionary events of 1964 and again in 1985 provided moments where it appeared the centre versus periphery binary might be overcome. On each occasion, the more radical professionals reached out to politicians representing the marginalised regions. The left-leaning first transitional government appointed Clement Mboro, one of the many southerners opposed to the former government's war in his region, as minister of interior. Mboro immediately began amnestying the rebel groups, purging senior police, and arranging trials to punish the abuses perpetrated in the south.[57] However, he departed with the first transitional government, the war continued, and no one was ever punished for the November Regime's atrocities in the South.

In 1985, leftists in the National Alliance reached out to the leader of the Sudan People's Liberation Army (SPLA), John Garang, hoping to entice him to participate in the transitional process. Garang drew a great deal of his backing from Marxist Ethiopia, and his 'New Sudan' vision drew heavily on Marxist formulas in insisting that the rebel movement should fight not just to emancipate southern Sudan but to liberate all the country's marginalised regions and bring an end to the economic dominance of the riverain centre. In theory, Garang made a perfect ally for the northern left, who hoped to use the SPLA's considerable constituency in the south in a post-transitional left-wing electoral alliance against the more conservative parties. Nevertheless, even though the northern left continued to remain committed to the democratic transition despite the interim regime's hostility to organised labour, the SPLA denounced the TMC unreservedly, describing it as a reinvention of Nimeiri's May Regime and intensifying its military campaign against it. In what many northern leftists lamented as a self-fulfilling prophecy, Garang correctly foresaw that the transitional government would not be viable; what he failed to anticipate was that what followed would be even more hostile to the cause of the marginalised. Garang thereby missed a historic opportunity to play a major role in the uprising by bringing the foremost rebel movement into the civilian transitional process.[58]

The failure of the 1964 and 1985 uprisings to end Sudan's conflicts and prevent the return of military rule led to much soul-searching among the country's urban revolutionaries, who were desperate to break the cycle of uprising, transition, conflict, failed democracy and military authoritarianism. Yet there are multiple new dimensions to Sudanese politics in, during and after the 2019 revolution that could mitigate against the persistence of this cycle.

Popular mobilisation has been far more sustained and continuous than was the case in 1964 or 1985, when it dissipated after achieving its immediate goal. In part, this reflects the expansion of the educated class and the growth and empowerment of the urban periphery. In 1965, the urban left attempted to call a second general strike to prevent the rightwards shift in the transitional regime engineered by the Umma Party. However, divested of the support of most of the political parties, it could not mobilise enough support to match the Ansar marching on Khartoum.[59] In 1985, Siwar al-Dahab and the TMC were able to impose a ban on further protests within a month of taking over. However, in 2019 the protests continued even after the formation of the TMC, and despite the efforts of the National Umma Party to deter them. On 30 June, tens of thousands marched in protests that the National Umma Party boycotted.[60] This was possible because the base for popular mobilisation now went well beyond the professional and labour unions, incorporating youth groups, the informal economy, organisations representing the marginalised regions, the urban lumpenproletariat, Facebook activists and women's groups. As such, it appears a lot harder for the National Umma Party to capture the 'near periphery' and use it against the radical urbanites than was the case in 1965.

One particular factor that militates against a conservative transition is Sudan's young population. More than 60% of the population is below 24 years of age, and the median age is just under 20.[61] The majority of this generation did not witness the previous transitions or the previous parliamentary eras and are not wedded to the old pragmatisms. The revolutionary youth established their own organisations, like *Shabab al-Thawra*, formed at the sit-in site.[62] The National Umma Party's youth wing was outspoken in challenging the conciliatory approach of Sadiq al-Mahdi towards the military in the years before the Intifada, and was among the first to clash with the security forces as it began.[63]

Three further factors have changed the dynamics of the 2018–19 uprising and subsequent transition. First of all, the marginalised periphery has become nearer to Khartoum than was the case in 1964 and 1985, suggesting an end to the old dichotomy between armed rebellion in the peripheries and civil protest at the centre.[64] Second, women have mobilised even more effectively than during the previous Intifadas, challenging their gendered marginalisation both under the al-Bashir regime and in society at large, as well as the patriarchal modes of authority that have underpinned authoritarian politics in Sudan. Third, 30 years of Islamists in power have both engendered widespread popular hostility to them, and also exposed the flaws in the Islamist project.

Cycles of Conflict in the Peripheries

From the perspective of Khartoum's urbanites, the rebellious periphery is now a lot closer to home than was the case in either 1964 or 1985. In that era fighting was restricted largely to the now seceded southern region, with the notable exception of the 1976 raid by the Islamist–sectarian National Front forces from their bases in Libya, which reached as far as Omdurman. That, however, was a military strike by unseated members of an excluded political elite, not a provincial insurgency encroaching on the riverain centre. Only after the 1985 uprising did civil war penetrate northern Sudan, beginning when the SPLA dispatched battalions into the Nuba Mountains later that year and escalating with attacks in Blue Nile, backed by Ethiopia. In the 1990s, the opposition National Democratic Alliance threatened to encircle Khartoum with an Eritrean-backed insurgency in eastern Sudan. In November 2000, the SPLA briefly took the eastern town of Kassala with Eritrean support. But it was the Darfur war of 2003 that most disturbed the regime, not least because one component of the Darfurian opposition—the Justice and Equality Movement (JEM)—was comprised of former senior cadres of the Islamic Movement, and al-Bashir feared they had sympathisers in Khartoum. In 2008 the JEM took the fight to Khartoum itself for the first time, as the Darfur-based JEM raided Omdurman with Libyan and Chadian backing and was turned back only after fierce fighting on the bridges crossing the Nile.

A threat re-emerged after the failure of both Khartoum and Juba to agree on the status of the northern Sudan-based divisions of the SPLA at the time of South Sudan's independence in 2011. Renewed war broke out in the Nuba Mountains in the weeks before the secession, and in Blue Nile a few months later. After the Sudanese SPLA battalions joined with the Darfur rebels to form the Sudan Revolutionary Front (SRF) in 2011, they tried once more to bring the battle closer to the capital, occupying Abu Kershola on the border between North and South Kordofan in 2013. However, geography and logistics proved to be obstacles to mounting a march on Khartoum from South Kordofan, and efforts to do so faltered in the face of the regime's superior airpower and the redeployment of the RSF to the battlefront.[65] At the time of 2018 uprising, the rebels were still challenging the regime's hegemony in rump Sudan, but they did not pose an existential threat.

The formation of the SRF in 2011, and its subsequent alliances with Khartoum-based parties, raised hopes of a unified revolutionary movement that would finally force the political centre to address the grievances of the marginalised regions. Yet the SRF's revolutionary ambitions were limited by its factiousness and the intense contestation over its collective leadership.[66] A number of the rebel factions have pursued a highly transactional approach towards dealing with the Khartoum regime, seeing peace negotiations as an opportunity to purchase a stake in the system, rather than overthrowing it.[67] When the 2018–19 uprising gathered momentum, the rebel movements gave their vocal support to it, and committed themselves to abstaining from peace negotiations till it had run its course. Yet after the rise of the TMC, Hemedti was quick to turn the transactional approach of the rebel groups against the revolutionary alliance. In May 2019 Yasir Arman, the northern leftist and SPLA veteran, arrived symbolically in Khartoum, auguring the emergence of an alliance between urban and rural revolutionaries like that which failed to materialise in 1985. In a matter of days the TMC arrested Arman and deported him to Juba—then went into talks with representatives of JEM and Minni Minawi's faction of the Sudan Liberation Movement.[68] Later that year, with Abdalla Hamdok in place as transitional prime minister and committing himself to a more inclusive peace process, Arman returned to Khartoum, bringing with him hopes of a more inclusive transition.

While the rebel groups themselves have not always acted as the most reliable revolutionaries, the impact of the conflict on the marginalised regions, and the increasing migration from those marginalised regions to the riverain centre, has led to the emergence of a new generation of urban revolutionaries who share a similar aspiration to challenge the hegemony of the Khartoum elites. Groups like the Darfur Student Association and Nuba Mountains Student Union have challenged the centre-focused politics of other activists.[69] They have also begun to shape the agenda of new political parties, like the Sudanese Congress Party. The mass public support for Arman's ultimately aborted presidential campaign in 2010 seemed to augur the possibility that the former rebels could effect change via electoral politics at the riverain centre.[70] In contrast to the 1964 and to some extent the 1985 uprising, the 2013 protests were dominated by Khartoum's peri-urban population, which demonstrated en masse against economic retrenchment by the regime, leading to a lethal campaign of repression by the RSF in the shanty towns.[71]

Initially, it was not the informal economy of the peri-urban areas but the affluent economy of the riverain centre and other northern towns that drove the 2018–19 uprising. Inflation affected the urban middle classes more than previous downturns, and it was these urban middle classes that had the technological know-how and organisational capacity to mount a sustained campaign of civil disobedience at the centre. In contrast with the 2013 uprising, the vast majority of the protests occurred in the city centres rather than the peri-urban areas. This has been attributed to the distrust of the marginalised populations who fled to the capital to escape wars in Darfur, the Nuba Mountains and the south, towards the more privileged populations of riverain descent, whose economic privileges are directly tied to the exploitation of the periphery.[72]

Yet the social gulf between the urban middle classes and the marginalised populations of the shanty towns has never been absolute. The middle-class protestors responded to security service efforts to provoke fear of rebel activity in the peri-urban zones with the slogan—aimed at al-Bashir—'You arrogant racist, we are all Darfur!' While the protests may not have had a marked impact on the most marginalised urban zones, the contribution of the most marginalised sectors towards protests at the urban centre was highly visible. This was particularly the case at the army headquarters sit-in, which was described by the psychologist, Mustafa Adam Suleiman, interviewed by *al-Sharq al-Awsat* at a makeshift clinic at the sit-in, as a scene of 'unintentional social melting'.[73] A special camp was established for *shamasa* children, some of whom gave interviews to the regional media, expressing their solidarity with the protestors.[74] Meanwhile, Awadiyya Mahmoud Kuku, herself from South Kordofan and the head of the Tea Sellers' Union that had sought to empower the women at the heart of Khartoum's informal economy, became the 'first lady of the revolution' at the sit-in, overseeing the operation to feed the thousands of protestors encamped there.[75] While the origins of the initial protests were middle class, as the Intifada developed further and the protestors at the sit-in began to embrace the spirit of *communitas* it appeared that every social sector had a stake.

While it was educated professionals and activists from riverain backgrounds who gave the Intifada its leadership, the Salvation Regime's underfunded expansion of the universities has given the citizens of the peripheries a partial stake in the higher education sector. Although students from Darfur and the Nuba Mountains are still relatively marginalised within the educated class, student bodies representing them can deploy far greater numbers than was the case in 1964 and 1985. Darfuri student organisations had been clashing with the security services at universities throughout central riverain Sudan in the decade leading up to the Intifada, resulting in several deaths;[76] it was no surprise, when the Intifada initially broke out, that the government crackdown particularly targeted Darfuri students in Khartoum's universities.[77] Given the close ties between the narrow educated elite and the core institutions of the state, the student groups of 1964 acted as vehicles for the transfer of power within an elite;[78] when the Salvation Regime expanded the higher education sector without providing concomitant resources or opportunities for post-graduation employment,[79] it created the potential for a much more sizeable revolutionary class.

While the politics of the periphery is increasingly shaping the politics of protest at the riverain centre, the methods and goals of civil protest are penetrating the periphery, altering the old dichotomy between peaceful opposition at the centre and armed rebellion at the margins.[80] There is a long, under-recognised history to this connection. There were substantial protests in Darfur in 1964—indeed, the first Darfuri regionalist organisation, the Darfur Renaissance Front, emerged out of the protests that broke out in the region during the October Revolution.[81] There were protests in al-Fashir again in 1981 and 1983. However, in those days there were few working phone lines and it took nearly a week to travel from Darfur to the Nile, which mitigated against provincial protest shaping what were rapid Khartoum-centred transitions. Today, 21st-century communications technology has shortened distances, which gives demonstrations in peripheral regions more opportunity to have an impact. Resistance committees in Nyala established camps to educate the youth in modes of civil protest,[82] and clashes with government security forces there led to solidarity marches in the cities on the Nile.[83] Meanwhile, locally based campaigns against the environmentally detrimental effects of gold mining in South Kordofan, where the use of toxic chemicals was poisoning land and water, received support from the communists,[84] and were able to force the cabinet to ban the use of mercury and cyanide in gold mining.[85] Hemedti tried to head off rural dissent by exploiting the FFC's emphasis on meritocratic empowerment of the riverain professional class to buy in rural elites who felt excluded from this particularist riverain vision.[86] However, this form of marketplace politics does not offer a means to disarm the rural-to-urban migrants of Khartoum and the other major towns and cities, who stand behind the most militant of the resistance committees.[87]

Women and Revolutions

Another novel dynamic is the intensity with which urban women mobilised during the 2018–19 Intifada. In and of itself, the mobilisation of women during the uprising is hardly novel. Female professionals were at the heart of the march to the palace that initiated the general strike of October 1964, and, as was the case in 2018–19, they chanted *zagharid* (ululations) to galvanise the popular mobilisation.[88] However, the demands that were made for women's political, social and economic emancipation were limited in contrast to today. One female protestor from 1964 recalls: 'Women mobilized without feeling that they were women, but rather as an inseparable part of the [whole] people.'[89] The nationalist politics of the early independence era did not offer women the same opportunities to present separate demands for gender liberation as are available today.[90] Political emancipation did extend to the granting of suffrage and candidature rights to women, and the Sudan Women's Union leader, Fatima Ahmad Ibrahim, duly became Sudan's first female MP in 1965. A campaign by the Sudan Women's Union in 1968 succeeded in guaranteeing equal pay for female teachers, albeit that the legislation was later reversed by Nimeiri.[91] However, the overall representation of women in the post-1964 and post-1985 parliaments was highly restricted. The Islamist project has been widely condemned for its marginalisation of women, but the pre-1989 parties did not do much better. Ironically, the only two female representatives in the 1986–89 democracy were members of the Islamist National Islamic Front.[92] The Turabist project had achieved a great deal of success in promoting women's access to education—including universities—while the dress code it established also enabled a new generation of middle-class women to enter the public sphere and compete alongside men.[93] In general, as was the case elsewhere in the region,[94] winning some political and economic rights did not entail social emancipation. Women like Fatima Ibrahim were able to progress politically precisely because they publicly adhered to conservative social mores, including the association of femininity with domesticity.[95]

By 2018 much of the caution of the earlier women's activists had been abandoned. There were several reasons for this. First of all, women became far more integrated into the public sphere, both through the formal and the informal economy. Whereas only a tiny minority of women had achieved university and secondary-level educations in 1964, today the figure is far greater, although full parity has not yet been achieved and women are more likely to remain unemployed after graduation.[96] Nevertheless the targeting of women, whether street-side tea ladies or trouser-wearing journalists like Lubna Hussein, by the Islamist regime's various para-police units (the Public Order Police, the Security of Society Police and the Popular Police) was a response to the increasing public visibility of women, whether it be women who were economically emancipated by Sudan's capitalist transformations or marginalised women who had fled from the wars in the periphery into the core urban zones.[97] Also, given the hyper-securitisation of the economy under al-Bashir, and given that recruits to the army, police and militias are predominantly male, it is unsurprising that women are proportionately more substantially represented in the civilian sectors of the education system and economy and that they have a related commitment to taking up a protest movement that makes the reduction of the security budget one of its principal demands.[98]

In 2018–19, women activists made more comprehensive political demands and also broke taboos by challenging perceived gender roles and raising awareness about sexual violence. A few weeks after the fall of al-Bashir, activists organised a well-attended march to the sit-in site to demand that the new government allow women to be granted 50% representation throughout the public sphere.[99] Women's groups went on to criticise the domination of the subsequent FFC–TMC talks by men,[100] although the eventual transitional government did grant women two seats in the Sovereign Council and four in the cabinet, making a contrast with the entirely male-dominated interim governments of 1964 and 1985. These women included the foreign minister, Asma Mohamed Abdalla, and the 33-year-old youth and sports minister, Walaa al-Boushi, who instantly angered Salafi ultraconservatives by overseeing the creation of a national women's football team.[101]

Women's activism has subverted societal gender norms in new and provocative ways. Once again, the lengthy revolutionary moment at the sit-in site contributed to this. Educated female protestors married and formed relationships with men encamped alongside them at army headquarters, often breaking convention by 'loudly proclaiming their desires' and choosing partners with little attention to their parents' class sensibilities.[102] Whereas the female protestors who ululated in support of the October Revolution were often portrayed as facilitators of male heroism,[103] in 2018–19 they were themselves the *kandakas*, or 'warrior queens'.[104] The most iconic of the *kandakas* was 22-year-old student, Alaa Salah, whose image went viral after being photographed atop a car, towering over an enormous crowd of demonstrators. Some Sudanese commentators criticised the adoption of Alaa Salah as the emblem of women's revolutionary agency, pointing to the white *tob* that marked her out as part of the riverain professional elite and arguing that the image contributed to the exclusion of socially marginalised women.[105] Subsequent calls to honour the Tea Sellers' Union chief, Awadiyya Mahmoud Kuku, who hails from the marginalised region of South Kordofan, for her role in supporting the sit-in, may serve as an important corrective here.[106]

On 8 April 2021, almost two years after the revolution, 200 women and girls with no prior knowledge of each other and whose networks barely intersected previously, congregated at the doorsteps of the justice ministry to contest the phenomenon of 'unsafe homes'. Demands for laws on gender-based violence to protect women against increasing incidents of abuse in the public and private spheres were common in the post-revolution setting. The women's procession manifesto included calls to activate regional and international women's rights frameworks, such as the UN Convention on the Elimination of All Forms of Discrimination Against Women, of which Sudan was a signatory (though it had not ratified it). This surge in political mobilisation was instigated by the murder of a 14-year-old girl, Samaha, at the hand of her father[107] and the subsequent collusion of state officials with patriarchal norms that ensured impunity for all. The murder and the cover-up were scandalous in themselves, but the women gathered because the incident exposed continuity with long patterns of injustice. The slogan of the women protestors continued to shape the contours of an unfinished revolution: 'we will wrestle what's ours ... from the prevailing order we will snatch it ... within the haram [space of domestic seclusion] and out on the streets'. The gathering was the beginning of a series of women's rights-based protests across Khartoum in the late spring of 2021.[108]

Expanded digital connectivity in Sudan had political implications beyond the ways in which democracy activists organised themselves and their relations with the public. Throughout 2019, women's groups on Facebook worked hard at networking, producing and exchanging knowledge, and organising in support of the 2019 call for civil disobedience by the SPA.[109] Until that point, Sudanese social media had been overwhelmingly non-political and indeed had amplified messages that underwrote customary norms that reaffirmed women's domestic and family roles. By dissolving the boundaries of private spaces, most women's social media in practice reinforced conformity with public Islamic performances, as those posting messages and images had to be alert to who might view them and how they might react. In revolutionary Sudan, this was subverted: the social media space was also transformed. Furthermore, during the most intense confrontations with the authorities, social media platforms became the only form of connective networks for women to perform politics with a degree of safety. A young female respondent stated that online presence was twice-over a useful tool of political mobilisation.[110] The anonymity availed while advocating for rights served to shield women from direct violence of the state and males in the public domain. Meanwhile, inside their homes, women were able to use public exposure and public opinion to shame male guardians who abused them. Fear of public rebuke reportedly served as an effective deterrent against at least some threats of violence by husbands and fathers. The internet meant that women's presence became at once private—that is, beyond reach—and public. As a result, new forms of feminism based on shared experiences and formulated around the revolutionary discourse of the post-Islamist era have begun to take shape.

Three generations of mostly educated women produced well-informed and highly ambitious female cadres, who were empowered by the employment opportunities of the 2000s and emboldened by the increased visibility of women in public life. These trends reached their climax in the uprising. Stories of brazen attitudes and frankness, openness in social relations and striking personal friendships with male counterparts, freedom of political association and voicing demands and opinions on financial dependency, were both common and widely circulated.

What were the tangible gains for women in the revolution? This has been a topic of fierce debate among Sudanese women and scholars of Sudan. Anecdotal impressions are now being revised or substantiated by surveys and research. One study found that, following the revolution, a significant percentage of women in the al-Nasr district, Khartoum, reported being more willing to express opinions in front of their families, seek financial independence, and demand men contribute to the housework.[111] Discussions with women activists suggest that these accelerated changes in social norms came at a cost, which was increasing tension and even violence inside homes, as conservative families struggled to exert control over their daughters.[112] Meanwhile, many men who continued to dominate the political arena have pushed back against the larger number of women who demand voice and power. One woman spoke about society's fear of women's 'active presence' making women more vulnerable to scrutiny and at increased risk of violence, especially as basic security on the streets has crumbled. Whether they be individual disapproving males or security agents and militiamen acting with impunity, men have latitude to harass and even assault women.[113]

The logic of the political marketplace—material, coercive and transactional—is highly masculine. It reduces people to tradeable commodities. Nonetheless, the disruptive potential of the marketplace logic in social relations can undermine old forms of patriarchy. Marriage has historically been a crucial means for patrilineal families to acquire wealth and establish authority, and women have had little say in the bargaining over their future and their status. This order has been irrevocably destabilised as a precarious middle class struggles to adapt marriage practices to its predicament. A younger and more liberal generation has come to the fore. For them, personal choice in a life partner is more important than the values and preferences of their parents. Moreover, women aspire to financial independence and men expect to acquire wealth through a professional career rather than through inheritance and brideprice, both as personal choice and as practical expectation.

Younger women are also uninterested in the formulae for political representation that dominated the women's rights agenda of the previous generation. The 40% quota for women is no longer persuasive. Young women speak the language of a hardened feminist stance, with increased political association at work and among social networks.

There remains a marked divide between centre and periphery, which continues to define the experience of Sudan's revolutionary women. The main agendas for women in the northern riverain have been matters such as challenging practices of female genital mutilation and child marriage, while women in the peripheries have focused on overcoming extreme poverty, displacement and insecurity.[114] Provincial women find it harder to get a stake in their local politics, which are even more profoundly dominated by men, whether they are government-aligned security chiefs, armed rebels, or the sons of chiefly families. In spite of extensive demands for participation by the Darfur Women's Protection Network and other women's groups in the transitional peace process,[115] they were allowed only brief involvement in the talks that generated the September 2020 Juba Peace Agreement.[116] Those groups that did attend were able to ensure that the interim government's commitment to 40% representation of women in national and regional governments was included in the agreements reached with the rebel groups, but the ongoing role of the RSF in the transitional process, particularly in Darfur, left them with serious concerns about redress for victims of sexual violence.[117]

It is too early to assess the outcome of women's activism during the revolution. Women's gains were uneven and uncertain, but there is no doubt that the status quo of patriarchy was shaken. There is no doubt that the vision of wide-ranging transformation of the gender order put forward by many of the activists added impetus to the revolutionary moment and increased the chances that the country might avoid the kind of conservative or Islamist transition that ultimately occurred in 1964 and 1985.

A Post-Islamist Uprising?

Another novel factor in the 2019 transition is the fact that the uprising raised the possibility of an outright eclipse of Islamist politics. Many of the Intifada's slogans were anti-Islamist in character. Both within Sudan and regionally the 2019 uprising was unprecedented in that it represented the first popular movement to successfully unseat a regime that was, in name and in its leading personnel, Islamist. Whether the al-Bashir government could truly be described as still pursuing an Islamic project had long been in doubt. Almost 20 years earlier, al-Turabi and many of his followers had split off and condemned those who remained in government as driven by a greed for money and power only—a charge that resonated. Meanwhile, the public flourishes that paid deference to Islamist ideals and quotidian repressions of the police enforcing the public order codes were little more than reminders of the halcyon days of passionate Islamist internationalism. Following a trajectory charted by Islamist 'neo-fundamentalists' elsewhere in the Arab and Muslim world, the Islamists that remained with the regime fixated upon the policing of public morality, abandoning the quasi-revolutionary agendas of earlier years.[118]

The civic revolutionaries wanted those tired old Islamists swept away and most of them had no time for the avowedly democratic Islamists who had joined the protests. Elsewhere in the region, Islamists presented themselves as the only alternative to military authoritarianism.[119] In Sudan this carries no credibility, as they were themselves succoured by military authoritarians for 30 years. The Islamists also have far less of a stake in the revolutionary organisations and the transitional government than was the case in 1964 and 1985, which will make it harder for them to engineer a conservative transition that protects the core elements of the Islamist project. The SPA, unlike the professional bodies of 1964 and 1985, had no significant Islamist component. Indeed, it refused to acknowledge the transitional proposals of the non-partisan 'Peace and Reform Initiative' group of academics and professionals headed by al-Jizouli Dafa'allah, the Islamist engineer of the last conservative transition.[120] When the 'Peace and Reform Initiative', which involved al-Bashir overseeing a broad-based transition, was first floated in 2016, it received broad support across the political and ideological spectrum; in 2018–19, when Dafa'allah attempted to revive it, a number of its secular and leftist signatories disowned it, recognising that the popular uprising had created the possibility for a more radical break with Islamist politics and fearing accusations that they were undermining the Declaration of Freedom and Change.[121] The only group with Islamist credentials that has had a stake in the transitional government is JEM, which has from the outset of the Darfur war subsumed its politics within the common demands made by secular provincial revolutionaries.

It is unlikely that the old mode of Islamist politics, which drew heavily on totalistic ideologues such as Qutb and Mawdudi, will return. The old Qutbist and Mawdudist language on battling the age of ignorance (*jahiliyya*), instituting divine sovereignty (*hakimiyya*), and fighting for the party of God against the party of Satan, has disappeared from most of the Islamists' rhetoric. Many, like Ghazi Salahuddin al-Atabani of Reform Now, are hoping that they can position themselves as 'Muslim democrats' akin to the al-Nahda Party of Rashid al-Ghannushi, who was awarded a Nobel Peace Prize on account of his willingness to participate in the post-Arab Spring parliamentary democracy in Tunisia.[122] Al-Ghannushi distanced himself from political Islam, agreed upon a constitution that did not make reference to sharia, and repositioned al-Nahda as a party of conventional social and economic conservatism.[123] Many of the Sudanese Islamists had begun a similar process of reinventing themselves as 'Muslim democrats' well before the regime fell. After al-Bashir threw al-Turabi out of power in 1999, many within the Islamist media denounced the 'totalitarian' character of the project they had initially backed.[124] As leader of the Popular Congress Party, al-Turabi distanced himself from many of the ideological tenets of the regime he had engineered, signing a 'Memorandum of Understanding' with the SPLA and entering the National Consensus Forces opposition coalition. Yet, in another twist of Sudan's turbulent politics, al-Turabi went on to abandon those alliances before his death in 2016, and at the time of the Intifada the PCP was participating in a parliament which resulted from a national dialogue process eschewed by the mainstream opposition.

During the Intifada, dissident Islamist intellectuals and the Islamist youth took to the streets. Uthman al-Mirghani, a former Turabist whose *al-Tayyar* newspaper had many run-ins with the regime's security services, was arrested during the uprising and went on to give speeches from the heart of the sit-in at army headquarters.[125] One of the uprising's most prominent martyrs was Ahmad Kheir, a PCP-affiliated teacher tortured to death by NISS agents in Kassala.[126] However, the uprising received only lukewarm backing from the leaderships of the 'reformist' Islamist parties, Ghazi Salahuddin of Reform Now and Ali al-Haj of the PCP. Ali al-Haj even gave his public blessing to al-Bashir's state of emergency declaration.[127] While these men were willing to strike deals with non-Islamist factions when they were in a position of relative strength, the risk for them was that a genuine popular uprising would empower those willing to hold them to account for their role in the 1989 coup and what followed. Indeed, soon after the uprising a group of opposition lawyers targeted both al-Haj and al-Atabani, alongside other leading Islamists, with an action seeking to put them on trial for overthrowing democracy. During the Intifada itself, there was a virtual civil war within the PCP, with the younger generation refusing to accept the reactionary approach of the leadership.[128] After the arrest of Ali al-Haj in November 2019, the PCP looked set to refrain from participating in the December 2019 'Green March' being called for by the NCP, hard-line Islamist factions and the older generation of the PCP that supported al-Bashir during the Intifada.[129] However, it changed its position at the last minute and called on its members to join.[130]

Can the Islamists still command enough popular support to prevent their movement being resigned to 'oblivion'?[131] Sudan has witnessed unprecedented levels of urbanisation, and most have been taking to the streets since 2018. Each of these factors makes a political sea-change in Sudan plausible. The problem for Sudan's urban leftists and liberals is that, even with the rise of cyberspace, the Islamists still dominate a huge portion of the conventional media—al-Mirghani's *al-Tayyar*, as well as other Islamist papers such as *al-Sudani* and *al-Sayha,* continued to publish during the transition. Al-Bashir's ultraconservative uncle, al-Tayyib Mustafa, whose brief arrest in 2020 drew protests from international human rights groups, carried on using his column in *al-Intibaha* to denounce the secular outlook of the transitional regime.[132] The official state media, including the Sudan News Agency (SUNA), although it became a vehicle for the transitional government, remained under the operation of old regime cadres. The Islamists might benefit from being excluded from the transitional government, and turn any economic failures against it in the post-transitional elections.[133] While the Islamists' pretensions to offer a coherent theory of modern Islamic statehood may now have been discredited by their experience in power, they can still resort to their classic negative tactics of discrediting their opponents by presenting them as the dupes of Western liberalism, secularism and neo-colonialism. Calling for a new protest movement to topple the transitional regime in March 2021, the regime's former foreign minister, Ali Karti, mocked its leaders for having 'flown in from Western capitals, where they lived as refugees, reared by [international] organizations'.[134]

If the urban revolutionaries of the riverain centre are unable to avoid the failures of the last two uprisings and consolidate their movement by extending it to western Sudan, they may yet face a challenge there. It is an uncomfortable fact for the FFC that until his arrest the only Darfuri leader of a major Khartoum-based civilian party was al-Haj of the PCP. Back in the 1960s al-Haj was the deputy head of the regionalist Darfur Renaissance Front, which formed after the urban protests that broke out in Darfur during the 1964 October Revolution.[135] From the 1960s to the 1980s, the Islamists had considerable success at co-opting Darfuri students into their movement, playing on their hostility towards the secularised riverain elites and tactically embracing the Western region's desire for decentralisation to establish a power base there.[136] The 1981 regionalist Intifada in Darfur was largely led by elite Islamists.[137] Once al-Bashir split with al-Turabi over the question of regional decentralisation in 1999, most Islamist Darfuris joined the PCP and al-Haj was widely believed to be a go-between with Darfur's rebel Justice and Equality Movement (JEM), itself established by a former Islamist militia leader.[138] The leader of JEM, Jibril Ibrahim, appointed as finance minister in the 2021 cabinet reshuffle, has historically been very close to both al-Turabi and al-Haj.[139] At the apparent instigation of the pro-Islamist Qataris, he came close to being a spoiler of the TMC–FFC talks in Addis Ababa in July 2019, causing so much disruption that the Ethiopian government briefly arrested him.[140]

Being forced to enter into government with a former Janjaweed commander has put the FFC in a difficult position with regard to Darfur, and al-Haj was quick to exploit this by drawing attention to Hemedti's position on the Sovereign Council.[141] Given the generals' affiliation to the Saudi–Emirati–Egyptian axis, and the proximity of the JEM and PCP leaderships to Turkey and Qatar, there was a real risk that the Islamists' opposition to the transitional arrangement might suck Sudan into the conflicts within the Middle East. The PCP attempted to further capitalise on resentment of the transitional military's regional affiliations by mobilising demonstrations against the interim government's normalisation of relations with Israel in late 2020.[142] Although the PCP hoped to capitalise on the sidelining of the NCP following the revolution to establish itself as the pre-eminent Islamist party, it still remains open to question whether it or any other Islamist faction has the capacity to re-unite the Islamic Movement and make it a credible political force once more.[143]

One factor that may mitigate against the Islamists returning is the fact that, unlike Tunisia, Sudan already has pre-made 'Muslim democrat' parties in a position to capture the same political base among rural–urban migrants and business elites. The Islamists entrenched themselves in western Sudan after 1989 by taking over militias and networks of patrimonial authority that had been building blocks of the Umma Party hegemony in that region.[144] If today's National Umma Party is able to recapture those networks, it could deal the Islamists a killer blow. Yet it is unclear whether the grandees of the National Umma Party, shorn of their stewardship of the pre-1989 cotton economy, possess the financial clout to outbid the Islamists in this region. This is another reason for turning to

Hemedti, the gold baron of Darfur, and his Gulf sponsors. If the National Umma Party does re-emerge as a major player, it is unclear whether this will mark an outright break with religious politics. Sadiq al-Mahdi formed parliamentary alliances with al-Turabi in both the previous democratic periods, and frequently vacillated over the removal of Jafa'ar Nimeiri's 'Islamised' legislation in the third democratic period.[145] In late 2019, he rejected calls for secularism, echoing the post-2011 Mohamed Morsi by observing that 'we are Islamists (*Islamiyyun*), and our interpretation (*ijtihad*) is that Islam supports the five principles of human rights: honour, justice, freedom, equality and peace'.[146] When al-Burhan and al-Hilu signed a deal in 2021 endorsing the separation of religion and state, it divided the National Umma Party. The leadership proposed deferring the issue to the end of the transitional period,[147] although the minister for religious affairs, himself a member of the party, began to draw up legislation banning the formation of parties on a religious basis, which brought about conflicting statements from party officials. The new secretary general, al-Wathiq Bireir, denied that his party was established on a religious basis,[148] although another party official subsequently issued a statement to the effect that it followed the principles of the 1881 Mahdist revolution, which 'was established with both religious and national aspects'.[149]

Throughout the transitional period, there has been evidence that many of the Islamists have begun to rethink their strategic position. Many have recognised the failure of their grandiose ideological project and have been compelled to accept that they are therefore in a weaker position. Rather than aggressively pursuing the goal of an Islamic state, they are returning to their more conservative strategy from the 1960s of attempting to support the 'sectarian' parties as a bulwark against a resurgent political left. This strategy in effect began with al-Turabi's vision shortly before his death in 2016 of a 'successor state' embracing representatives of other religiously orientated parties.[150] It was very much visible in the joint declaration criticising the transitional arrangement made by the PCP and the National Umma Party, and the ongoing demands of these parties for early elections.[151]

Some non-Islamists were also wary that attempting to efface religious politics outright might cause the transition to fail. For instance, Shafie Khidir, an ex-communist and Hamdok ally formerly affiliated with al-Jizouli Dafa'allah's non-partisan Peace and Reform Initiative, called for a 'historic bargain to satisfy the ambitions of the partisans of the Islamic choice, and the ambitions of those who call for secularism and a civil state' to ensure that the interim period would be successful.[152] Former members of the defunct Peace and Reform Initiative were well placed to influence the transitional process: information minister, Faisal Muhammad Salih, an unabashed secularist and long-term journalistic critic of the al-Bashir regime, resisted calls from revolutionary radicals to shut down Islamist outlets;[153] the attorney Nabil Adib was awarded the delicate task of overseeing the investigation into the sit-in massacre, which risked upsetting the delicate civil–military power-sharing agreement.

In spite of the widely acknowledged complicity of the RSF in the sit-in massacre and earlier war crimes in Darfur, they and senior intelligence officials were not targeted by interim judicial processes in the same manner as the Islamists. This is in itself an irony of history. During the 1985–86 transition, the interim regime tried the Arab nationalist and leftist officers who had conducted the 1969 coup along with some of the regime's most corrupt civilian profiteers; the Islamists, who had upheld the May Regime in its last years before turning on it in its dying moments, were left largely untouched. Interim justice in 1964 and 1985 was often both transactional and tied to wider politics, enabling those with sufficient political or financial capital to buy themselves out of accountability. In 1985 the Islamists had purchased a huge stake in the media and security sector; in 2019, the RSF and the other Saudi-aligned generals drew on their position within the interim regime, control over the gold economy, and a massive public relations campaign aimed at establishing themselves as the guardians of the revolution, to escape justice. Given the regional alignment of the generals and the personal proximity of both al-Burhan and Hemedti to the atrocities committed in Darfur, it is unsurprising that the transitional regime moved forward with the trials of the Islamist putschists a lot quicker than with the investigation into the sit-in massacre or war crime tribunals. The Islamists were quick to highlight the inconsistency: before his own arrest, al-Haj condemned the presence of Hemedti in the government and called on Sudan to work with the International Criminal Court.[154] The trial of the killers of Ahmad Khair gave the Islamists the opportunity to highlight the prominent role of the PCP in the fight for justice, and the role of the as yet unrepealed Islamist Penal Codes in avenging his death. Twenty-nine security officers were sentenced to death in accordance with the wishes of Khair's family, in line with the Islamic principle of *qisas* (retribution), which the PCP proposed should be invoked in the cases of all the revolutionary martyrs.[155] In its handling of the process of transitional justice, the interim government tried to balance a range of potential risks: alienating the citizens of Sudan's peripheries, provoking a military counter-revolution, enabling the Islamists to use its failings against it.

Sudan's Revolution in Theory

There are theories of revolutions—why they happen, the trajectories they take, and their ultimate outcomes. As we mentioned in Chapter 1, the Sudanese use of the term *thawra* is protean and neither the country's civic uprisings nor its military takeovers fits the classic mould of the total social revolution. Nonetheless, social science theories of revolution can be pressed into service to ask whether they can help us explain Sudan's civilian uprisings.

Models that emphasise the role of a charismatic leader or revolutionary vanguard would seem to fail;[156] in fact, they would better seem to explain the military coups of 1969 and 1989, which were led respectively by Marxist/Arab socialist and Islamist factions in the military along with their civilian counterparts. There was no leader in 1964, 1985 or 2019 as charismatic or influential as Hasan al-Turabi, the organisational mastermind of the 1989 coup. Al-Turabi himself did exercise charismatic agency in 1964, but could never hope to acquire as much power through this movement as he did through his initial role in al-Bashir's regime.

What of the ideological projects of the movements that led the uprisings? The three uprisings, which witnessed far more substantial popular participation than the 1969 and 1989 coups, are referred to as *thawrat* far more frequently and consistently, but were never dominated by a single ideological faction. It is true that in 1964 and

1985 Ba'athist, Communist and Islamist factions in the military, professional and student movements attempted to act as vanguards, but ultimately in every instance the students and professionals worked in coalition with groups such as the Umma, DUP and independents (including latterly the Sudanese Congress Party) that were less than ideologically revolutionary.[157] The dominant factor unifying the civilian leadership of the popular uprisings from 1964 to 2019 has been a shared commitment to a civic ideal and rejection of authoritarianism. Sudan's *thawrat* were led by coalitions that were united enough to defeat the military, but which broke up following the uprising due their different visions of Sudanese society and disagreements as to the merits of parliamentary democracy as a vehicle for social change.

The Sudanese Communists had, of course, a theory of revolution, which coloured their practices both in preparing their role in uprisings and in what followed. However, they were neither so dominant nor so doctrinaire as other Marxists: for example, the Ethiopian student radicals, whose commitment to Marxist–Leninist practice focused their energies and limited their imaginaries, and foreclosed the space for any form of non-violent civic republicanism in their country.[158] Sudan's civic revolutionaries, by contrast, have developed their own distinctive praxis, rich in vernacular framing and deliberately eschewing the rigours of political-economic theorising in favour of untheorised consensus on the need for democratic change.

Turning to the structural determinants of revolution, Theda Skocpol, prominent theorist on the issue, argued that the most credibly 'revolutionary' movements in modern history—France in 1789, Russia in 1917 and China in 1949—occurred in principally agrarian societies. She was later forced to reconsider her model following the Iranian Revolution of 1979, which toppled a rentier state that had neglected its agrarian economy.[159] Sudan does not fit the agrarian model neatly, because of the dominance of mercantile capitalist farming. Nor, by 2019, was it a conventional rentier state on the Iranian model, because of the collapse of its oil revenues. And of course, while Shia Islamism unified the Iranian revolutionaries in 1979, [160] in the recent Sudanese case an eclectic range of actors revolted against an Islamist regime.

Do postcolonial models of revolution explain the 2019 movement? For the pioneering postcolonial theorist, Frantz Fanon, such a revolutionary movement occurs when the rural populace and urban lumpenproletariat overthrow the intermediary elite that has profited from the extraction of the country's resources.[161] However, Sudan's movements do not neatly fit the Fanon model—they were led, if not necessarily initiated, by unions, the revolutionary potential of which Fanon decried due to what he perceived as their symbiotic relationship with colonial economic structures.[162] The urban bias of each of Sudan's revolutionary movements distinguishes them from the classic Fanon model, as does their emphasis on peaceful protest, since Fanon saw violence as an inevitable function of genuine anti-colonial revolution.[163] Moreover, most of Sudan's provincial movements, while drawing on deep-seated grievances among the agrarian poor, have failed to translate their transformational aspirations into practical programmes. We can see this most clearly in peace talks, in which the armed movements that pursued a transactional rather than a transformational form of rural politics were those that came to the fore, despite the emergence of civic mobilisation in the main provincial towns. As noted above, the disenfranchised rural-to-urban migrants played a major role in street mobilisation in 1985 and 2019, and subsequently stood behind some of the most active resistance committees; they have not, however, been able to shape the ultimate outcome of the 2019 revolution. The SPLM–North of Abdel Aziz al-Hilu, the armed group most resolutely committed to principles such as secularism and self-determination for the marginalised, has been marginal in the transitional process. Meanwhile, the transitional government has hewed more closely to international precepts for economic management than its predecessor, which was only just beginning to shed its pariah status.

Prior to 2019, Sudan's experience hardly figured in the international literature on non-violent movements, despite its rich history of civic protest. In some classic comparative texts it was mentioned in passing at best[164] and in studies of civic uprisings in the Middle East it warranted only a single reference[165] or none at all.[166] Sudan was, it seems, a marginal concern for scholars and practitioners of non-violence. Why so?[167] Possibly because the revolutions appeared *sui generis* when they happened and took place counter-cyclical to global democratisation trends. Given that they occurred in the Cold War period, there was a mistaken tendency to conflate Sudan's historic civilian uprisings with the military-led 'revolutions' that were so common in that era.[168] Scholarship on the country focused on ongoing civil wars. The neglect of Sudan's uprisings was also likely due to the fact that Africa, apart from South Africa, was also marginalised in the canon on civil protest. After 2019—perhaps precisely because the revolution provided a welcome moment of democratic hope at a time when so much of the world was shifting in an authoritarian direction—the Sudanese example was taken as an inspiration across Africa and the Middle East and even further afield. The Sudanese tactical repertoire of protests, the creative use of social media along with music and art, and the gender dynamics evident on the streets, are fast becoming part of the folklore of the worldwide community of practitioners of non-violence. This is part of bringing sub-Saharan African civic movements, along with their creative range of methods, contexts and goals, out of the scholarly and activist shadows and into the mainstream of studies of non-violence.[169] This in turn will in due course contribute to a richer theorisation of non-violence as a set of tactics and as a revolutionary strategy, but it is still too early to assess how the academic community will place Sudan in its emerging theory, and how this will influence practitioners. Undoubtedly, Sudanese democracy activists, both at home and in the diaspora, learned from others, but ultimately they always did it themselves, in their own unique ways.

In short, Sudan's revolutions do not fit any template other than their own imperfect one. Insofar as the civic protest movements of 1964, 1985 and 2019 were 'revolutions', we can agree only on the following: 'they are complex conjunctures of unfolding conflicts involving differently situated and motivated (and at least minimally organized) groups'.[170]

6

NOT THE LAST CHAPTER

A Scripted Coup

There sat General Abdel Fattah al-Burhan, his eyes fixed on the paper in front of him, reading in a measured way. It was 25 October 2021, and al-Burhan was comfortable. Unlike the patricide of April 2019, the general was parlaying a familiar script: the army had stepped in to save the nation from civil war and chaos. He was brushing aside a feckless civilian government that had failed the country, to assert strong and stable leadership. Nobody believed him.

This was the fourth time Sudan had been through the cycle of military–civilian–military rule since self-government almost seventy years earlier. It was a familiar narrative to the older generation: between 1956 and 1990 Sudan had more coups and coup attempts than any other country in Africa.[1] Also, it was not the first mutiny or attempted coup since Hamdok took office. The cycle of civil uprising, fractious democracy, popular disillusion, and military coup is known to all. All previous coups had been mounted against parliamentary governments, and all had a civilian constituency and an ideology. Al-Burhan's coup had neither of these features.

'This is not a coup,' said al-Burhan. He described it as a 'correction' to the course of the transition. That morning, he had asked Hamdok to join him as prime minister of a reconstituted government—in effect to legitimise the takeover. Hamdok refused, and the general removed the prime minister and his wife to his own residence, ostensibly for their protection.

It was a coup foretold. Just a month earlier, on 21 September, as if to test the waters, the army announced it had foiled a coup attempt. Following unrest in Eastern Sudan, including a blockage on the road from Port Sudan that interrupted imports of essential goods to Khartoum, there was a half-hearted mutiny by an army unit. According to the reports from the military, armed men in uniform entered the national radio station and demanded to play patriotic music on the TV. In a previous era, capturing the national radio gave an instant monopoly over information in the country, but that era had long passed. In this case the soldiers did not even carry guns and were rebuffed by staff.[2] It was a curiously shambolic effort for a group of men trying to take over a state. The following day, al-Burhan and Hemedti reassured the Sudanese public that they had acted quickly and decisively to crush the coup, and that in fact their intelligence had known about it but had chosen to wait until the plotters showed their hand. They were oddly reluctant, however, to name the guilty men. Instead, they chose to describe the event as an illustration of civilian failings and military patriotism. The two generals appeared on the podium addressing newly graduating special forces at the Wadi Sayidna military base near Omdurman. In his speech, al-Burhan intimated that he was keeping his options open for staying on beyond the expiry of his term as chair of the Sovereign Council—a date that had already once been postponed. 'We are the guardians of the unity, security, construction and future of Sudan, despite anyone's objection,'[3] he said. Al-Burhan also complained that the army had been excluded from Hamdok's recent 'Way Forward' initiative and that he would never accept 'a monopoly of certain political forces ruling Sudan'.

Taha Osman Ishag, who represented the SPA on the Removal of Tamkeen Committee, said the general's words 'are more dangerous than the coup itself'. The FFC said they were a 'direct threat to the transition' and the Sudanese Congress Party blamed the military itself for the growing insecurity in the country.[4] If the drama had been staged to test popular sentiment, it showed at least that the revolutionaries were alert to the dangers. In an emergency session of the cabinet, Hamdok blamed the coup on 'remnants of the previous regime', but also pointedly spoke out against the military and, in particular, their penetration of commerce and the institutions of government. He said that the coup attempt 'clearly indicates the need to reform the security and military apparatus'.[5]

The FFC and the resistance committees had immediately seen through the generals' stratagem. They mobilised protests in support of a civilian government. However, the reaction of provincial powerbrokers and foreign governments was something between quiet endorsement and disinterest. Two of the Juba Peace Agreement (JPA) signatories, Minni Minawi and Jibril Ibrahim, split from the FFC to form their own breakaway faction, the 'FFC-National Accord'. The army sponsored a somewhat farcical sit-in outside the Republican Palace in which demonstrators blamed the civilians for the crisis and called for the military to save the nation. The US Special Envoy for the Horn, Jeffrey Feltman, flew to Khartoum to signal American commitment to the Constitutional Declaration. In a meeting with al-Burhan on 24 October, he spelled out the punitive measures that Washington DC would take if the general went ahead with his widely rumoured coup. In parallel, Egyptian president Abd al-Fattah al-Sisi and Israeli intelligence were sending the opposite message.

The deeper issues behind the coup were the paralysis of the democratic transition, due in part to the direct and indirect obstruction of the military men. The transition would succeed only if it could dismantle what the revolutionaries called the 'deep state'. The Removal of Tamkeen Committee was finally pushing this agenda forward, to the dismay not only of the remnants of the former regime but also the generals and paramilitaries who had not only protected but actually expanded their business empires over the previous two years.

The Removal of Tamkeen Committee had compiled extensive documentation exposing the networks of corruption, especially military owned companies. It angered senior military officers by targeting gold-smuggling rings in which they were involved.[6] In September the army removed the soldiers who had been protecting the committee's buildings and 22 other properties they had taken over. It was a clear message that they were leaving the committee exposed. In the days before the coup, members of the committee together with an array of prominent civilian leaders, including Mohamed al-Faki, a civilian member of the Sovereign Council, held a press conference to make public some of their findings. They also spoke about their disputes with the military wing, whom they accused of blocking reform. Ministry of information spokesperson Jaafar Khalid accused al-Burhan and Hemedti of utilising the military as a political vehicle to push through their agendas. In his speech on the morning of the coup, al-Burhan singled out these men's disrespect and disregard for the military as a national institution, claiming that their instigated campaign of hatred against the army and armed forces could have resulted in a national security crisis.

The dismantling of the military–commercial complex was quietly emerging as Hamdok's priority agenda, which he would be in a position to push energetically once the military majority on the Sovereign Council was removed, which was due to happen when a civilian took the post. Exactly when this handover should happen was a matter on which al-Burhan was fastidiously ambiguous. The transitional clock had been reset by the Juba Peace Agreement, giving al-Burhan an extension as *de facto* head of state. The military, and many diplomats, believed that the 18-month term of al-Burhan should be considered to start anew from the October 2020 signature in Juba, giving him an extra 14 months. However, the FFC demanded that the handover should be no later than November 2021. This demand was spearheaded by the cabinet affairs minister, Khalid Omar Yousif. The generals called him a troublemaker. On the morning of 25 October, Khalid was arrested. Security officers came to his house in the early hours and he was ferried into an unknown location wearing his white cotton pyjamas. Reports of his torture and hospitalisation reached the public, with no means of verification.

The technocrats and the civilian parties had not fully grasped the political dynamics of the Juba Peace Agreement. The immediate reason was that they were not sufficiently organised to run peace talks. They did not appreciate the professional skills needed for setting the agenda for negotiating a ceasefire nor the political path that would be set as soon as those talks were set up. A ceasefire is far more than ceasing to fire guns: it sets the parameters for how the security sector is to be organised in the future, which in turn shapes political authority. Negotiating a ceasefire stealthily gives political privileges to those who are at the table. At root, perhaps the civic revolutionaries saw the question of peace in the peripheries as a technical matter rather than a political one, and hence they failed to foresee how the generals would exploit the peace process to more fully embed themselves in power. The hard-bitten armed groups' leaders knew this dynamic from the outset. They lost confidence in the civilians' capacity and may also have sensed that the new civilian government would be around for long enough to matter.

The incorporation of the armed groups into key Sovereign Council, cabinet and gubernatorial positions following the JPA worried the civilian parties. Most of the former rebels were at home in the political marketplace. Minawi could not expect many votes in a competitive election but had sufficient fighters and commercial connections to be a player in a transactional political system. Jibril's Justice and Equality Movement (JEM) was similar with the added element of its Islamist links. While they were rivals to Hemedti, they shared an interest with the RSF leaders in the status quo. They also worried that the Removal of Tamkeen Committee would dismantle their networks and block them from creating new ones—part of a wider phenomenon whereby anti-corruption efforts created only losers among the provincial elites because rural governance had been so completely sown up by soldiers, crony businessmen and tribal chiefs. Minawi used his position as governor of Darfur to close down the local branch of the committee.[7] Jibril was also at odds with the committee in his new post-JPA role as finance minister, claiming that the finance ministry had never received the funds it had sequestered.[8]

The FFC-National Accord of Minawi and Jibril distanced themselves from the civilian members of the coalition. They threw their weight behind a military-backed sit-in outside the Republican Palace and called for the dissolution of the cabinet and a return to an executive of technocrats—a formula that would at one stroke reduce the influence of the civilian parties and set up a politically weak executive that could be more readily controlled by the military majority in the Sovereign Council. Distrust between the rebels from the marginalised regions and the civilian Khartoum politicians increased. The urbanites were unhappy about the presence of the armed groups in the capital. The provincial leaders smelled the habitual disdain of the metropolitans. The organiser of the army-organised sit-in accused Wajdi Salih, a Ba'athist and leading member of the Removal of Tamkeen Committee, of having made racist remarks about the sit-in participants during a speech in Wad Medani.[9] Meanwhile, Hamdok's former advisor, Shafie Khidir, wrote a piece warning of 'the disaster that is expected to happen in Sudan', acknowledging that the Removal of Tamkeen Committee had acted excessively and at times unaccountably, but maintaining that it should be reformed not abandoned.[10]

The unrest in Eastern Sudan highlighted the issue most acutely. A series of conflicts and protests in Kassala and Port Sudan brought to the surface a tension that has been present throughout Sudan's revolutionary history, a tension between revolutionary forms of urban politics that seek to dissolve tribalism, and forms of rural politics that embrace neo-traditionalism and seek fairer representation on a regional or ethnic basis.[11] This tension erupted when the radicals of 1964 attempted to dissolve the Native Administration. In the 1985–86 transition, the re-empowerment of the riverain technocrats caused significant unrest in the East, where Nimeiri had been buying off Beja regionalists by bringing senior Beja from the old Native Administration into the Sudan Socialist Union. When the transitional technocrats targeted corrupt Nimeiri-era politicians, people in Eastern Sudan came to see this through an ethno-regional lens, as a reassertion of centralised 'Arab' power at their expense.[12] In countries like Sudan, anti-corruption efforts are invariably seen as selective political crackdowns, regardless of motive. So, too, in 2020–21, when efforts at dismantling the Islamist–security networks and prosecuting corruption also entailed targeting leaders of the provincial aristocracy. This was not the only reason for the unrest in Eastern Sudan—the orchestrated destabilisation by Eritrea was another factor—but it served as a background to the unrest that preceded the coup. Among the principal brokers in the Eastern Sudan turmoil was, it appeared, the NCP-era Beja Nazir, Muhammad al-

Amin Tirik, who demanded the formation of a new military council and an end to the Removal of Tamkeen Committee.[13] Tirik's Higher Council for the Beja Nazirates was angry that the committee had dismissed from the justice ministry a number of 'sons of the East' who had come into government following the 2006 Eastern Sudan Peace Agreement.[14]

The Islamists also saw an opportunity for leverage in the unrest. The newspapers owned by al-Tayyib Mustafa, *al-Intibaha* and *al-Sayha*, were banned for their efforts in fomenting disruption.[15] And in any such situation, those with the funds and networks to de-escalate the crisis also had an interest in allowing it to rumble on until they could gain the political credit from stepping in to solve it. This element became obvious when, immediately after 25 October, the blockade on Port Sudan was lifted, a deal was struck with the Beja, and food and fuel suddenly reached the market.

The Kleptocrats' Coup

Feltman spent the weekend of 23–4 October in Khartoum. He met with al-Burhan on the Sunday evening before leaving for the airport to fly to Qatar. In that meeting he made it clear to the general what would happen if he went ahead with the rumoured coup: a cut-off in US assistance, an end to debt relief and World Bank programmes and, possibly, financial sanctions. When Feltman landed in Doha in the early hours of Monday and switched on his cellphone he read the headline in disbelief.

Others had apparently assured al-Burhan that they would cover his back. Egypt's President al-Sisi was among them, and shortly afterwards he refused to sign a joint statement with the USA, Britain, Saudi Arabia and the UAE calling for a return to the Constitutional Declaration. The Israeli government said nothing publicly but security delegations visited Khartoum before and after the takeover.

In the days after the coup, al-Burhan did not look secure. His initial press conference, in which he claimed to have taken Hamdok to his house to give him a place to work in peace, brought widespread derision. Al-Burhan's greatest weakness internally was that nobody in Sudan believed his story. It was transparently an attempt to protect the exorbitant privileges that he and the military enjoyed. Previous Sudanese military takeovers had a civilian constituency ready to support their programme: not so al-Burhan. Mass protests began at once.

However, al-Burhan could call upon several constituencies unhappy with the prospect of an institutionalised civic democracy. The military itself is huge and its influence is far-reaching, including the expanding profile of the RSF. As well as the middle and upper ranks of the dissolved National Congress Party, he had the open sympathies of many government bureaucrats who owed their posts and privileges to the former regime and who were threatened by the Removal of Tamkeen Committee. While the Islamists were united in their fear of the anti-Tamkeen process, politically they remained divided. The revolutionary Islamists who challenged Saudi Arabia in Egypt in the 1990s and who reacted furiously to Sudan's normalisation of relations with Israel were unlikely to support al-Burhan. The Islamists who supported al-Bashir's post-1999 Islamism were social conservatives opposed to the left, as well as those seeking a means for social control, and a veil for all manner of corrupt practices. They formed a natural albeit dispersed group in favour of al-Burhan. Moreover, al-Burhan's regional allies had become comfortable with these pallid Islamists before 2019 and remained so, provided that they did not join forces with their radical brethren—and they saw authoritarian leaders who espouse conservative social Islam as a bulwark against such a threat.

The National Umma Party, bereft of its historic leader Sadiq al-Mahdi and divided between pro- and anti-military factions, did not reprise its role from 1964 and 1985 as an enabler of conservative transition. Its acting head, Fadlallah Burma Nasir, would later help to mediate the 21 November deal with Hamdok and announced it to the press,[16] only for his party through its energetic new secretary general, al-Wathiq al-Bireir, to reject it outright.[17]

Al-Burhan's greatest weakness externally was his financial dependence on Western support. Back in 2019, the Transitional Military Council had been bailed out by Saudi Arabia and the UAE, but that had been a short-term measure. The Gulf states knew that the amounts needed to stabilise the Sudanese economy were simply too large, and that debt relief along with aid from the World Bank and IMF would be needed, and for those it was essential to obtain US and European support. The direct snub to Feltman added insult to the already injurious coup, and the US promptly suspended $700 million in aid with the indication that further macroeconomic support was in jeopardy. The World Bank and Germany also paused their assistance. Jibril—still minister of finance—admitted that all Western financial aid had stopped, and continued: 'but I am very optimistic that things will be back to normal'.[18] He was assuming that the Western donors would simply accept that military leadership is normal and would consider the status quo better than a slide into further turmoil. He overlooked that 'normal' had been precisely the problem that the transitional government was trying to solve.

Western demands were modest: a return to the 2019 Constitutional Document and Juba Peace Agreement as the guiding principles, the reinstatement of Hamdok as prime minister and the release of political prisoners. The US and Europe fell short of explicitly calling for al-Burhan to step down as chair of the Sovereign Council, let alone for the removal of the military from politics altogether, which was the demand of the street. Speaking at the US Institute of Peace, Feltman said that the American priority for the Horn of Africa was 'stability'.[19] The overriding concern of the US and others was with Ethiopia, where a combination of war, mass atrocity, famine and state collapse threatened to take the Horn of Africa back a generation. International diplomats were not in the mood for making maximal demands and they wanted a conflict-resolving compromise in short order.

There were several initiatives to resolve the crisis—by leading Sudanese figures, by the United Nations special representative and even by the World Food Programme.[20] The US approach was to lead from behind, bringing the key Arab states into line, rather than by intervening directly. After two weeks, al-Burhan spurned these initiatives and, on 11 November, he crossed the Rubicon: he announced the formation of a new Sovereign Council. Once this was a *fait accompli*, al-Burhan and Hemedti were ready to fall in line with the specific headline demands put forward by the internationals. According to US Assistant Secretary of State for African Affairs Molly Phee: 'Sudanese military leaders went from refusing to discuss Hamdok's status, to saying "they had no objection to his return".'[21]

The New Rural Sudan

Potentially, the backbone of Sudan's military-led government are the provincial elites, estranged from the civic revolutionaries. From the first days of the 2019 revolution, Hemedti had made a bid for the allegiance of the tribal aristocracy, who had become enmeshed within the mercenary patrimonialism of the al-Bashir era. The RSF had tightened its grip on the rural political economy, becoming both enforcer of production from farms and mines, and provider of essential services, including health and subsidised sugar and wheat.[22]

The role of Hemedti and his Rapid Support Forces (RSF) represented something new in Sudanese politics. In the three generations since independence, every transition in power had been decided at the centre, resolved between the metropolitan civilian elite and its counterpart among the officer corps of the national army. Sudan's peripheries at best provided the chorus. In 2019–21, it was different: the Darfurians became powerbrokers, too, though not in the expected way. Sudan's civic revolutionary leaders had long assumed that the people of the peripheries shared their agenda of a modern, institutionalised democracy. Many indeed did—including the Sudan Liberation Movement (SLM) of Abd al-Wahid Nur, with its passionate following in the displaced camps, and the growing number of resistance committees in the towns of the region. But Hemedti represented a twist in that narrative. His ascent was a manifestation of the rise of the ruthless but capable transactional politicians, getting their way through the astute use of coercion and cash. With four stars on the lapel of his uniform, the fresh-faced general was the personification of this political marketplace, no longer so peripheral. Most crucially, he was the tangible representation of that system of rule transplanted to the centre of state power, and, although he adapted his public political style to the demands of the national stage, the brute reality is that real politics in Khartoum were conducted according to the rules that he had mastered. Hemedti's ascendancy was the blowback from Khartoum's calamitous mismanagement of Darfur, the sorcerer's apprentice of decades of brutal counter-insurgency and militarised tribalism. He was Darfur's revenge. This fact was better appreciated by the Darfurians, including his rivals and enemies (including Minawi and Jibril), than by the elites of the Nile. Under al-Bashir, both army and party leaders pretended that Hemedti and his working methods were an aberration, but in truth mercenarised militarism was the norm. Al-Burhan, while representing the face of the traditional military establishment, was playing the same political game as the upstart militia chief.

The New Urban Street

Across every town and city in Sudan, resistance committees and the unions that comprised the SPA were prepared. The pro-democracy movement had a horizontal structure without leaders, to a greater extent even than during 2018–19. They were not content with a civilian-led government that shared power with the military: they wanted the army out of politics altogether. In the words of analyst Kholood Khair: 'The civilians on the streets made their core demand clear: They want a fully civilian government to be set up immediately to take the country out of this crisis.'[23]

Superficially the confrontation resembled the aftermath of the June 2019 massacre, with escalating street protests—named 'million-person' marches—meeting with deadly responses from the police and military. More than 40 protestors died in Khartoum during four huge marches and numerous other confrontations. Strikes across many sectors shut down trade and services, including blockades targeting exports to Egypt. There were, however, critical differences. The protestors did not reach out to the army, asking them to stand with the people. They no longer trusted the military to keep its promises and discounted the prospect that progressive army officers might be the midwives for a democratic transition. What the street democrats now demanded was an immediate revolution. *Madaniyya* now entailed escalating the challenge and, if need be, bearing the human price of radical change, rather than an incremental and an uncertain process of reform.

This demand was dismissed by diplomats as naive. 'It's not realistic to think that you're going to sideline the military entirely from the transitional period,' said Feltman.[24] He explained his more modest goal: 'You have to have a more of a level playing field between the civilians and the military if there's ever going to be the start of a conversation again.' Having seen the chaos that followed the disbanding of the Iraqi army and Ba'ath Party in 2003 and the overreach of revolutionaries and reformers in several Arab Spring countries and in Ethiopia, no foreign power was going to support a political settlement that did not have at minimum the reluctant consent of the generals.

The military strategy was to play for time and use divide-and-rule. It used a well-rehearsed set of tactics to undermine the protests. This began with a complete blackout of both phone networks and internet, intended to weaken the organisational capacity of protestors who relied on the internet to communicate their directives to the public. It also made it hard to document atrocities and organise international lobbying. Occasionally, the security services switched the internet back on so as to monitor and track activists and to watch the few locations that had landline internet access in Khartoum, such as certain office buildings and the Salam Rotana Hotel that were being used to upload pro-democracy online content. Thousands of local activists were arrested and detained.

Despite the violence and the targeted crackdowns, the numbers of demonstrators did not decline, and new resistance committees emerged in towns that had previously been relatively quiet, such as Nyala and al-Fashir. However, the physical and virtual crackdown meant that it was difficult for the movement to develop a structure that could detail its demands and could open negotiations. The protestors also made a tactical error, albeit a very human one. In celebrating Hamdok's refusal to accept al-Burhan's offers, they made the deposed prime minister into a symbol of the resistance, implying that he was the one to negotiate on their behalf.

Destined to Disappoint?

If the coup had been foreshadowed so, too, was its deflating denouement. Sudan's previous coups had all represented a decisive upending of democratic possibility. Al-Burhan's statement that 'this is not a coup' provided just enough of an opening for a face-saving compromise that—as Jibril promised—provided a return to 'normality'. Al-Burhan insisted that his takeover was a 'corrective' in line with the Constitutional Declaration, which was enough of a hook for domestic and international mediators to hang a purported compromise.

On 21 November, a shaky and disoriented-looking Hamdok appeared alongside al-Burhan and Hemedti on national television, behind them a huge blue banner describing the purpose of the meeting: 'ratification of the political deal.' It was a brief event. First, the announcer read the provisions of the agreement that highlighted the commander-in-chief's decision to amend the constitutional charter to end the current political crisis and the deadlock it created, as well as averting threats to the country's stability and national unity. He continued by outlining a number of provisions that were clearly aimed at defusing public anger and claiming legitimacy. These included the formation of a new cabinet of technocrats, the transition to an elected government in a period of no longer than two years, and the setting up of investigative committees to look into the use of excessive violence against protestors. Hamdok followed up with a brief statement that made use of some his old slogans: a recognition of the Sudanese people's resolve, the complexity of the transition, his belief in a breakthrough, and the importance of not shedding any more blood. Al-Burhan thanked all those involved in the reconciliation and praised Hamdok for his willingness to end to the deadlock.

The democracy movement and civilian parties were disconcerted for a moment, assessing the surprise deal—taken aback by its content and by the fact that the FFC had not been involved in the negotiations. Although the acting National Umma Party leader had been a mediator, the party dissociated itself. The street was more forthright, adding Hamdok's name to the list of the disgraced. New chants echoed loudly in Khartoum's early evening air, such as 'In life and in image, Hamdok turned out to be a liability.'[25] Samahir Mubarak, spokesperson of the SPA, dismissed the deal as a capitulation. 'Hamdok chose his side,' she said.[26] Samahir found relief in clarity: it was better to live with the brute reality of the military takeover than with the false pretence of a cooperative with the military. Later in the day she added in an interview with Al Jazeera: 'This partnership for us is done. It has collapsed. It has totally collapsed and there is no way of reforming it.'[27]

Hamdok had been kept in isolation from Sudanese civic activists during his time under house arrest, with security officers constantly present, able only to speak to diplomats and Sudanese mediators. Even those closest to him conceded that he had signed a bad deal. Hamdok himself struggled to regain his composure, demanding that all the hundreds of detained activists must be released, and emphasising those parts of the agreement that gave him room for manoeuvre; but he could not paper over the sad fact that he had accepted a role and a political vision far different to that of August 2019. On 3 January 2022, Hamdok resigned as Sudan's prime minister. His Sudanese model to transition Sudan into a democracy ended with a complete military takeover.

The lessons of the missed opportunities of previous civic revolutions were no mystery. In 1999, in the darkest days of war and repression, A. H. Abdel Salam, then chair of the Sudan Human Rights Organization, spoke at the opening of a civil society conference:

> Sometime in the coming months and years, Sudan will face a transition to peace and democracy. This will be a huge opportunity to create a new Sudan in which it will be possible for all Sudanese citizens to have their basic human rights respected, and for political opponents to settle their differences by dialogue and electoral competition, rather than through violence. But there are no guarantees on the successful outcome of this process. Three times before, Sudan has had transitional governments, holding out high promises of democracy, peace and development … Each time, the high hopes have been dashed.[28]

Abdel Salam insisted first that democracy activists should never give up hope, and second, that they must not only struggle for freedom but must carefully prepare the agenda for what to do when they achieved that immediate goal. His first enjoinder was heeded, his second was not.

For many Sudanese, there was a moment in which the sense of limitless revolutionary potential seemed within grasp. This was the extraordinary spirit of the sit-in around the army headquarters during April and May 2019. For the passionate activists who put their bodies on the line to challenge al-Bashir and his securocrats, the promise of the sit-in was that Sudan would be transformed in their image. The protests were a display for how a new country should be governed—a new, perfect social contact.

This was a moment of Utopian revolution in Sudan, an inspiring promise that a different world was possible. For a few weeks, in one place, the fog of politics cleared enough for a remarkable congregation of Sudanese to create a space for a festival of a popular republic. It was euphoric: a generation's worth of ideals and aspirations released in an explosion of pride, protest and patriotism. It was a moment and a place where everything that divided Sudanese citizens was set aside, when citizenship and participation took on a heightened sense. Sudanese and non-Sudanese who joined the sit-in revelled in how the ordinary became extraordinary: the mazes of tea shops offering minty brew to resting revolutionaries; the chants and songs; the street art; the freedom of speech and association; and the sense of community. The sit-in coalesced around an egalitarian system of solidarity that stood in stark contradiction to the hierarchies and deal-making that still dominated the world outside its barricades. Anyone with human feelings was inspired. There was a democratic Sudan and it lasted 53 days—between the challenge to a dictator and a massacre.

One of the most remarkable features of the sit-in was the extent to which it was capable of uniting, in the moment, ideological and socially disparate factions. Historically, professional and student groups made the University of Khartoum the 'shrine' to their 'civil religion'.[29] The cotton landlords of the Umma Party followed Sadiq al-Mahdi's call for 'civil jihad'.[30] Protestors in urban Sudan called for *madaniyya*: civic values. Even some of the Islamists who recognised the failure of their hubristic 'civilizational project' (*al-mashru' al-hadhari*) of the 1990s tried to rescue the ideal of common citizenship that lay somewhere in the ruins of that project and reinvented themselves as protestors.

For many activists, the revolution was an opening to resolve the dilemma of Sudan's 'multiple marginality'[31] by firmly asserting the 'African' character of their movement. This was no shadow of the 'Arab spring'—Sudan was, despite its lost South, still an African nation and Sudan's nationalism still bore the African genealogy now almost a century old. Since Sudan's putative Arab or African dichotomy has often been mapped onto configurations of power and class, many among the protestors celebrated an African character in the uprising. Led and enacted by activists from the very geographical centre of the country, fully members of the community of the state, the revolutionaries nonetheless expressed their determination to wipe away all those hierarchies of race and class that had disfigured their country.

There is a direct line between this idealistic *communitas* of the sit-in and the essentially apolitical vision of a Sudan governed by an impartial, honest meritocracy. Those who led both had faith in the state as a social contract forged anew, moulded into modern institutions of administration and development. They saw raw, transactional politics as a fault to be swept away rather than a reality to be reformed. This was a recurrent failing in a new guise. Past revolutions were undone in part by Sudan's deeply embedded status hierarchy, with its panoply of geographical, social and racial divides. At independence in 1956, and again in 1964 and 1985, the metropolitan civilian elite, irrespective of political leaning, lacked the concern, courage or imagination to treat the leaders of the peripheries as their equals. Those failures were coloured by racism, outright or implicit. In 2019, the revolutionary sentiment was far more egalitarian, but a parallel condescension emerged along the status gradient of development versus under-development, or institutionalised governance versus the political market.

Focused on what Sudan's politics *should be*, the revolutionaries often neglected how those politics *actually* operated. The civilian parties were rivalrous when outside government and were equally divided and ineffective after joining it alongside the signatories to the Juba Peace Agreement. For two years the party leaders failed to agree on the formation of the Transitional National Legislative Assembly. The FFC could not broker agreement on this crucial issue. They bargained incessantly over the allocation of posts as much as their different ideologies and policies. The Ba'athists, the Communists and SPA focused on their long-standing concerns of wage increases and keeping subsidies in place, while the armed groups' leaders wanted a thorough-going restructuring of the wealth of the country. All the radical disagreements over the identity of Sudan and the causes of its chronic ailments surfaced again and again. While they talked, the generals accumulated power.

In July 2019, discussing whether to take the position of prime minister, Hamdok had said that he did not want to be reduced to the role of a cashier in a convenience store, selling groceries while drug dealers carried out the real business in the back room. He knew that his best chance of avoiding that fate was swift international action to lift sanctions and provide debt relief and concessionary aid. These actions, taken fast, would not only stabilise the economy but give the technocrats a chance to level the economic playing field for legitimate businesses to drive an economic turnaround, wrenching the economy out of the grasp of the kleptocrats.

Technocrats in government always have a weak hand to play. In Sudan, as elsewhere, the reason why they accepted to join the cabinet was a touching belief that their time in office could be a holiday from the real politics of week-to-week deal-making, during which they could apply their expertise in an apolitical manner. They had their theories of economic reform, justice and state-building, but they lacked practical theory of the practice of politics. Sudan's technocrat–democrats were let down by the leisurely pace with which Sudan's international donors, led by the US, removed sanctions and provided debt relief and other forms of assistance, as well as being hit hard by the economic repercussions of the Covid-19 pandemic. Their wager that economic stability would gain them political credit did not pay out. It took a year and a half for Washington DC to remove sanctions and provide financial support.[32] When the money finally was pledged in October 2020 it was not because the Trump administration cared about democracy in Sudan, but was the by-product of a deal to bolster the president's re-election campaign through extending the Abraham Accords whereby Arab states recognised Israel.[33] And, when money from the Western donors was finally delivered, it came in the form of programmatic aid that was slow, often ineffective, and did not win political credit for its architects. Hamdok needed cash to compete in Sudan's political marketplace. Instead he got an army of consultants and UN officials who sat in air-conditioned rooms in Khartoum.

The delay did not merely postpone the moment at which the new policies could begin to work: it provided a crucial period during which al-Burhan, Hemedti and their circles lost no time in consolidating their position as inheritors of the Islamist–security state, taking over the instruments of real power and patronage. The official holiday from real politics ended with the cabinet reshuffle of February 2021. No technical magic had solved Sudan's political–economic problems. The civilian politicians now had to carry the can and, in due course, they became the public face of economic austerity and political compromise. Behind the scenes, the military majority on the Sovereign Council blocked reform measures simply by failing to act on the decisions passed to them by the cabinet. Shortly before the coup, Hamdok averred privately that the laws of the political marketplace still dictated the fate of Sudan's revolution.[34]

Under al-Bashir, the transactional system of governance penetrated every element of political life. Even a stronger and more capable civilian government could not abolish this by dictat. Neither institutionalised democracy nor economic development can sweep away a political market overnight. The soldiers, who continue to wield far more power than they should, possess the keenest sense of how this shadowy system works. They are resolute counter-revolutionaries, but they are surely aware that even with far greater resources and skills than they possess, they could not run a centralised autocratic system without sending Sudan into new spirals of deadly conflict.

There is a long-standing joke about Sudanese politics: that it changes every week but if you come back after ten years it is exactly the same. This captures the turbulence that is a feature of Sudan's political life, that normality is instability, and that there is no permanent political settlement, rather a constantly renegotiated political unsettlement. At its best, Sudanese politics is a vibrant, civil and unfinished conversation over national identity and the different forms that government and society should take. At its worst, it is intolerant, greedy and cruel. But it is constantly in motion, a perpetually unstable state.[35]

During the 2018–19 revolution a new generation came of age politically, idealistic and unbowed by repression and repeated disappointment, determined to reinvent their nation. Sudan's democratic activists have tasted freedom and change and they will not give up. They are learning democracy in the practice of the non-violent struggle. Let us give the last word to Samahir Mubarak, with whom we opened this book, wondering whether the call for protest would be answered. After nearly three years of alternating triumph and despair, angry at al-Burhan's October coup and disillusioned by Hamdok's compromise, and vowing to continue to protest, she said: 'I strongly believe in Sudan and the Sudanese people. This is definitely not the last chapter.'[36]

NOTES

CHAPTER 1. FREEDOM AND CHANGE

1. El-Gizouli, 2020.
2. Andrew Yaw Tchie and Jihad Salih Mashamoun, 'Sudan's deep state still poses a threat to the democratic process', The Conversation, August 2020, available at: https://theconversation.com/sudans-deep-state-still-poses-a-threat-to-the-democratic-process-130243
3. De Waal, 2015.
4. De Waal and Abdel Salam, 2004.
5. Berridge, 2017.
6. Berridge, 2015.
7. Africa Watch, 1990.
8. Gallab, 2008.
9. Lesch, 1998: 154–5.
10. Young, 2012: 327–31.
11. Interview with SPA official SPA 1, Khartoum, August 2019. Interview with SPA official SPA 2, Khartoum, October 2020. Interview with SPA official SPA 3, Khartoum, October 2020. Most interviews of current and former government officials, protest leaders and diplomats have been anonymised to protect sources.
12. Interview with government figure 1, Khartoum, May 2019. Ibid., SPA official SPA 1.
13. Luke Patey, 'Oil, gold, and guns: The violent politics of Sudan's resource booms', World Peace Foundation, 2021.
14. 'Sudan escalates mass arrests of activists after protest lockdown', Amnesty International, 2 October 2013, available at: https://www.amnesty.org/en/latest/press-release/2013/10/sudan-escalates-mass-arrests-activists-amid-protest-crackdown/

15. Interview with SPA official SPA 4, location withheld, April 2019.
16. World Bank, 2007; Sidahmed, 2014.
17. International Labour Organization, 'Statistics on the informal economy', ILOSTAT, available at: https://ilostat.ilo.org/topics/informality/
18. Tajammu al-Mihniyyin al-Sudaniyyin, 'Dirasa hawla wada'a al-ujur fi al-Sudan' (November 2018). See Musa'ab al-Sharif, 'Mihniyyin al-Sudaniyyin: al-ma'aishiyya al-shahriyya li-5 afarid taklaf akthar min 15 ilf', *al-Hadag*, 11 November 2018, available at: https://www.sudaress.com/alhadag/140460
19. Sikainga, 2002.
20. Interview with SPA official SPA 4, interview with SPA official SPA 5, Khartoum, June 2019.
21. Noah Salomon, 'New histories for an uncharted future in Sudan', Africa is a Country, 17 May 2019, available at: https://africasacountry.com/2019/05/new-histories-for-an-uncharted-future-in-sudan; Elia El Khazen, 'Uprising in Sudan: Interview with Sudanese comrades', Historical Materialism Blog, 27 May 2019, available at: https://www.historicalmaterialism.org/blog/uprising-sudan-interview-with-sudanese-comrades
22. Gallab, 2014.
23. Elnur, 2009: 100–1, 109.
24. Ibid.: 109.
25. Mahmoud, 1984; Elnur, 2009: 57–8.
26. Duffield, 1981.
27. For a comparison of the 'Closed District Ordinances' with South Africa's Bantustan system, see Mamdani, 2020: 215–18.
28. On the ecological impacts, see Elnur, 2009: 57.
29. Calkins and Ille, 2014.
30. Ille, 2016: 198–200.
31. Amar Jamal, 'Nonviolent guerilla cartographers', Africa is a Country, 18 November 2020, available at: https://africasacountry.com/2020/11/nonviolent-guerrilla-cartographers
32. 'Declaration of Freedom and Change', 1 January 2019, available at: http://www.sudaneseprofessionals.org/en/declaration-of-freedom-and-change/
33. Gresh, 2010.
34. Magdi El-Gizouli, 'Sudan's days of rage', *Sudan Tribune*, 24 December 2018, available at: https://sudantribune.com/article64958/
35. Hale, 1986: 25; Fadlallah, 2018.
36. Transitional justice refers to the range of tools to call members of the former regime to account for their past violations through

both judicial and non-judicial means, including trials, truth-telling, reparations and institutional reforms.

37. Vezzadini, 2015.
38. Idris, 2005; Vezzadini, 2015.
39. Deng, 1989.
40. Daly, 1991.
41. Young, 2017.
42. Ibrahim, 2004.
43. Sharkey, 2003; Beshir, 1969.
44. Young, 2017.
45. Berridge, 2015; Mahjub, 2015.
46. 'Marches mark 55th anniversary of the October Revolution across Sudan', Dabanga, 21 October 2019, available at: https://www.dabangasudan.org/en/all-news/article/marches-mark-55th-anniversary-of-october-revolution-across-sudan
47. Mubarak, Samahir, interview with the author, Khartoum, May 2019.
48. 'Protestor's funeral becomes new flashpoint in Sudan unrest', VOA News, 18 January 2019, available at: https://www.voanews.com/africa/protesters-funeral-becomes-new-flashpoint-sudan-unrest
49. Bain did not respond to an interview request in 2019.
50. Justin Lynch and Robbie Gramer, 'How two US Presidents reshaped America's policy towards Sudan', *Foreign Policy*, 8 April 2019, available at: https://foreignpolicy.com/2019/04/08/how-two-us-presidents-reshaped-americas-policy-towards-sudan-bashir-protests-calling-for-removal-diplomacy-east-africa-us-intelligence-cooperation/
51. Ibid. Interview with former senior US intelligence official 1, Washington DC, January 2019.

CHAPTER 2. REAPING THE WHIRLWIND

1. This draws on Alex de Waal's discussions with officials in the Republican Palace, during the period 2009–12, when he was an advisor to the African Union High-Level Implementation Panel for Sudan.
2. Khalid Abdelaziz, Michael Georgy and Maha El Dahan, 'Abandoned by the UAE, Sudan's Bashir was destined to fall', *Reuters*, Special Report, 3 July 2019, available at: https://www.reuters.com/investigates/special-report/sudan-bashir-fall
3. Abdel Hai himself has neither confirmed nor denied the story, on one occasion claiming that his words were intended as rhetoric only.

4. 'Al-Jazeera net tunshir asrar inqilab al-Sudan…madha dar bayna generalayn fi ijtima'a bi-sayyara askariyya?', Al Jazeera, 26 June 2019, available at: https://tinyurl.com/6khtum8
5. 'Al-Jazeera net tunshir al-asrar'.
6. De Waal, 2015, 2019.
7. Brown, 1990.
8. De Waal, 1993; Salih and Harir, 1994.
9. El-Battahani, 2013: 38.
10. De Waal and Abdel Salam, 2004.
11. De Waal, 2015.
12. Sidahmed, 2013.
13. Patey, 2014.
14. Berridge, 2017.
15. De Waal, 2015.
16. Interview, Sudan business official 1, Khartoum, May 2019.
17. World Bank, 2007.
18. Adapted from de Waal, 2015.
19. James, 2015.
20. UNSCR 2046 (2012), available at: https://digitallibrary.un.org/record/726444?ln=en#record-files-collapse-header
21. Tubiana, 2014.
22. Asmar Marwan, 'Sudan's gold boom', *Gulf News*, 28 November 2015, available at: https://gulfnews.com/uae/environment/sudans-gold-boom-1.1626644
23. 'Darfur gold concession winner warned-off by Hilal', Dabanga, 17 April 2014, available at: https://www.dabangasudan.org/en/all-news/article/darfur-gold-concession-winner-warned-off-by-hilal
24. UN Security Council, 2016.
25. McGregor, 2017.
26. African Centre for Justice and Peace Studies, 2018; Tubiana et al., 2018.
27. 'Second phase of disarmament campaign to begin next week across Sudan', Dabanga, 11 November 2018, available at: https://www.dabangasudan.org/en/all-news/article/second-phase-of-disarmament-campaign-to-begin-next-week-across-sudan
28. Mohamed Amin, 'Blood and gold: Now Sudan's land wars have spread to mining', Middle East Eye, 21 April 2018, available at: https://www.middleeasteye.net/news/blood-and-gold-now-sudans-land-wars-have-spread-mining
29. Elbadawi and Suliman, 2018.
30. Ibid.: 4.

31. Ibid.: 5.
32. Magdi El-Gizouli, Arab Reform Initiative, 12 April 2019, 'The fall of Al-Bashir: Mapping contestation forces in Sudan', available at: https://www.arab-reform.net/publication/the-fall-of-al-bashir-mapping-contestation-forces-in-sudan/; El-Gizouli, 2019a; Chaillou-Gillette, 2019.
33. Mohamed Vall, 'How bread has emerged as the main symbol of Sudan unrest', Al Jazeera, 27 January 2019, available at: https://www.aljazeera.com/news/2019/01/sudan-revolution-hungry-persists-crackdown-190127124859617.html
34. Chevrillon-Guibert, 2019.
35. McSparren et al., 2015: 120.
36. Peter Schwartzstein, 'One of Africa's most fertile lands is struggling to feed its own people', Bloomberg Businessweek, 2 April 2019, available at: https://www.bloomberg.com/features/2019-sudan-nile-land-farming/?srnd=businessweek-v2
37. 'PAX Sudan alert: Actor map', PAX, 20 June 2019, available at: https://www.paxforpeace.nl/publications
38. World Bank data, GDP per capita (currency US$)—Sudan, available at: https://data.worldbank.org/indicator/NY.GDP.PCAP.CD?locations=SD
39. Porch, 2013.
40. Salmon, 2007: 12.
41. Salih and Harir, 1994: 198.
42. Flint and De Waal, 2008.
43. Haggar, 2007.
44. Flint, 2008; 2010.
45. UNAMID Force Commander General Martin Agwai, quoted in de Waal, 2009.
46. De Waal et al., 2014: 373.
47. Fadul and Tanner, 2007.
48. Andrew Carter and Nima Albagir, 'Meet the Janjaweed', Channel 4 News, 2008, available at: https://www.dailymotion.com/video/xtxd8n; see also Flint, 2008.
49. Holt, 1958.
50. Khalid, 1985.
51. Tubiana et al., 2018.
52. Ibn Khaldun, 1967.
53. Magdi El-Gizouli, 'Himedti and his president: War as a livelihood', *Still Sudan*, 8 May 2015, available at: https://stillsudan.blogspot.com/2015/05/himeidti-and-his-president-war-as.html

54. McCutcheon, 2014.
55. 'Ahali Janub Kordofan yarfuduun bi-shidda da'wa al-Bashir li'l-difa'a al-Sha'abi wa'l-Jihad', Dabanga, 8 March 2012, available at: https://tinyurl.com/e93hpeer
56.. Magdi El-Gizouli, 'Another coup in Sudan: The politics of temptation', *Sudan Tribune*, 27 November 2012, available at: https://sudantribune.com/spip.php?article44665

    'Al-Muhawala al-inqilabiyya...kashafat hujm khilafat al-Islamiyyun', *al-Intibaha*, 23 November 2012, available at: https://www.sudaress.com/alintibaha/25976
57. One of its members was the United Front for Change, in French, *Front uni pour le changement*, giving rise to the acronym FUC, which was indicative of the haste with which it was put together, no member having considered its connotations to Anglophones.
58. Abd al-Salam, 2010: 31–2; Gallab, 2014; Berridge, 2017.
59. 'Salah Gosh', Profile, on *Sudan Tribune*.
60. Ken Silverstein, 'Official pariah Sudan valuable to America's War on Terrorism', *Los Angeles Times*, 29 April 2015, available at: https://www.latimes.com/archives/la-xpm-2005-apr-29-fg-sudan29-story.html
61. De Waal, 2013a.
62. Justin Lynch, 'Why is Sudan's genocidal regime a CIA favorite?', *Daily Beast*, 9 January 2019, available at: https://www.thedailybeast.com/why-is-sudans-genocidal-regime-a-cia-favorite
63. Magdi El-Gizouli, 'Another coup in Sudan: The politics of temptation', *Sudan Tribune*, 27 November 2012, available at: https://sudantribune.com/spip.php?article44665
64. 'Tajammu al-Mihniyyin yarfud mubadara "al-Islah wa'l-Salam", allati ra'asaha al-Jizouli Dafa'allah, wa yatamassak bi-isqat Nizam bidun shuruut', *Kush News*, 11 February 2019, available at: https://kushnews.net/2019/02/134942
65. Ibrahim Abu Jamal, 'Qiyadi ittihadi yakshaf li-Kush News...siinario tansiib "Gosh" fi qiyada al-hizb', *Kush News*, 3 October 2019, available at: https://kushnews.net/2019/10/195761
66. Mark Perry, 'Saudi Arabia's blood pact with a genocidal strongman', *The American Conservative*, 5 December 2018, available at: https://www.theamericanconservative.com/articles/saudi-arabias-blood-pact-with-a-genocidal-strongman-houthis-bashir-sudan-yemen-uae/
67. 'Sudan airlifts hundreds of Darfuri recruits to UAE bound for the Yemen war', Radio Dabanga, 18 April 2018, available at: https://www.dabangasudan.org/en/all-news/article/sudan-airlifts-hundreds-of-darfuri-recruits-to-uae-bound-for-the-yemen-war

68. Bel Trew, '"It's our biggest employer": How a lucrative war in Yemen fuels conflict in Darfur 2,000km away', *The Independent*, 22 December 2019, available at: https://www.independent.co.uk/news/world/africa/darfur-yemen-civil-war-sudan-soldiers-conflict-employment-a9256046.html

CHAPTER 3. COUNTER-REVOLUTION AND COMPROMISE

1. Bell and Pospisil, 2017.
2. Turner, 1969.
3. Agamben, 1995.
4. This theme will be revisited in Chapter 5.
5. Berridge, 2015: 108.
6. Interview with Sudan activist 1, August 2019, Khartoum.
7. Y. Arman, 'Ma'aloumat jadida…'an thawra wa al-thawra al-mudada wa majlis al-askari', Dabanga, 19 April 2019, available at: https://tinyurl.com/2huztx2v
8. Sudan business official 1.
9. Abdullah Alaqam, 'Kharij iqaa al-'asr', *Sudan Post*, 9 July 2020, available at: https://tinyurl.com/dec8rjuv
10. 'Wifa ahad abraz mu'aridi nizam al-Bashir…Ali Mahmoud Hassanein', al-Khaleej Online, 24 May 2019, available at: https://tinyurl.com/k6wvpzpc; Abd al-Basit Idris, 'Inqilab al-Inqadh…jadal al-muhakama wa'l tawqif', *al-Rakoba*, 26 November 2019, available at: https://tinyurl.com/3ndnzu7z
11. 'Allaqat Ittihadi wa Gosh…ila ayna taqud al-safina?', *al-Sayha*, 26 September 2019, available at: https://www.assayha.net/17126/; 'al-Hizb al-Ittihadi al-Dimuqrati al-asl yanfi tadakkhal Gosh li'l-islah fi ajhizathu', *al-Nilin*, 19 September 2020, available at: https://www.alnilin.com/13144682.htm; 'al-Qutb al-Ittihadi Taj al-Sir Muhammad Salih: Shaksiyyan ubarik wa urahhib bi-indimam Salah Gosh li'l-Hizb al-Ittihadi al-Dimuqrati', *al-Nilin*, 29 September 2019. available at: http://www.alnilin.com/13082185.htm
12. See Chapter 5 and Berridge, 2015: 108, 178.
13. Interview with a civilian negotiator, July/August 2019, Khartoum.
14. 'Sudan's livestream massacre', BBC Africa Eye documentary, 12 July 2019, available at: https://www.youtube.com/watch?v=dR56qxM4kHA
15. Jason Patinkin, 'US Sudan envoy criticized for dining with Darfuri warlord', VOA News, 19 May 2019, available at: https://www.

voanews.com/africa/us-sudan-envoy-criticized-dining-darfuri-warlord

16. Interviews with participants who prefer to remain anonymous.
17. Human Rights Watch, 2019.
18. 'Mass grave found in search for Sudanese "missing" after December 2018 Revolution', Dabanga, 12 November 2020, available at: https://www.dabangasudan.org/en/all-news/article/mass-grave-found-in-search-for-sudanese-missing-after-december-2018-revolution
19. Chenoworth and Stephan, 2011.
20. Donham, 2006.
21. A first-hand account of the massacre by a protagonist at the scene on the day, who managed to escape despite being chased and held hostage in one of the adjacent hospitals for more than a day, can be read here: Amar Jamal, 'Thousands of mockingbirds', Africa is a Country, 2 December 2021, available at: https://africasacountry.com/2021/02/thousands-of-mockingbirds
22. Parker, Najja, 'Rihanna brings awareness to ongoing Sudan massacre', *The Atlanta Journal-Constitution,* 13 June 2019. Also 'Rihanna brings awareness to ongoing Sudan massacre', *Boston 25 News*, 13 June 2019, https://www.boston25news.com/news/trending-now/rihanna-brings-awareness-to-ongoing-sudan-massacre/957842343/
23. Nouwen et al., 2020.
24. Available at: https://twitter.com/IrfanUKAmb/status/1148161782260948997
25. Yousif, Mohamed, interview with author, summer 2019, Khartoum.
26. 'Hizb al-Sadiq al-Mahdi yarfud al-da'wa li'l-idrab al-aam', Al Jazeera.net, 26 May 2019, available at: https://tinyurl.com/yrpxfa4z
27. Justin Lynch, 'Women fueled Sudan's revolution, but then they were pushed aside', *The Independent*, 4 August 2019, available at: https://www.independent.co.uk/news/world/africa/sudan-revolution-women-uprising-democratic-transition-army-bashir-a9038786.html
28. Ibid.
29. Alnagar, 2010.
30. 'Statement by Ms Hala Al-Karib to the UN Security Council, 14 September 2021', *Sudan Tribune*, 15 September 2021, available at: https://sudantribune.com/spip.php?article70073
31. Amjad Farid, interview with author, August 2019, Khartoum.
32. SPA official, SPA 4, interview with author, Spring 2019, location withheld.
33. Abd al-Jalil, Sara, interview with author, August 2019, telephone.

34. Ben Naimark-Rowse, 'Liberating "Insidious Enemy" in our nation', *The Atlanta Journal Constitution*, 4 August 2018, available at: https://www.ajc.com/news/opinion/opinion-liberating-insidious-enemy-our-nation/mTJgib0sadcIJgiTmxlktO/

CHAPTER 4. POLITICAL BUSINESS AS USUAL

1. Berridge, 2015: 161.
2. Ibid.: 179–81.
3. Xuxin, 'Sudan gov't announces 10 priorities for transitional period', Xinhua, 10 September 2019, available at: http://www.xinhuanet.com/english/2019-09/10/c_138381809.htm
4. Abdalla Hamdok, interview with author, December 2020, Khartoum.
5. Adil al-Baz, 'Tahaluf al-thawra mudada ma' quwwat al-hubut al-na'im!', *al-Youm al-Tali*, 8 September 2019, available at: https://tinyurl.com/y4fvlwp4. For Amjad Farid's departure from the party, see 'Majmoua min abraz al-attiba al-shiyu'iyyin tastaqil min al-hizb', *al-Hurriyat*, 16 October 2016, available at https://www.sudaress.com/hurriyat/211090, and for Shafie Khidir's dismissal from the party see *al-Rakoba* 12 July 2016, available at https://www.sudaress.com/alrakoba/240275
6. Abdalla Hamdok, interview with author, December 2020, Khartoum.
7. Interview with Abdalla Hamdok, Khartoum, 25 August 2019.
8. 'Sudan rebel leader deported as military steps up street patrols', *The Guardian*, 11 June 2019, available at: https://www.theguardian.com/world/2019/jun/11/sudan-rebel-leader-deported-as-military-steps-up-street-patrols
9. Senior Sudanese government official, interview with author, October 2020, Khartoum.
10. '70+ dead or injured in bloody West Darfur tribal violence', Dabanga, 31 December 2019, available at: https://www.dabangasudan.org/en/all-news/article/70-dead-or-injured-in-bloody-west-darfur-tribal-violence
11. Ibid.
12. 'West Darfur attacks: Death toll rises to 80+, more than 8,000 families displaced', Dabanga, 3 January 2020, available at: https://www.dabangasudan.org/en/all-news/article/west-darfur-attacks-death-toll-rises-to-80-more-than-8-000-families-displaced
13. International Crisis Group, 2021a: 6–7.
14. Various interviews with diplomats, summer 2019 and January 2020, Khartoum and Washington DC.

15. Abdalla Hamdok, interview with author, December 2020, Khartoum.
16. Interview with Abdalla Hamdok, Khartoum, 16 December 2020.
17. United Nations, 'UN mission responding to evolving needs in Sudan transition process', 14 September 2021, available at: https://news.un.org/en/story/2021/09/1099842
18. Internal Displacement Monitoring Centre, annual conflict and disaster displacement figures 2021, available at: https://www.internal-displacement.org/countries/sudan
19. Gallopin et al., 2021.
20. Interview with Abdalla Hamdok, Khartoum, 25 August 2019.
21. Thomas and El-Gizouli, 2020.
22. Gallopin et al., 2021.
23. International Crisis Group, 2020.
24. World Bank, 2019.
25. International Monetary Fund, 2020.
26. World Bank, 2019.
27. Interview with Abdalla Hamdok, Khartoum, December 2020. The GoS can implement a reform package that will gradually increase the tariff and strengthen the social security net for those affected.
28. Yousif, Mohammad, interview with author, December 2019, Khartoum.
29. Interview with Abdalla Hamdok, Khartoum, 16 December 2020.
30. Interview with Abdalla Hamdok, Khartoum, 25 August 2019.
31. Mohamed Amin, 'Sudanese Government bows to pressure and backtracks on plan to lift subsidies', Middle East Eye, 30 December 2019, available at: https://www.middleeasteye.net/news/sudanese-government-bows-pressure-and-backtracks-plan-lift-subsidies
32. Interview with Abdalla Hamdok, Khartoum, 16 December 2020.
33. Telephone interview with an advisor to Hamdok, October 2020.
34. Various US government officials, interviews with co-author, autumn 2019, 2020, 2021, telephone and Washington DC.
35. Justin Lynch and Robbie Gramer, 'Sudan's new prime minister grapples with his country's past', *Foreign Policy Magazine*, January 2019.
36. Richard Downie, 'Sudan needs much more than upgraded US ties to rebuild itself after Bashir', *World Politics Review*, December 2019.
37. Mohamed Amin, 'U.S. to loan World Bank $1 Billion to clear Sudan debt', Bloomberg, 15 December 2020, available at: https://www.bloomberg.com/news/articles/2020-12-15/u-s-to-help-sudan-clear-world-bank-arrears-with-1-billion-loan

38. Jean-Baptiste Gallopin, 'Bad company: How dark money threatens Sudan's transition', European Council on Foreign Relations, 9 June 2020, available at: https://ecfr.eu/wp-content/uploads/bad_company_how_dark_money_threatens_sudans_transition.pdf
39. 'Sudan confiscates $4 bln of assets from ex-president Bashir', Al Arabiya News, 23 May 2020, available at: https://english.alarabiya.net/en/News/middle-east/2020/05/23/Sudan-confiscates-4-bln-of-assets-from-ex-president-Bashir; Zdravko Ljubas, 'Sudan's anti-graft body to seize property of the Bashir family', Organized Crime and Corruption Reporting Project, 8 May 2020, available at: https://www.occrp.org/en/daily/12304-sudan-s-anti-graft-body-to-seize-property-of-the-bashir-family
40. Mohamed Alamin, 'Warlord-linked Sudanese firm hands over gold mines to government', Bloomberg, 5 May 2020, available at: https://www.bloomberg.com/news/articles/2020-05-05/warlord-linked-sudanese-firm-hands-over-gold-mines-to-government
41. '"Unacceptable": Sudanese PM criticises army's business interests', Al Jazeera, 15 December 2020, available at: https://www.aljazeera.com/news/2020/12/15/unacceptable-sudanese-pm-criticises-armys-business-interests
42. 'Ifraj an 'Muammar Musa bi'l-damana aadiya', *al-Sudani*, 10 July 2021, available at: https://www.sudaress.com/alsudani/1130352
43. 'Al-Asam yutalib bi-itlaq sarah mu'ammar musa', *Kush News*, 15 September 2020, available at: https://www.sudaress.com/kushnews/256452
44. On the *tamkeen* process, see, for example, 'Sudan's Islamist regime: The rise and fall of the Civilization Project', Sudan Democracy First Group, 10 July 2014, available at: https://democracyfirstgroup.org/2014/07/10/sudans-islamist-regime-the-rise-and-fall-of-the-civilization-project/
45. Al-Majidi was detained simultaneously for criticising the RSF and Empowerment Elimination Committee. See 'A Sudanese female human rights defender faces "Defamation" charges for criticising the Rapid Support Forces on Facebook', African Centre for Peace and Justice Studies, 21 September 2021, available at: http://www.acjps.org/a-sudanese-female-human-rights-defender-faces-defamation-charges-for-criticising-the-rapid-support-forces-on-facebook//
46. The document appears to be a memorandum from the attorney general's office dated 7 September 2021, and is in wide circulation online.
47. 'Sudan: shabakat murtabita bi-jamaat irhabiyya tuharid 'ala al-Unf', AA News, 8 July 2021, available at: https://tinyurl.com/jdsfv4ju.

48. 'Outcry as Sudan blocks El-Sudani newspaper and 30 other websites', Radio Dabanga, 6 July 2021, available at: https://www.dabangasudan.org/en/all-news/article/outcry-as-sudan-blocks-el-sudani-newspaper-and-30-other-websites
49. Interview between Robbie Gramer and Abdalla Hamdok, 5 December 2019, Washington DC.
50. Interview with Abdallah Hamdok, Khartoum, December 2020.
51. Hamdok, Abdallah, interview transcript with Robbie Gramer for *Foreign Policy* shared with authors, December 2019, Washington DC.
52. The political skill of strategic delay. See page 90.
53. Mat Nashed, 'How a human rights report could upend Sudan', *New Lines Magazine*, 4 May 2021, available at: https://newlinesmag.com/reportage/how-a-human-rights-report-could-upend-sudan/
54. Interview with Abdallah Hamdok, Khartoum, December 2020.
55. Abdalla Hamdok tweet, 9 March 2020, available at: https://twitter.com/SudanPMHamdok/status/1236957491482832898?ref_src=twsrc%5Etfw%7Ctwcamp%5Etweetembed%7Ctwterm%5E1236957491482832898%7Ctwgr%5E%7Ctwcon%5Es1_&ref_url=https%3A%2F%2Fwww.bbc.com%2Fnews%2Fworld-africa-51800278
56. 'Sudanese Professionals Association withdraws from FFC Alliance', Darfur 24, 25 July 2020, available at: https://www.darfur24.com/en/2020/07/25/sudanese-professionals-association-withdraws-from-ffc-alliance/
57. 'Istiqala jama'iyya li-attiba al-shiyu'i al-Sudani', ahewar, 18 October 2016, available at: https://www.ahewar.org/debat/show.art.asp?aid=535038
58. Ibrahim, 1996.
59. Musa'ab Muhammad Ali, 'Khilafat dakhil tajumma al-Mihniyyin al-Sudaniyyin…fasl al-'ada wa ittihamat mutabadila', *al-Quds al-Arabi*, 28 October 2019, available at: https://tinyurl.com/y2ep2vm4
60. El-Gizouli, 2020.
61. Ashraf Alhassan, 'Guardians of the barricades: Fading dream and confusion of resistance in Sudan', African Arguments 15 July 2021, available at: https://africanarguments.org/2021/07/guardians-of-the-barricades-fading-dream-and-confusion-of-resistance-in-sudan/
62. Mohamed Amin, 'Protests erupt in Sudan as calls mount to "correct" the revolution', Middle East Eye, 30 June 2020, available at: https://www.middleeasteye.net/news/protests-sudan-correct-revolution-path-hamdok
63. Watson et al., 2020.

64. De Waal, 2021a.
65. 'Sudan', International Monetary Fund, available at: https://www.imf.org/en/Countries/SDN
66. De Waal, 2004.
67. Marcus, 1963; Nur, 1971.
68. International Crisis Group, 2021b.
69. The term is used to refer to borders that are open for local people to cross easily to maintain livelihoods and community ties and where official demarcation of boundaries does not disrupt existing settlement patterns.
70. Wubneh, 2015.
71. Dereje Asefa, 'The Tigray–Amhara boundary should be resolved by constitutional means', World Peace Foundation, Reinventing Peace blog, 16 July 2021, available at: https://sites.tufts.edu/reinventingpeace/2021/07/16/the-tigray-amhara-boundary-should-be-resolved-by-constitutional-means/
72. IGAD, 'Communiqué of the 38th Extraordinary Assembly of IGAD Heads of State and Government. Djibouti, Republic of Djibouti, 20th December 2020'.
73. Interview with Abdallah Hamdok, Khartoum, December 2020.

CHAPTER 5. MORE THAN HISTORY REPEATING ITSELF

1. Mitchell, 1993: 331.
2. For the 1964 funeral procession of Ahmad al-Qurayshi, see Berridge, 2015: 21–2.
3. James Copnall, 'Sudan civil disobedience: Why are people staying at home?', BBC News, 19 December 2016, available at: https://www.bbc.co.uk/news/world-africa-38364197
4. Berridge, 2015: 27.
5. See, for example, 'Sudan protestors plan new march on Presidential Palace amid nationwide demos', France 24, 24 January 2019, available at: https://www.france24.com/en/20190124-sudan-protesters-plan-new-march-palace-nationwide-demos
6. Pascucci, 2014.
7. Rolandsen and Daly, 2016: 81; Johnson, 2006: 31.
8. Wai, 1981.
9. For example, Johnson, 2006, Idris, 2005.
10. Sharkey, 2003: 29.
11. Nur Hamad, 'al-Taghyir wa qaid al-'aql al-ri'awi', *al-Taghyeer*, 11 September 2016, available at: https://tinyurl.com/jvnykp2b.

In a follow up piece Hamad maintains conflicts between various Arab groups, including the Battahin, Kababish and Shukriyya, can be understood with reference to this 'pastoral mentality', and characterises fighting in Darfur in similar terms. Al-Nur Hamad, 'Tashrih bunya al-'aql al-ri'awi', *al-Hurriyat*, 8 December 2016, available at: https://www.sudaress.com/hurriyat/214317

12. See, for instance, Hale, 1999: 381.
13. Al-Sawi, 2015: 229.
14. See, for example, Pantuliano, 2010 for a discussion of the pressures that force Misseriyya communities into militia-isation.
15. Jizouli, 2006: 238. See also discussion in Berridge, 2011: 238.
16. Wehr, 1994: 59–60.
17. De Waal, 2015.
18. Branch and Mampilly, 2015: 196–9.
19. Gallab, 2014.
20. Ibrahim, 1996: 106–8.
21. Berridge, 2015: 103–6, 158–62.
22. Ibrahim 2015.
23. Ibid.
24. Berridge, 2012.
25. Berridge, 2015: 109–16, 182–4.
26. Magdi El-Gizouli, Arab Reform Initiative, 12 April 2019, 'The fall of al-Bashir: Mapping the contestation forces in Sudan', available at: https://www.arab-reform.net/publication/the-fall-of-al-bashir-mapping-contestation-forces-in-sudan/
27. El-Gizouli, 'The fall of al-Bashir'.
28. 'Restrictions, fines on Darfur tea sellers cause suffering: union', *Dabanga,* 27 October 2017, available at: https://www.dabangasudan.org/en/all-news/article/restrictions-fines-on-khartoum-tea-sellers-cause-suffering-union
29. For the history of Mustafa's father, Yousif Ahmad al-Mustafa, who was the first secretary general of the Gezira Tenants' Union upon its founding in 1953, see Hassan Warag, 'Sira munadil usturi li-haraka al-muzari'in fi Sudan hazza 'arsh malika al-Baritaniyya al-uzma!', *al-Rakoba*, 9 September 2012, available (4 parts) at https://www.sudaress.com/alrakoba/71026
30. Berridge, 2015: 121–31; Nur, 2002: 529. The *ahliyya* schools were originally founded in the 1920s with funding from the nationalists of the era and provided an alternative political dialectic to that associated with the colonial regime's schools, such as Gordon Memorial College. They still remain an important reference point for civil society activists today.

31. Berridge, 2015: 131–46.
32. Woodward, 1990; Berridge, 2015: 119.
33. Berridge, 2015: 131–46; al-Mirghani, 2002; Sa'id, 2001.
34. Ahmed Hassan, 'The rise and fall of the Sudanese Alliance Forces (1)', African Arguments, 8 October 2009, available at: https://africanarguments.org/2009/10/08/the-rise-and-fall-of-the-sudan-alliance-forces-1/
35. International Crisis Group, 2019.
36. 'Man huwa Abu Bakr Demilab mudir al-mukhabarat al-Sudaniyya al-jadida?', *al-Khalij al-Jadid*, 15 April 2019, available at: https://tinyurl.com/ytu642w9
37. International Crisis Group, 2019.
38. Berridge, 2013b: 862, 865.
39. International Crisis Group, 2019.
40. Johnson, 2006: 81–2; Salmon, 2007.
41. Mitchell, 1993 describes the Muslim Brotherhood in Egypt as a party of 'conservative transition'. In Sudan the term might perhaps be more appropriately attached to the Umma.
42. Niblock, 1987: 51–2, 58; Warburg, 2003: 95.
43. Berridge, 2015: 129.
44. Ibid.: 168.
45. Warburg, 2003.
46. Johnson, 2006: 83.
47. 'Al-Mahdi yuwajjih jamahirahu li'l-musharaka fi muzaharat 6 April wa yu'tabirha 'fard al-'ayn", *al-Sharq al-Awsat*, 3 April 2019, available at: https://tinyurl.com/y2v5f6ss
48. Gallab, 2008: 58.
49. I. Al-Madu, 'al-Mahdi: la li-tasa'aid wa al-askari sa yastamirr fi al-hukm', *Akhir Lahza*, 27 June 2019, available at: http://akhirlahza-sd.com/18605/
50. 'Al-Mahdi yada'uu 'aada' al-majlis al-askari li-dukhuul hizbhu', *al-Tayyar*, 10 July 2019, available at: https://tinyurl.com/y74pmrnc
51. 'Al-Shiyu'i: al-thuwwar lan yasmahu bi-qiyaam intikhabat mukbira', *al-Jareeda*, 16 December 2019.
52. 'Al-Harrak al-Siyasi: al-Umma al-Qawmi yada'u li-ta'ayiin wula askariyyin fi manatiq al-hashasha', *Baj News*, 20 April 2021, available at: https://www.sudaress.com/bajnews/123707
53. See the discussion of Gallab in Berridge, 2017.
54. El-Affendi, 1991.
55. Berridge, 2015.
56. Ibrahim, 1996: 103.

57. Berridge, 2015: 169–70.
58. Ibid.: 184–7.
59. Ibid.: 161, 183.
60. Zeinab Mohammed Salih, 'Scores of protestors wounded and seven dead on Sudan's streets', *The Guardian*, 1 July 2019, available at: https://www.theguardian.com/world/2019/jun/30/fears-of-violence-as-sudan-gets-ready-for-million-man-march-khartoum
61. 'Sudan', *The World Factbook*, CIA, available at: https://www.cia.gov/the-world-factbook/countries/sudan/#people-and-society; 'Human development reports -Sudan', United Nations Development Programme, available at: http://www.hdr.undp.org/en/countries/profiles/SDN
62. 'Ialan tahaluf jadid tahta musamma Shabab al-Thawra', *Al-Sudan al-Youm*, 16 April 2019, available at: https://tinyurl.com/yamdze29; 'Tahaluf al-shabab fi maqarr al-iatasam tahta musamma 'shabab al-thawra', *Al-Sudani*, 16 April 2019, available at: https://tinyurl.com/yaz2azzc
63. 'Bayyan min tullab al-Ansar wa Hizb al-Umma al-Qawmi bi'l-ja'amat wa al-ma'ahid al-ulya', *al-Rakoba*, 2 June 2013, available at: https://tinyurl.com/yaqrx7pp; 'al-Amn ya'ataqal majmoua min Shabab al-Umma al-Qawmi', *al-Tahrer*, 14 December 2018, available at: https://www.alttahrer.com/archives/24044
64. De Waal, 2013b: 214.
65. McCutcheon, 2014: 23.
66. Magdi El-Gizouli, 'The Sudan Revolutionary Front: Comrades in squabble', African Arguments, 9 November 2015, available at: https://africanarguments.org/2015/11/the-sudan-revolutionary-front-comrades-in-squabble/
67. De Waal, 2015.
68. 'Sudan's TMC, two armed groups, agree to uphold ceasefire in Darfur', *Sudan Tribune*, 28 June 2019, available at: http://www.sudantribune.com/spip.php?article67692
69. Branch and Mampilly, 2015: 194.
70. Branch and Mampilly, 2015: 188.
71. Bakhit et al., 2019.
72. Ibid.; Chevrillon-Guibert and Deshayes, 2019.
73. Muhammad Amin Yasin, 'Al-Thawra tudammij 'abtal al-shawari'a' fi mujtama al-iatisam', *al-Sharq al-Awsat*, 24 April 2019, available at: https://tinyurl.com/wc47j6dp
74. Ibrahim Habbani, 'al-Sudan: Iatasam al-qiyada yansif 'awlad al-shams', Sky News Arabiyya, 24 April 2019, available at: https://tinyurl.com/nyh3pdx6; Yasin, 'Al-Thawra tudammij'.

75. Khalid Mahmoud, 'Awadiyya Kuku...ba'ia al-shay wa sayyida al-thawra al-uula fi al-Sudan', *al-Emarat al-Youm*, 12 July 2019, available at: https://www.emaratalyoum.com/politics/weekly-supplements/beyond-politics/2019-07-12-1.1232182
76. '"Istihdaf tullab Darfur"...hal asbabhu siyasiyya am ansariyya?', *Al-Taghyeer*, 19 November 2017, available at https://tinyurl.com/y9k5s48e
77. Tariq Al-Shaikh, 'Al-Sudan...thawra wa tuhum unsuriyya', *al-Araby*, 2 January 2019, available at: https://preview.tinyurl.com/ybf3yn8r
78. Branch and Mampilly, 2015.
79. See, for example, Lesch, 1998: 144.
80. See Willow Berridge, 'The Sudan uprising and its possibilities: Regional revolution, generational revolution, and an end to Islamist politics?', *Sudanalysis,* 14 October 2019, available at: https://blogs.ncl.ac.uk/willowberridge/2019/10/14/the-sudan-uprising-and-its-possibilities-regional-revolution-generational-revolution-and-an-end-to-islamist-politics/; For a discussion of this dichotomy, see De Waal, 2013b.
81. Berridge, 2015: 37.
82. 'South Darfur students coached in peaceful resistance after Nyala violence', Dabanga, 26 September 2019, available at: https://www.dabangasudan.org/en/all-news/article/south-darfur-students-coached-in-peaceful-resistance-after-nyala-violence
83. 'Sudan paramilitaries attack, detain public after anti-mining protests', Dabanga, 8 October 2019, available at: https://www.dabangasudan.org/en/all-news/article/sudan-paramilitaries-attack-detain-public-after-anti-mining-protests
84. 'Solidarity marches for Darfur all over Sudan', Dabanga, 24 September 2019, available at: https://www.dabangasudan.org/en/all-news/article/solidarity-marches-for-darfur-all-over-sudan
85. 'Sudan cabinet outlaws use of mercury, cyanide in mining', Dabanga, 9 October 2019.
86. Magdi El-Gizouli, 'Sudan's season of revolution', *Review of African Political Economy*, 5 July 2019, https://roape.net/2019/07/05/sudans-season-of-revolution/
87. Ibid.
88. Berridge, 2015: 34.
89. Uthman, 2015.
90. For a discussion of how 'feminist agency' was 'subordinated to and contained by national agency' in the politics of the era, see McClintock, 1995: 367.

91. Al-Amin, 2001: 13, 17.
92. Hale, 1999: 380.
93. Willemse, 2011.
94. al-Ali, 2000: 68.
95. Brown, 2017: 136.
96. Interviews conducted by Raga Makawi and Yousra Mohammed. Raga Makawi and Yousra Mohammed conducted a dozen informal interviews between 26 July and 6 August 2021 with female members of women's groups participants of the Women's Procession to examine their demands, political agenda and forms of mobilisation.
97. On the various public order units, see Berridge, 2013a.
98. Justin Lynch, 'Women fueled Sudan's revolution, but then they were pushed aside', *The Independent,* 4 August 2019, available at: https://www.independent.co.uk/news/world/africa/sudan-revolution-women-uprising-democratic-transition-army-bashir-a9038786.html
99. Medani and Aziz, 2019.
100. Justin Lynch, 'Women fueled Sudan's revolution, but then they were pushed aside'.
101. 'Women football aimed at distracting Sudanese from crises: Radical Islamists', *Sudan Tribune*, 5 October 2019, available at: https://www.sudantribune.com/spip.php?article68240
102. Medani and Aziz, 2019.
103. See, for example, Shamouq, 2008.
104. Medani and Aziz, 2019.
105. Nesrine Malik, 'She's an icon of Sudan's revolution. But the Woman in White obscures vital truths', *The Guardian*, 24 April 2019, available at: https://www.theguardian.com/commentisfree/2019/apr/24/icon-sudan-revolution-woman-in-white/. The *tob* is a dress worn by Sudanese women.
106. Khalid Mahmoud, 'Awadiyya Kuku…ba'ia al-shay wa sayyida al-thawra al-uula fi al-Sudan', *al-Emarat al-Youm*, 12 July 2019, available at: https://www.emaratalyoum.com/politics/weekly-supplements/beyond-politics/2019-07-12-1.1232182
107. Zeinab Mohammed Salih, 'There is a war on women in Sudan: Women demand protection against violence and harassment', *The New Arab*, 20 April 2021, available at: https://english.alaraby.co.uk/features/sudanese-women-demand-protection-against-domestic-violence-and-harassment
108. 'Sudanese women protest gender discrimination, demand legal reform', Dabanga, 9 April 2021, available at: https://www.

dabangasudan.org/en/all-news/article/sudanese-women-protest-gender-discrimination-and-demand-legal-reform

109. Ali, 2019.
110. Nour, 2014.
111. Adam and WagiAlla, 2021: 38.
112. Interviews conducted by Raga Makawi and Yousra Mohammed.
113. 'Sudan Public Order Law still being implemented: SIHA network', Dabanga, 3 September 2021, available at: https://www.dabangasudan.org/en/all-news/article/sudan-public-order-law-still-being-implemented-siha-network
114. Abdel Aziz and Alfaki, 2021.
115. 'UN, African Union officials discuss peace with Sudan's prime minister', *Sudan Tribune*, 10 October 2019, https://www.sudantribune.com/spip.php?article68271
116. Dame Rosalind Marsden, Expert Comment, 'Is the Juba Peace Agreement a turning point for Sudan?', Chatham House, 9 September 2020, https://www.chathamhouse.org/2020/09/juba-peace-agreement-turning-point-sudan
117. Nazik Awad, 'Sudanese women show that peace requires participation not just representation', *OpenDemocracy*, 17 December 2020.
118. Berridge, 2017: 305. On the concept of 'neo-fundamentalism', see Roy, 1994: 75.
119. See, for example, Berridge, 2019b: 218–21; Hamid, 2015.
120. 'Tajammu al-mihniyyin yarfud mubadara 'al-Islah wa'l-Salam', allati ra'asaha al-Jizouli Dafa'allah, wa yatamassak bi-isqat nizam bidun shuruut', *Kush News*, 11 February 2019, available at: https://kushnews.net/2019/02/134942
121. 'Mubadara al-52 tatajaahal mawja al-naqd wa tashra' ittisalat siyasiyya waasi'a', *Kush News*, 13 February 2019, available at: https://kushnews.net/2019/02/135587
122. Hamid et al., 2017.
123. Cavatorta and Merone, 2015.
124. Gallab, 2008.
125. 'Sudan authorities release al-Tayyar editor Osman Mirghani', Dabanga, 30 March 2019, available at: https://www.dabangasudan.org/en/all-news/article/sudan-authorities-release-detained-el-tayyar-editor-osman-mirghani; 'El-Tayyar editor: Al-Bashir ordered massacre before coup', Dabanga, 21 April 2019, available at: https://www.dabangasudan.org/en/all-news/article/el-tayyar-editor-al-bashir-ordered-massacre-before-coup

126. 'Ba'ad ightiyal ahad a'ada'aha…al-mu'atamar al-sha'abi…imtihan al-khuruj min "anq 'al-sharaka"', *al-Rakoba*, 9 February 2019, available at: https://tinyurl.com/y9w9v8al
127. 'al-Mu'atamar al-Sha'abi: Ali al-Hajj atla'a ala kull al-qarrarat al-ri'asiyya al-akhira wa waaqafa aleiha bi-shidda', *al-Sudan al-Youm*, 4 March 2019, available at: https://tinyurl.com/y9oeef48; see also Berridge, 2019a.
128. Abd al-Nasir al-Haj, 'Masadir Sudaniyya li-"al-Watan": bawadir inshiqaqat fi "Hizb al-Turabi"', *al-Watan*, 18 March 2019, available at: https://tinyurl.com/3jpu427v
129. 'Yada'amha ansar al-Bashir: taraqqub hadhr li-milyuniyya al-zahf al-akhbar bi'l-Sudan', Al Jazeera, 13 December 2019, available at: https://tinyurl.com/y8ybk862
130. 'Al-Sha'abi yu'lin rasmiyyan musharikathu fi milyuniyya al-zahf al-akhdar', *al-Youm al-Tali*, 14 December 2019, available at: https://tinyurl.com/yawbjheh
131. Gallab, 2014.
132. 'Al-Tayyib Mustafa yaktub: bayna ialan al-ilmaniyya wa ilgha' nizam al-aam!', *al-Intibaha*, 4 April 2021, available at: https://www.sudaress.com/alnilin/13177219. For his arrest, see 'Sudan: Arbitrary detention of writer contradicts democratic transformation principles' Euro-Mediterranean Human Rights Monitor, 3 June 2020, https://euromedmonitor.org/en/article/3583/Sudan:-Arbitrary-detention-of-writer-contradicts-democratic-transformation-principals
133. International Crisis Group, 2019.
134. 'Bi'l-Video: Ali Karti yutalib bi'l-Khuruj bi'l-Khuruj li'l-sharia wa'l-iltizam bi'l-silmiyya li-isqat al-Nizam', *Nilin*, 15 February 2021, available at: https://www.alnilin.com/13169613.htm
135. Berridge, 2015: 37; 2017: 271.
136. Berridge, 2017: 270–2; Flint and de Waal, 2008: 19–20.
137. Harir, 1994: 159.
138. Flint and de Waal, 2008: 106.
139. Ibid.
140. 'Qatar yuwazzif adhra'aha li-takhrib al-ittifaq al-siyasi fi al-Sudan', *Al-Arab*, 23 July 2019, available at: https://tinyurl.com/y8dlfxvw
141. 'Ali al-Haj yu'lin takwin hukuumat zill li-isqat nizam', *Intibaha*, 22 August 2019, available at: https://www.sudaress.com/alnilin/13072075
142. 'Al-Sudan: Hizb al-Turabi yada'u ila al-nuzuul li'l-sharia li-isqat al-tatbi'a ma' Isra'il', *al-Quds al-Arabi*, 25 October 2020, available at: https://tinyurl.com/ycfv2pap

143. 'Al-Mu'atmar al-Sha'abi yujayyish 'al-Ansar' li'l-isqat al-hukuma al-intiqaliyya fi al-Sudan', *Al-Arab*, 12 December 2019, available at: https://tinyurl.com/ycbkgpw4
144. International Crisis Group, 2008: 14.
145. Lesch, 1998.
146. 'Al-Mahdi: al-Islam aqida ghalabiyya al-Sudaniyyin wa narfud al-'ilmaniyya wa taqrir al-masir', *al-Sudani*, 22 December 2019, available at: https://tinyurl.com/yd4jl9j3
147. 'Mawaqif ba'ad al-ahzab min ialaan Burhan-Hilu', *Nilin*, 4 April 2021, available at: https://www.sudaress.com/alnilin/13177297
148. 'Al-Wathiq Bireir yarfud idraj al-Umma al-Qawmi bi-qa'ima al-ahzab al-munshi'a ala asas ala asas diniyya', alnwrs.com, 4 April 2012, available at: https://alnwrs.com/2021/04/78068/
149. 'Ahzab tu'lin rafdha qanun hazr al-ahzab diniyya fi Sudan', *Independent Arabiyya*, 8 April 2021, available at: https://www.sudaress.com/alrakoba/31548972
150. Ahmed Kodouda, 'Sudan's Islamist resurrection: al-Turabi and the successor regime', African Arguments, 24 February 2016, available at: https://africanarguments.org/2016/02/sudans-islamist-resurrection-al-turabi-and-the-successor-regime/
151. Najda Bushara, 'Ittifaq al-Umma wa'l-Sha'abi…ma jadid!', *al-Rakoba*, 3 September 2020, available at: https://tinyurl.com/3d4h5zcd
152. Al-Shafie Khidir Sa'id, 'al-Sudan wa al-musawama al-tarikhiyya', *Sudanile*, 25 November 2019, available at: https://www.sudaress.com/sudanile/120100
153. Rebecca Hamilton, 'The enemies of Sudan's democracy are lurking everywhere', *Foreign Policy*, 6 December 2019, available at: https://foreignpolicy.com/2019/12/06/sudan-democracy-enemies-everywhere-bashir/
154. 'Al-Sha'abi yutalib bi-taslim al-Bashir li'l-jina'iyya', *al-Sudani*, 12 November 2019, https://www.sudaress.com/alsudani/1047030
155. Salah Mukhtar, 'al-Sha'abi—akhtar min risala!', *al-Sayha*, 1 January 2019, available at: https://www.sudanakhbar.com/645464
156. See, for example, Tilly, 1975: 525, cited in Skocpol, 1994: 109.
157. Berridge, 2015.
158. Zeleke, 2020.
159. Skocpol, 1994: 240–4.
160. Ibid.: 1994: 247–50.
161. Fanon, 2001.
162. Ibid.

163. Ibid.
164. Sharp, 2005; Ackerman and Duvall, 2001.
165. Zunes, 1999.
166. Stephan, 2009.
167. De Waal, 2013b.
168. Kamrava, 2005: 301, for instance, refers to the 'so-called October Revolution' in Sudan in the same breath as Ba'athist and Free Officer coups in Syria, Egypt, Libya and elsewhere.
169. Branch and Mampilly, 2015; de Waal and Ibreck, 2013.
170. Skocpol, 1994: 104.

CHAPTER 6. NOT THE LAST CHAPTER

1. McGowan, 2003.
2. Witness interview, Khartoum, September 2021.
3. Radio Dabanga, 'Sudan military, politicians exchange accusations over coup attempt', 23 September 2021, available at: https://www.dabangasudan.org/en/all-news/article/sudan-military-politicians-exchange-accusations-over-coup-attempt
4. Radio Dabanga, 'Sudan revolutionaries urge reform of the armed forces', 24 September 2021, available at: https://www.dabangasudan.org/en/all-news/article/sudan-revolutionaries-urge-reform-of-the-armed-forces
5. Radio Dabanga, 'Sudan PM on foiled military coup: "What happened is a lesson learnt"', 21 September 2021, available at: https://www.dabangasudan.org/en/all-news/article/sudan-pm-on-foiled-military-coup-what-happened-is-a-lesson-learnt
6. 'Inqilab al-Sudan: la yumkinhum qatlna jami'an', *al-Rakoba*, 8 November 2021, available at: https://www.sudaress.com/alrakoba/31639174.
7. Uthman al-Tahir, 'Ta'tiil lajna al-tamkin bi'l-Fashir', *al-Jareeda*, 24 October 2021.
8. 'Zahir Bakhit al-Faki yaktub: bayna Wajdi wa Jibril taha al-dalil!', *al-Jareeda,* 15 June 2021, available at: https://www.sudaress.com/kushnews/290199
9. 'Lajna iatasam al-qasr tutahhim Wajdi Salih bi-taqdim khitab Ansari khilal nadwa fi Wad Medani', *Baj News*, 20 October 2021, available at: https://www.sudaress.com/bajnews/141880
10. 'Karitha mutawaqqa'a huduthha fi al-Sudan', *al-Quds al-Arabi*, 17 October 2021, available at: https://tinyurl.com/2e8m9s9n

11. Abd al Wahab Abdalla, 'On the Reactionary Nature of Sudanese Provincial "Revolutions": Liberating the Bantustans?', African Arguments, 8 September 2009, available at: https://africanarguments.org/2009/09/liberating-the-bantustans-on-the-futility-of-sudanese-provincial-revolutions/
12. Morton, 1989.
13. Sky News Arabiyya, 'Za'im al-Beja yarfa'a saqf matalibhu wa yaghlaq matar burtsuudan', 23 September 2021 available at: https://www.sudanakhbar.com/1055238
14. 'Azima sharq al-Sudan…al-hukuma fi qafs al-ittiham', 30 July 2021, *al-Taghyeer*, available at: https://www.sudaress.com/alsudani/1132390
15. *The New Arab*, 'Sudan temporarily suspends two newspapers for publishing protest announcement', 20 September 2021, available at: https://english.alaraby.co.uk/news/sudan-suspends-two-newspapers-over-protest-announcement
16. 'Sudan military to reinstate PM Hamdok after New Deal: Mediators', Al Jazeera 21 November 2021, available at: https://www.aljazeera.com/news/2021/11/21/sudan-military-to-reinstate-ousted-pm-hamdok-after-deal-reports
17. 'al-Umma al-Qawmi: lan nakun tarafan fi ayy ittifaq la yulabbi tatalla'at al-sha'ab al-Sudani', *Baj News*, 21 November 2021, available at: https://www.sudaress.com/alnilin/13217120
18. *The National*, UAE, 'Sudan minister hopeful that "things will be back to normal"', 9 November 2021, available at: https://www.thenationalnews.com/world/africa/2021/11/09/sudan-minister-hopeful-that-things-will-be-back-to-normal/
19. Interview with an official familiar with the government of Sudan's Central Bank activities, November 2021, Khartoum.
20. US Institute of Peace, 'Taking stock of U.S. policy on Ethiopia: A conversation with Ambassador Jeffrey Feltman', 2 November 2021, available at: https://www.usip.org/events/taking-stock-us-policy-ethiopia-conversation-ambassador-jeffrey-feltman
21. Debating Ideas/African Arguments, '"This is not a coup": Sudan's mediators need a mediator', 2 November 2021, available at: https://africanarguments.org/2021/11/this-is-not-a-coup-sudans-mediators-need-a-mediator/
22. Nick Shiffrin (PBS) on Twitter, 18 November 2021, available at: https://twitter.com/nickschifrin/status/1461351773994553354?s=20
23. Edward Thomas and Magdi El-Gizouli, 'Creatures of the deposed: Connecting Sudan's urban and rural struggles', African Arguments,

11 November 2021, available at: https://africanarguments.org/2021/11/creatures-of-the-deposed-connecting-sudans-rural-and-urban-struggles/

24. Kholood Khair, 'Sudan's coup is on Shaky Ground', Al Jazeera, 19 November 2021.
25. 'What we know about Sudan's ongoing civil disobedience after military coup', PBS, 28 October 2021.
26. Translated from Arabic. One of the many new chants critical of Hamdok.
27. Interview with Samahir Mubarak, Khartoum, 21 November 2021.
28. Live interview with Samahir Mubarak, Al Jazeera English TV, 21 November 2021.
29. Abdel Salam and de Waal, 2001: 'Introduction', xi.
30. Gallab, 2008: 57.
31. Ibid.: 58.
32. Mazrui, 1971.
33. 'Trump says US will remove sanctions on Sudan in historic new chapter in relations', ABC News, 20 October 2020.
34. Colum Lynch and Robbie Gramer, 'The World Food Program's freelance diplomacy', *Foreign Policy*, 16 November 2021.
35. Interviews with Abdalla Hamdok, Addis Ababa, July 2019 and by phone, August 2021.
36. Cf. Woodward, 1990.
37. Interview with Samahir Mubarak, Khartoum, 21 November 2021.

REFERENCES

Abd al-Salam, Mahbub (2010), *Harakah al-Islamiyya al-Sudaniyya: Da'irat al-Daw'–Khuyut al-Zalam* (Cairo: Madarik).

Abdel Aziz and Ahmed Azza (2019), 'The third Sudanese revolution reinstates women from all walks of life onto the map of Sudanese public life', May, Noria Research, available at: https://www.noria-research.com/the-third-sudanese-revolution-reinstates-women/

Abdel Aziz, Ahmed, Azza and Alfaki, Aroob (2021), *Shifting Terrains of Political Participation in Sudan: Elements Dating from the Second Colonial (1898–1956) Period to the Contemporary Era* (Stockholm: International Institute for Democracy and Electoral Assistance).

Abdel Salam, A. H. and de Waal, Alex (eds) (2001), *The Phoenix State: Civil Society and the Future of Sudan* (Trenton, NJ: Red Sea Press).

Ackerman, Peter and Duvall, Jack (2001), *A Force More Powerful: A Century of Non-Violent Conflict* (London: Palgrave Macmillan).

Adam, A. H. M. and WagiAlla, F. A. (2021), 'The state of awareness of women's rights among ordinary Sudanese women and the impact of the 2018 revolution on that awareness: A case study of women of the Al-Nasr District', *Journal of Studies in Social Sciences and Humanities*, 7 (1), 31–41.

Africa Watch (1990), *'Denying the Honor of Living,' Sudan: A Human Rights Disaster* (New York: Human Rights Watch).

African Centre for Justice and Peace Studies (2018), 'Study on the war economy in Darfur: The cross-border automobile trade: January 2014–March 2017' (Khartoum: African Centre for Justice and Peace Studies).

Agamben, Giorgio (1995), *Homo Sacer: Sovereign Power and Bare Life* (Stanford, CA: Stanford University Press).

Al-Ali, Nadje (2000), *Secularism, Gender and the State in the Middle East: The Egyptian Women's Movement* (New York: Cambridge University Press).

Al-Amin, Nafisa Ahmed and Magied, Ahmed Abdel (2001), 'A history of the Sudanese women organizations and the strive for liberation and development', *Ahfad Journal*, 18 (1), 2–23.

Al-Mirghani, Isam (2002), *al-Jaysh al-Sudani fi Siyasa* (Cairo: Afro wa Naji li-tasmiya wa'l-tiba'a).

Al-Sawi, Abd al-Aziz Hussein (2015), 'Al-Yasar al-Sudani wa Oktober: Istikmal al-Muhimma bi-Istikmal al-Muraaja'a al-Nuqdiyya li'l-Dhat', in H. A. Ibrahim, *Khamsun 'Aaman Ala Thawrat Uktubir al-Sudaniyya, 1964–2014: Nuhud al-Sudan al-Bakir*, pp. 217–34 (Khartoum: Markaz al-Dirasat al-Sudaniyya).

Ali, Nada (2019), 'Sudanese women's groups on Facebook and #Civil_Disobedience: Nairat or thairat? (radiant or revolutionary?)', *African Studies Review*, 62 (2), 103–26.

Alnagar, Samia (2010), 'Patriarchy, politics and women's activism in post-revolution Sudan', Sudan Brief 02 (Bergen: Chr. Michelsen Institute).

Bakhit, Mohamed A. G., Ibrahim, Sherein and Madani, Rania (2019), 'The spatial dimension of the four months long Sudanese uprising', in Clément Deshayes, Etienne Margaux and Khadidja Medani (eds), '"Down with the rule of thieves": Investigating the revolutionary trends in Sudan Part II', Special Issue on Sudan, Noria Research.

Bell, C. and Pospisil, J. (2017), 'Navigating inclusion in transitions from conflict: The formalised political unsettlement', *Journal of International Development*, 29 (5), 576–93.

Berridge, W. J. (2012), 'Nests of criminals: Policing in the peri-urban regions of northern Sudan, 1949–1989', *Journal of North African Studies*, 17 (2), 239–55.

Berridge, W. J. (2013a), 'The ambiguous role of the popular, public order and society police in Sudan, 1983–2011', *Middle Eastern Studies*, 49 (4), 528–46.

Berridge, W. J. (2013b), 'Sudan's security agencies: Fragmentation, visibility and mimicry, 1908–1989', *Intelligence and National Security*, 28 (6), 845–67.

Berridge, W. J. (2015), *Civil Uprisings in Modern Sudan: The 'Khartoum Springs' of 1964 and 1985* (London: Bloomsbury).

Berridge, W. J. (2017), *Hasan al-Turabi: Islamist Politics and Democracy in Sudan* (Cambridge: Cambridge University Press).

Berridge, W. J. (2019a), 'Briefing: The uprising in Sudan', *African Affairs*, 119 (474), 164–76.

Berridge, W. J. (2019b), *Islamism in the Modern World: A Historical Approach* (London: Bloomsbury).

Beshir, Mohamed Omer (1969), *Educational Development in the Sudan, 1898–1956* (Oxford: Clarendon Press).

Branch, Adam and Mampilly, Zachariah (2015), *Africa Uprising: Popular Protest and Political Change* (London: Zed Books).

Brown, Marie (2017), *Khartoum at Night: Fashion and Body Politics in Imperial Sudan* (Stanford, CA: Stanford University Press).

Brown, Richard P. C. (1990), *Sudan's Debt Crisis: The Interplay between International and Domestic Responses, 1978–88* (Durban: Beboren).

Calkins, Sandra and Ille, Enrico (2014), 'Territories of gold mining: International investment and artisanal extraction in Sudan', in Jorg Gertel, Richard Rottenburg and Sandra Calkins (eds), *Disputing Territories: Land, Commodification and Conflict in Sudan*, pp. 52–76 (Woodbridge, UK: James Currey).

Carter, Andrew and Albagir, Nima (2008), 'Meet the Janjaweed', Channel 4 News, available at: https://www.dailymotion.com/video/xtxd8n

Cavatorta, Francesco and Merone, Fabio (2015), 'Post-Islamism, ideological evolution and "La *Tunisianité*" of the Tunisian Islamist Party *al-Nahda*', *Journal of Political Ideologies*, 20 (1), 27–42.

Chaillou-Gillette, Claire (2019), 'The Sudanese popular uprising: From the first demonstration to the state of emergency', in Clément Deshayes, Etienne Margaux and Khadidja Medani (eds), '"Down with the rule of thieves": Reflections on the Sudanese revolutionary dynamics', Special Issue on Sudan, Noria Research, available at: https://noria-research.com/the-sudanes-popular-uprising/

Chenoweth, Erica and Stephan, Maria (2011), *Why Civil Resistance Works: The Strategic Logic of Non-violent Conflict* (New York, NY: Columbia University Press).

Chevrillon-Guibert, Raphaëlle (2019), 'Cronyism, asymmetry, and injustice in the dynamics of the protest', in Clément Deshayes, Etienne Margaux and Khadidja Medani (eds) '"Down with the rule of thieves": Reflections on the Sudanese revolutionary dynamics', Special Issue on Sudan, Noria Research, available at: https://noria-research.com/political-economy-of-the-regime-and-revolt/?

Chevrillon-Guibert, Raphaëlle and Deshayes, Clément (2019), 'Political economy of the regime and revolt', May 2019, Noria Research, available at: https://www.noria-research.com/political-economy-of-the-regime-and-revolt/.

Daly, M. W. (1991), *Imperial Sudan: The Anglo-Egyptian Condominium, 1934–1956* (Cambridge: Cambridge University Press).

De Waal, Alex (1993), 'Some comments on militias in contemporary Sudan', in M. W. Daly and A. A. Sikainga (eds), *Civil War in the Sudan*, pp. 142–57 (London: British Academic Press).

De Waal, Alex (2004), 'The politics of destabilization in the Horn, 1989–2001', in Alex de Waal (ed.), *Islamism and its Enemies in the Horn of Africa*, pp. 182–230 (London: Hurst).

De Waal, Alex (2009), 'UNAMID and the Security Council: Evidence for Policy', African Arguments, 29 April, available at: http://africanarguments.org/2009/04/29/unamid-and-the-security-council-evidence-for-policy/

De Waal, Alex (2013a), 'African roles in the Libyan conflict of 2011', *International Affairs*, 89 (2), 365–79.

De Waal, Alex (2013b), 'Civic mobilization, elusive democratisation, provincial rebellion, and chameleon dictatorships', *Journal of Contemporary African Studies*, 31 (2), 213–34.

De Waal, Alex (2015), *The Real Politics of the Horn of Africa: Money, War and the Business of Power* (Cambridge: Polity Press).

De Waal, Alex (2019), 'Sudan: A political marketplace framework analysis', World Peace Foundation. Occasional Paper no. 19, August, http://eprints.lse.ac.uk/101291/1/De_Waal_Sudan_a_political_marketplace_analysis_published.pdf

De Waal, Alex (2021a), *New Pandemics, Old Politics: Two Hundred Years of the War on Disease and its Alternatives* (Cambridge: Polity Press).

De Waal, Alex (2021b), 'Concluding reflections: Sudan's Comprehensive Peace Agreement and theories of change', in Sarah M. H. Nouwen, Laura M. James and Sharath Srinivasan (eds), *Making and Breaking Peace in Sudan and South Sudan: The Comprehensive Peace Agreement and Beyond*, ch. 17 (Oxford: Oxford University Press).

De Waal, Alex and Abdel Salam, A. H. (2004), 'Islamism, state power and jihad in Sudan', in Alex de Waal (ed.) *Islamism and Its Enemies in the Horn of Africa*, pp. 73–113 (London: Hurst).

De Waal, Alex and Ibreck, Rachel (2013), 'Hybrid social movements in Africa', *Journal of Contemporary African Studies*, 31 (2), 303–24.

De Waal, Alex, Hazlett, Chad, Davenport, Christian and Kennedy, Joshua (2014), 'The epidemiology of lethal violence in Darfur: Using micro-data to explore complex patterns of ongoing armed conflict', *Social Science and Medicine*, 120, 368–77.

Deng, Francis Mading (1989), 'What is not said is what divides us', in Abdel Ghaffar Mohamed Ahmed (ed.) *Management of the Crisis in the Sudan*, pp. 10–18 (Bergen: Centre for Development Studies).

Donham, Donald (2006), 'Staring at suffering: Violence as a subject', in Edna G. Bay, Donald L. Donham (eds), *States of Violence: Politics, Youth, and Memory in Contemporary Africa*, pp. 16–34 (Charlottesville, VA: University of Virginia Press).

Duffield, Mark (1981), *Maiurno: Capitalism and Rural Life in Sudan* (Exeter, NY: Ithaca Press).

El-Affendi, Abdelwahab (1991), *Turabi's Revolution: Islam and Power in Sudan* (London: Grey Seal).

El-Battahani, Atta (2013), 'The post-secession state in Sudan: Building coalitions or deepening conflicts?', in Gunnar M. Sørbø and Abdel Ghaffar M. Ahmed (eds), *Sudan Divided: Continuing Conflict in a Contested State*, pp. 25–44 (New York: Palgrave Macmillan).

El-Gizouli, Magdi (2019), 'Class dynamics, dissemination of the Sudanese uprising', in Clément Deshayes, Etienne Margaux and Khadidja Medani (eds), "'Down with the rule of thieves": Reflections on the Sudanese revolutionary dynamics', Special Issue on Sudan, Noria Research, available at: https://www.noria-research.com/class-dynamics-dissemination-of-the-sudanese-uprising/

El-Gizouli, Magdi (2020), 'Mobilization and resistance in Sudan's uprising: From neighbourhood committees to zanig queens', Briefing Paper January 2020, Rift Valley Institute.

Elbadawi, Ibrahim and Kabbashi Madani Suliman (2018), 'The macroeconomics of the gold economy in Sudan', Economic Research Forum Working Paper no. 1203, Khartoum: Economic Research Forum.

Elnur, Ibrahim (2009), *Contested Sudan: The Political Economy of War and Reconstruction* (New York, NY: Routledge).

Fadlallah, Amal (2018), *Branding Humanity: Competing Narratives of Rights, Violence and Global Citizenship* (Stanford, CA: Stanford University Press).

Fadul, Abdul Jabbar and Tanner, Victor (2007), 'Darfur after Abuja: A view from the ground', in De Waal, A., *War in Darfur and the Search for Peace: Studies in Global Equity*, ch. 12 (Cambridge, MA: Harvard University Press).

Fanon, Frantz (2001), *The Wretched of the Earth* (London: Penguin).

Flint, Julie (2008), *Beyond 'Janjaweed': Understanding the Militias of Darfur*, Small Arms Survey, Sudan Working Paper 17 (Geneva: Small Arms Survey).

Flint, Julie (2010), *The Other War: Inter-Arab Conflict in Darfur*, Small Arms Survey, Sudan Working Paper 22 (Geneva: Small Arms Survey).

Flint, Julie and De Waal, Alex (2008), *Darfur: A New History of A Long War. Second Edition* (London: Zed Books).

Gallab, Abdullahi A. (2008), *The First Islamist Republic: Development and Disintegration of Islamism in Sudan* (Aldershot: Ashgate).

Gallab, Abdullahi A. (2014), *Their Second Republic: Islamism in the Sudan from Disintegration to Oblivion* (Aldershot: Ashgate).

Gallopin, Jean-Baptiste, Thomas, Eddie, Detzner, Sarah and de Waal, Alex (2021), 'Sudan's political marketplace in 2021: Public and political finance, the Juba Peace Agreement and contests over resources', London School of Economics, Conflict Research Programme, Occasional Paper August 2021.

Gresh, Alain (2010), 'The free officers and the comrades: The Sudanese Communist Party and Nimeiri face to face, 1969–1971', *The South Atlantic Quarterly*, 109 (1), 9–30.

Haggar, Ali (2007), 'The origins and organization of the Janjawiid in Darfur', in Alex de Waal (ed.), *The War in Darfur and the Search for Peace*, pp. 113–39 (Cambridge, MA: Global Equity Initiative).

Hale, Sondra (1986), 'Sudanese women and revolutionary parties: The wing of the patriarch', *MERIP Middle East Report*, 138, 25–30.

Hale, Sondra (1999), 'Mothers and militias: Islamic state construction of the women citizens of northern Sudan', *Citizenship Studies*, 3 (3), 373–86.

Hamid, Shadi (2015), *Temptations of Power: Islamists and Illiberal Democracy in the New Middle East* (Oxford: Oxford University Press).

Hamid, Shadi, McCants, William and Dar, Rashid (2017), 'Islamism after the Arab Spring: Between the Islamic State and the nation-state', Brookings Project on Relations with the Islamic World, available at: https://www.brookings.edu/wp-content/uploads/2017/01/islamism-after-the-arab-spring_english_web_final.pdf/

Harir, Sharif (1994), '"Arab Belt" versus "African Belt": Ethno-political conflict in Darfur and the regional cultural factors", in Sharif Harir and Terje Tvedt (eds), *Short-cut to Decay: The Case of Sudan,* pp. 144–85 (Uppsala: Nordiska Afrikainstitutet).

Holt, P.M. (1958), *The Mahdist State in Sudan, 1881–1898* (Oxford: Clarendon Press).

Human Right Watch (2019), '"They were shouting 'Kill them'": Sudan's violent crackdown on protesters in Khartoum', 17 November, available at: https://www.hrw.org/report/2019/11/18/they-were-shouting-kill-them/sudans-violent-crackdown-protesters-khartoum.

Ibn Khaldun (1967), *The Muqaddimah: An Introduction to History*, translated and introduced by Franz Rosenthal, abridged and edited by N. J. Dawood (Princeton, NJ: Princeton University Press).

Ibrahim, Abdullahi Ali (1996), 'The 1971 coup in Sudan and the radical war of liberal democracy in Africa', *Comparative Studies of Africa, Asia and the Middle East*, 16 (1), 98–114.

Ibrahim, Haider Ali (2015), *Khamsun 'Aaman Ala Thawrat Uktubir al-Sudaniyya, 1964–2014: Nuhud al-Sudan al-Bakir* (Khartoum: Markaz al-Dirasat al-Sudaniyya).

Ibrahim, Hasabo (2015), 'Mugabala ma' Hasabo Ibrahim, an haraka al-muzaari'in wa nidaalatha', in H.A. Ibrahim, *Khamsun 'Aaman Ala Thawrat Uktubir al-Sudaniyya, 1964-2014: Nuhud al-Sudan al-Bakir*, pp. 403–15 (Khartoum: Markaz al-Dirasat al-Sudaniyya).

Ibrahim, Hassan Ahmed (2004), *Sayyid Abd al-Rahman al-Mahdi: A Study of neo-Mahdism in the Sudan, 1899–1956* (Boston, MA: Brill).

Idris, Amir H. (2005), *Conflict and Politics of Identity Sudan* (New York, NY: Palgrave Macmillan).

Ille, Enrico (2016), 'Complications in the classification of conflict areas and conflicts actors for the identification of "conflict gold" in Sudan', *Extractive Industries and Society*, 3 (1), 193–203.

International Crisis Group (2008), 'Sudan's Southern Kordofan problem: The next Darfur?', Africa Report No. 145, 21 October, available at: https://www.crisisgroup.org/africa/horn-africa/sudan/sudan-s-southern-kordofan-problem-next-darfur

International Crisis Group (2019), 'Safeguarding Sudan's revolution', Africa Report 281, 21 October, available at: https://www.crisisgroup.org/africa/horn-africa/sudan/281-safeguarding-sudans-revolution.

International Crisis Group (2020), 'Financing the revival of Sudan's troubled transition', Briefing no. 157, 22 June, available at: https://www.crisisgroup.org/africa/horn-africa/sudan/b157-financing-revival-sudans-troubled-transition

International Crisis Group (2021a), 'The rebels come to Khartoum: How to implement Sudan's new peace agreement', Briefing no. 168, 23 February, available at: https://d2071andvip0wj.cloudfront.net/b168-sudans-new-peace-agreement_0.pdf

International Crisis Group (2021b), 'Containing the volatile Sudan–Ethiopia border dispute', Briefing no. 173, 24 June, available at: https://www.crisisgroup.org/africa/horn-africa/ethiopia/containing-volatile-sudan-ethiopia-border-dispute

International Monetary Fund (2020), *Sudan: Selected Issues*, IMF Country Report No. 20/73, available at: https://www.imf.org/en/Home

James, Laura (2015), *Fields of Control: Oil and (in)Security in Sudan and South Sudan* (Geneva: Small Arms Survey).

Jizouli, Hasan (2006), *Unf al-Badiya* (Khartoum: Manshurat al-Madarik).

Johnson, Douglas (2006), *Root Causes of Sudan's Civil Wars* (Oxford: James Currey).

Kamrava, Mehran (2005), *The Modern Middle East: A Political History since the First World War* (Berkeley, CA: University of California Press).

Khalid, Mansur (1985), *Nimeiri and the Revolution of Dis-may* (London & Boston, MA: KPI).

Lesch, Ann Mosley (1998), *Sudan: Contested National Identities* (Bloomington, IN: Indiana University Press).

Mahjub, A. M. A. (2015), '"Aid Aid ya Oktober", qira'a tariq nahwa al-mustaqbal', in H. A. Ibrahim (ed.), *Khamsuun 'Aaman 'Ala Thawrat al-Oktobir al-Sudaniyya, 1964–2014: Nuhud al-Sudan al-Bakir*, pp. 255–64 (Khartoum: Markaz al-Dirasat al-Sudaniyya).

Mahmoud, Fatima Babiker (1984), *The Sudanese Bourgeoisie: Vanguard of Development?* (Khartoum: Khartoum University Press).

Mamdani, Mahmoud (2020), *Neither Settler nor Native: The Making and Unmaking of Permanent Minorities* (Cambridge, MA: Harvard University Press).

Marcus, Harold (1963), 'Ethio–British negotiations concerning the western border with Sudan, 1896–1902', *Journal of African History*, 4 (1), 81–94.

McClintock, Anne (1995), *Imperial Leather: Race, Gender and Sexuality in the Colonial Context* (New York, NY: Routledge).

McCutcheon, Andrew (2014), *The Sudan Revolutionary Front: Its Formation and Development* (Geneva: Small Arms Survey, Graduate Institute of International and Development Studies), available at: http://www.smallarmssurveysudan.org/fileadmin/docs/working-papers/HSBA-WP33-SRF.pdf

McGowan, Patrick (2003), 'African military coups d'état, 1956–2001: Frequency, trends and distribution', *Journal of Modern African Studies*, 41 (3), 339–70.

McGregor, Andrew (2017), 'Musa Hilal: Darfur's most wanted man loses game of dare with Khartoum … for now', Aberfoyle Security, AIS Special Report, 12 December, available at: https://www.aberfoylesecurity.com/?p=4096

McSparren, Jason, Tok, Mohamed Evren, Shaw, Timothy and Besada, Hany (2015), 'Inclusive growth, governance of natural resources and sustainable development in Africa from a Qatari perspective', in Rogaia M. Abusharaf and Dale F. Eickelman (eds), *Africa and the Gulf Region: Blurred Boundaries and Shifting Ties*, pp. 111–28 (Berlin: Gerlach).

Mitchell, Richard (1993), *The Society of Muslim Brothers* (Oxford: Oxford University Press).

Morton, John (1989), 'Ethnicity and politics in Red Sea Province, Sudan', *African Affairs*, 88 (350), 63–76.

Niblock, Tim (1987), *Class and Power in Sudan: The Dynamics of Sudanese Politics, 1898–1985* (Basingstoke: Macmillan).

Nour, S. M. (2014), 'Assessment of the gender gap in Sudan', *International Journal of Sudan Research*, 4 (1), 7–34.

Nouwen, S., James, L. and Srinivasan, S. (2020), *Making and Breaking Peace in Sudan and South Sudan: The Comprehensive Peace Agreement and Beyond* (Oxford: Oxford University Press).

Nur, Mahgub Bireir Muhammad (2002), *Mawaqif ala Darab al-Zaman (Volume 1)* (Khartoum: Sharika Mataabi' al-Sudan li'l-Umla).

Nur, Taha Hassan (1971), 'The Sudan–Ethiopia boundary: A study in political geography', Doctoral thesis, Durham University, UK.

Pantuliano, Sara (2010), 'Oil, land and conflict: The decline of Misseriyya pastoralism in Sudan', *Review of African Political Economy*, 37 (123), 7–23.

Pascucci, Elisa (2014), 'Beyond depoliticization and resistance: Refugees, humanitarianism, and political agency in neoliberal Cairo', PhD thesis, University of Sussex.

Patey, Luke (2014), *The New Kings of Crude: China, India, and the Global Struggle for Oil in Sudan and South Sudan* (London: Hurst).

Porch, Douglas (2013), *Counterinsurgency: Exposing the Myths of the New Way of War* (Cambridge: Cambridge University Press).

Rolandsen, Øystein H. and Daly, M.W. (2016), *A History of South Sudan: From Slavery to Independence* (Cambridge: Cambridge University Press).

Roy, Olivier (1994), *The Failure of Political Islam*, translated by Carol Volk (Cambridge, MA: Harvard University Press).

Sa'id, S. (2001), *al-Saif wa'l-Tugha: al-Quwwat al-Musallaha al-Sudaniyya: Dirasa Tahliliyya 1971–1995* (Cairo: Sharika 'Aalamiyya li'l-tiba'a wa'l-nushr).

Salih, M.A. Mohamed and Harir, Sharif (1994), 'Tribal militias: The genesis of national disintegration', in Sharif Harir and Terje Tvedt (eds), *The Short-cut to Decay: The Case of Sudan*, pp. 186–203 (Uppsala: Nordiska Afrikainsitutet).

Salmon, Jago (2007), *A Paramilitary Revolution: The Popular Defence Forces* (Geneva: Small Arms Survey, Graduate Institute of International Studies).

Shamouq, A. (2008), *Oktober al-Thawra al-Zafira. Third edition* (Khartoum: ha'ia al-Khartoum li'l-Shafa wa Nushr).

Sharkey, Heather (2003), *Living with Colonialism: Nationalism and Culture in the Anglo-Egyptian Sudan* (Berkeley, CA: University of California Press).

Sharp, Gene (2005), *Waging Nonviolent Struggle: 20th Century Practice and 21st Century Potential* (Boston, MA: Porters Sargent Publishers).

Sidahmed, Alsir (2013), 'Oil and politics in Sudan', in Gunnar M. Sørbø and Abdel Ghaffar M. Ahmed (eds), *Sudan Divided: Continuing Conflict in a Contested State*, pp. 103–20 (New York, NY: Palgrave Macmillan).

Sidahmed, Alsir (2014), *The Oil Years in Sudan: The Quest for Political Power and Economic Breakthrough* (Toronto: Key Publishing).

Sikainga, Ahmad Alawad (2002), *'City of Steel and Fire': A Social History of Atbara, Sudan's Railway Town, 1906–1984* (Woodbridge: James Currey).

Skocpol, Theda (1994), *Social Revolutions in the Modern World* (Cambridge: Cambridge University Press).

Stephan, Maria J. (1999), *Civilian Jihad: Nonviolent Struggle, Democratization and Governance in the Middle East* (London: Palgrave Macmillan).

Thomas, Edward and El-Gizouli, Magdi (2020), 'Sudan's grain divide: A revolution of bread and sorghum', Briefing Paper, February, Rift Valley Institute.

Tilly, Charles (1975), 'Revolutions and collective violence', in Fred I. Greenstein and Nelson W. Polsby (eds), *Handbook of Political Science. Volume 3: Macropolitical Theory*, pp. 483–555 (Reading, MA: Addison-Wesley).

Tubiana, Jérôme (2014), 'Out for blood and gold in Sudan', Letter from Jebel Amir, *Foreign Affairs*, 1 May, available at: https://www.foreignaffairs.com/arti-cles/sudan/2014-05-01/out-gold-and-blood-sudan

Tubiana, Jérôme, Warin, Clotilde and Saeneen, Gaffar Mohammud (2018), *Multilateral Damage: The Impact of EU Migration Policies on Central Saharan Routes*, The Hague: Clingendael, the Netherlands Institute of International Relations, 6 September, available at: https://www.clingendael.org/publication/impact-eu-migration-policies-central-saharan-routes.

Turner, Victor (1969), *The Ritual Process: Structure and Anti-structure* (Chicago, IL: Aldine Publishing).

UN Security Council (2016), 'Final report of the Panel of Experts submitted in accordance with paragraph 2 of resolution 2200 (2015)', S/2016/805, September 22.

Uthman, N.M. (2015), 'An dawr al-mara wa huququha', in H.A. Ibrahim, *Khamsun 'Aaman Ala Thawrat Uktubir al-Sudaniyya, 1964-2014: Nuhud al-Sudan al-Bakir*, pp. 417–22 (Khartoum: Markaz al-Dirasat al-Sudaniyya).

Vezzadini, Elena (2015), *Lost Nationalism: Revolution, Memory and Anti-colonial Resistance in Sudan* (Woodbridge, UK: James Curry).

Wai, Dunstan M. (1981), *The African–Arab Conflict in Sudan* (New York, NY: Africa Publishing Co.).

Warburg, Gabriel (2003), *Islam, Sectarianism and Politics in Sudan since the Mahdiyya* (London: Hurst).

Watson, O. J., Abdelmagid, N., Ahmed, A., Abd Elhameed, A., Whittaker, C., Brazeau, N., Hamlet, A., Walker, P., Hay, J., Ghani, A., Checchi, F., and Dahab, M. (2020), 'Report 39 – Characterising COVID-19 epidemic dynamics and mortality under-ascertainment in Khartoum, Sudan', Imperial College London, 1 December 2020.

Wehr, Hans (1994), *A Dictionary of Modern Written Arabic (Arabic–English)*, edited by J. Milton Cowan (Ithaca, NY: Spoken Languages Services).

Willemse, Karin (2001), 'A room of one's own: Single female teachers negotiating the Islamist discourse in Sudan', *Northeast African Studies* 8 (3), 99–127.

Woodward, Peter (1990), *Sudan: The Unstable State, 1898–1989* (Boulder, CO: Lynne Rienner).

World Bank (2007), *Sudan: Public Expenditure Review, Synthesis Report*, World Bank, Poverty Reduction and Economic Management Unit, Report No. 41840-SD, December (Washington, DC: World Bank).

World Bank (2019), 'From subsidy to sustainability: Diagnostic review of Sudan's electricity sector', Final Report 30 June (Washington, DC: World Bank), available at: https://openknowledge.worldbank.org/bitstream/handle/10986/33702/From-Subsidy-to-Sustainability-Diagnostic-Review-of-Sudan-Electricity-Sector.pdf?sequence=1&isAllowed=y.

Wubneh, Mulata (2015), 'This land is my land: The Ethio–Sudan boundary and the need to rectify arbitrary colonial boundaries', *Journal of Contemporary African Studies*, 33 (4), 441–66.

Young, Alden (2017), *Transforming Sudan: Decolonization, Economic Development and State Formation* (Cambridge: Cambridge University Press).

Young, John (2012), *The Fate of Sudan: The Origins and Consequences of a Flawed Peace Process* (London: Zed Books).

Zeleke, Elleni Centime (2020), *Ethiopia in Theory: Revolution and Knowledge Production, 1964–2016* (Chicago, IL: Haymarket Books).

Zunes, Stephen (1999), 'Unarmed resistance in the Middle East and North Africa', in Stephen Zunes, Lester R. Kurtz and Sarah Beth Asher (eds), *Nonviolent Social Movements: A Geographical Perspective*, pp. 41–51 (Oxford: Blackwell).

INDEX